GREAT WAR LITERATURE

NOTES

Written by W Lawrance

on

THE OXFORD BOOK OF WAR POETRY

AN ANTHOLOGY, EDITED BY JON STALLWORTHY

Great War Literature Notes on The Oxford Book of War Poetry, an anthology edited by Jon Stallworthy.
Written by W Lawrance

Published by:
Great War Literature Publishing LLP
Forum House, Stirling Road, Chichester PO19 7DN
Web site: www.greatwarliterature.co.uk
E-Mail: enquiries@greatwarliterature.co.uk

Produced in Great Britain

ISBN 978-1905378272 (1905378270) Paperback Edition

10 9 8 7 6 5 4 3 2 1

Design and production by Great War Literature Publishing LLP
Typeset in Neue Helvetica, ITC Berkeley Old Style and Trajan Pro

Great War Literature Notes on

The Oxford Book of War Poetry

CONTENTS

Introduction	5
Thomas Hardy	7
Rupert Brooke	16
Herbert Asquith	21
Julian Grenfell	25
John McCrae	29
Charles Sorley	33
A. E. Housman	37
Hugh MacDiarmid	41
Carl Sandburg	44
Robert Frost	46
Wallace Stevens	48
Guillaume Apollinaire	50
Benjamin Péret	52
W. B. Yeats	54
Siegfried Sassoon	61
Edward Thomas	72
Ivor Gurney	85
Isaac Rosenberg	95
Wilfred Owen	111
Robert Graves	134
Edmund Blunden	144
Richard Aldington	156
Edgell Rickword	161
E. E. Cummings	166
John Peale Bishop	173
David Jones	177
Laurence Binyon	180
Ezra Pound	186
T. S. Eliot	191
G. K. Chesterton	194
Rudyard Kipling	198
Elizabeth Daryush	213
May Wedderburn Cannan	216
Philip Larkin	220
Vernon Scannell	222
Ted Hughes	224
Douglas Dunn	226
Further Reading	229
Bibliography	163
Other Titles	237

INTRODUCTION

The Oxford Book of War Poetry was first published in 1984 by the much respected Jon Stallworthy. In an epic volume, he has charted the history of war poetry from The Bible, to the atomic age, which is no mean feat. The section of this anthology which covers the First World War, features 72 poems by 37 poets, of whom seven were born in America, eighteen were non-combatants and only two are women.

As a collection, there does seem to be an imbalance in the number of non-combatant poets given here, although the combatant poets are represented by a greater number of poems. However, it could be argued that Jon Stallworthy was trying to demonstrate as many different perspectives of the conflict as possible, given the limitations of space.

As to the choices of poet and poems, these are also somewhat surprising. There is, of course, the ubiquitous presence of Wilfred Owen, Siegfried Sassoon, Isaac Rosenberg et al, and I, for one, am pleased to see the inclusion of Ivor Gurney and G.K. Chesterton, whose work is often overlooked. I would, however, have preferred to see the work of Wilfrid Wilson Gibson over the likes of Ezra Pound or T.S. Eliot. Gibson was another non-combatant, but one who wrote some of the most realistic trench-life poetry of the conflict, purely from his imagination and whom I feel could have provided students of this topic with a greater spectrum of ability and vision.

For those studying the AQA A-Level syllabus, this anthology provides a challenge when answering the examination questions. Due to its format, it is unlikely that the question will revolve around a 'first' or 'last' poem providing a suitable introduction or conclusion to the collection. Questions are more likely to focus on themes, literary merit, a key poem or the variety of poems included. Most of these questions are purely a matter of opinion, and depend upon the student having a sound knowledge and understanding of the anthology. In addition, I would recommend that students also read some other collections, such as *Up The Line to Death* by Brian Gardner or *Voices of Silence* by Vivien Noakes. These will help students to formulate an opinion as to the quality and choices of the poems included in *The Oxford Book of War Poetry*.

In these notes, we have given biographies of all the poets, although some of these are briefer than others. These biographies are followed by analysis of the poems themselves. Again, the length of the analysis varies greatly, depending on many factors, including the quality and length of the poem concerned and its overall relevance to the anthology.

All of the analysis and perspectives given in this guide are a reflection of the opinions of the author of these notes.

THE OXFORD BOOK OF WAR POETRY

AN ANTHOLOGY EDITED BY JON STALLWORTHY

THOMAS HARDY

The two poems given by Thomas Hardy are probably the most common of his 'War' poems, other than his *Channel Firing* which was written in April 1914, but is often included in anthologies, to show the inevitability of the war. Here, however, Jon Stallworthy has chosen pieces which were composed during the conflict and which reflect Hardy's perception of war, and its effects on humanity and the countryside which he loved so much.

BIOGRAPHICAL DETAILS

Born in Dorset on June 2nd 1840, Thomas Hardy was the oldest child of Thomas and Jemima Hardy. His father was a master mason and bricklayer and young Thomas initially trained to become an architect. While he was undertaking a commission in Cornwall, he met Emma Gifford and they were married in 1874. By this time, Hardy had given up architecture and had decided to become a full-time writer and poet. The marriage, although happy to begin with, soon floundered and they lived essentially separate lives. Emma died suddenly in 1912 and it was only then that Hardy realised the depth of his former wife's unhappiness and his role in creating that. Two years later, Hardy married Florence Dugdale, who had been his secretary, but she always felt that she lived in Emma's shadow, due to Hardy's guilt. He is probably best known today for his novels, including *The Mayor of Casterbridge*, *Tess of the d'Urbervilles* and *Far from the Madding Crowd*, although poetry was really his first love. Hardy had a great influence on many of the war poets, especially Siegfried Sassoon, Edmund Blunden and Robert Graves. He died in January 1928 and his ashes were placed in Poet's Corner in Westminster Abbey. His heart, however, was removed prior to cremation and was buried alongside his first wife, Emma, at Stinsford in Dorset.

MEN WHO MARCH AWAY

This poem was written on September 5th 1914, less than five weeks after the First World War began. Many poems written at that time were fervently patriotic, either extolling the virtues of "England's cause", or cajoling men into enlisting and doing their "duty" for their country. Examples of this jingoistic poetry include pieces by poets such as Jessie Pope and Harold Begbie whose works now seem bloodthirsty and warmongering, but which were extremely popular at the time. Other poets in the early stages of the war, while still patriotic, were not so direct in their message, focusing instead on England's need and the desire of men to do their duty, regardless of the cost. This group includes poets such as W. N. Hodgson, Rupert Brooke and John Freeman. Then there were the early war poets who did not write so much of nationalism, pride or causes, but concentrated instead upon their personal reasons for enlisting or their own perspectives of gratitude towards those who were fighting on their behalf. This group includes some, perhaps, surprising names, such as Siegfried Sassoon, Wilfred Owen and Laurence Binyon. Hardy's *Men Who March Away* can, therefore, be seen to be a poem of and about its time; no more or less appropriate than most other verses that were being written in the early weeks of the conflict.

The "men" of the title would have referred to the regular soldiers of the British Expeditionary Force, not to the new recruits of Kitchener's Army or the Pals Battalions, as they were also known. These were being formed by volunteers from all over the country, but on 5th September 1914, these groups were still very much in their infancy and were certainly not in a position to "march away" to war. The subtitle "Song of the Soldiers" serves two purposes: it reinforces the title, reminding us that these men are in uniform and are marching away to fight; it also suggests something cheerful, however, since marching songs are rarely woeful. Therefore, the reader is immediately and simply informed that the "men" are not unhappy to be marching away.

Throughout the poem, Hardy makes significant use of alliteration and repetition, which enhance the effect of the marching men, with their feet moving in time to their song. In the opening verse, the first two lines are repeated at the end of the stanza. However, Hardy has changed the emphasis here by adding a question mark, thereby posing a query to the reader and also to the watcher, who will be introduced in the second verse. Hardy's reference to "faith" is not necessarily a religious connotation, but may refer more to the reason why the men are marching away, whether that be a belief in their cause, or themselves as serving soldiers, their duty or a trust in their country, or God. His reference to "fire" is an allusion to courage and conviction: a resolution to complete the task in hand. Hardy places himself alongside the "men who march away", using the word "us", suggesting that he empathises with the situation of the soldiers. This may, however, refer to the fact that Hardy felt there was just as much of a war to fight on the home front, as there was in Flanders. This is reinforced by the remainder of the verse, in which Hardy reminds the reader of some of the home front sights and sounds that the men are prepared to leave behind, even though these would ordinarily "win" them over, such is the "faith and fire" within their desire to march away to war.

In the second verse, Hardy poses a question to a single person standing the crowd of onlookers. Some critics have suggested that this "friend" might be Hardy himself and that in posing these questions, he is expressing his own doubts about the war. Personally, I dispute this suggestion: I believe that Hardy's questions are posed to those who wonder about the justification of Britain's involvement in the war and, at the time, there is no evidence to suggest that Hardy shared such an opinion. He wonders, in the poem, whether this watcher thinks the war is a blind joke, as he stands sighing sadly at the marching soldiers. Hardy suggests that this man has thought a great deal upon the subject, but has still been deceived into making the wrong decision - hence he stands on the roadside, rather than joining the soldiers and doing his "duty". His description of the onlooker suggests not only stupidity, but also complacency and arrogance, which are hardly characteristics which he would have attributed to himself.

At the beginning of the third verse, Hardy immediately refutes the notion that the watcher might be wiser than the soldiers, or that they are going blindly into war, without understanding its consequences. He refers to men like the onlooker as "dalliers", implying that they have been slow to understand and respond to their country's call. This word alone reinforces the notion that Hardy had little time for those who he perceived as shirking their responsibilities. The soldiers, he suggests, see themselves as "England's need" or as fulfilling their country's requirement, to save her from her present predicament. It is also worth noting that Hardy, in common with many other poets at theme, describes the country in female terms, implying that the men must protect and defend the women, both literally and metaphorically against the enemy. To see their women or the country in "distress" would be a thing of great regret for any man, according to Hardy's philosophy. Again, as in previous verses, he repeats the first two lines at the end of the stanza, although here the addition of the exclamation mark gives this a sense of triumph.

The fourth verse opens with the suggestion that deep down, the men believe in the justification of their cause and that they will be victorious. This was very common amongst poets and writers at the beginning of the war, who often refused to sanction the idea of defeat, believing wholeheartedly that as Britain (in their opinion) had right and justice on her side, she would naturally conquer all. Hardy goes on to reinforce this, stating that "braggarts" or egotists will always be defeated. Germany was thought of as being somewhat conceited and arrogant at the time, so this description is not really surprising. Hardy's suggestion that they will "bite the dust" is another way of saying that they will die: a harsh and bloodthirsty notion, but at the time, those in favour of the war, sought nothing less than total victory. Within this statement, there is also the implied suggestion that the British cannot "bite the dust", since they have right on their side and are not "braggarts". Nonetheless, Hardy goes on to state that the soldiers will push forward "ungrieving", which implies that they appreciate that they do have something to lose and that there could be some human cost involved in their supposedly inevitable victory. The end of this verse - again repeated from the first two lines - has an air of sadness about it, possibly due to Hardy's mention of grief, but also because the sounds of the words "heart", "field", "ungrieving", "believing" etc., are softer and longer than some of the harsher tones used earlier in this verse, forcing the reader to slow the pace of the poem, making it become more thought-provoking.

The final verse is an almost exact repetition of the first stanza, except that Hardy no longer asks any questions. He feels he has now explained the "faith and fire" within the marching men: they may have something, or even everything, to lose, but duty, courage, honour and "faith" are more important than any loss or cost.

Hardy's language throughout this piece can sometimes verge on the simplistic, especially when he appears to use it to make his rhyme schemes work, such as in verse four: "And that braggarts must/surely bite the dust", which seems almost childishly forced. Indeed, the overly repetitive nature of the poem as a whole, while it may serve some minor purpose in demonstrating the monotonous nature of marching, does little to enhance the poem itself.

The messages contained in this poem may seem out-dated or old-fashioned to 21st Century readers, but this is where context comes into play. Duty was an important factor in the decision of many enlisting men, and it must be remembered that the soldiers in this poem are regulars, so those to whom the poem is addressed are the doubters in the crowds; those whose duty waivers; they are the ones towards whom Hardy is directing his piece. Hardy had grown up through many conflicts, including the Crimean War, the Indian Mutiny, the American Civil War, the Franco-Prussian War and the Boer War, which were all very different types of conflict to the First World War which, having barely started, was still an unknown quantity at the time Hardy wrote this piece. For the first few months of the conflict, most people firmly believed that it would be "over by Christmas" and many men enlisted simply because they did not want to miss out on the "fun". Hardy was, therefore, basing his perspective on these previous conflicts and general opinion, rather than the much more costly attritional trench warfare that we all know the 1914-18 campaign would become.

Many writers and poets wrote positively about the war in the early stages, not just the non-combatants like Hardy, who was seventy-four years old when he wrote this piece, but also those who would go on to serve in the conflict, like Rupert Brooke, Siegfried Sassoon and Wilfred Owen. In later months and years, these serving soldiers who survived generally changed the tone of their poetry, while many non-combatants ceased writing war poetry altogether, presumably unable to reconcile the realities of the First World War with their previously held ideals.

IN TIME OF 'THE BREAKING OF NATIONS'

This poem was first published on January 29th 1916 in the Saturday Review. It was, however, written at some point during the previous year and had its beginning even earlier than that. In his book *The Poetry of Thomas Hardy*, by James Osler Bailey, the author quotes from Hardy as follows: "... the poem entitled "The Breaking of Nations" contains a feeling that moved me in 1870, during the Franco-Prussian war, when I chanced to be looking at such an agricultural incident in Cornwall. But I did not write the verses until the war with Germany of 1914 and onwards."

The title of the piece refers to the Bible: in Jeremiah, Chapter 51, verse 20, it says: "Thou art my battle axe and weapons of war: for with thee will I break in pieces the nations, and with thee will I destroy kingdoms;". However, this poem is littered with double-meanings and contrasts, and the title is no exception, so this is not merely a Biblical quotation, but also a reference to the literal breaking of the ground caused by war: the physical damage done to the land and the countryside as a result of conflict. Hardy is also referring to the fact that, after wars have been fought, nations may tumble and be "broken", but this he will contrast in his poem, with the continuity of life in a rural community, which continues, unaffected by wars.

This is a poem of irony and implied contrasts, the contrasts made greater by not being explicit: Hardy's silence on the subject of the war is supposed to make it more significant. So when the first verse opens with the word "Only", Hardy's meaning is somewhat ambiguous. He is implying here that the man is more important than someone "only" ploughing the land and, through contrast, he is also suggesting that this man and his role are worthy of comparison with the soldiers who are fighting in the war. He reiterates this contrast and comparison, informing us that the man is "harrowing clods", which is only really another way of saying that he is ploughing the field ready for sowing the seeds. However the contrast between this suggestion of new life and the destruction of the Western Front is enormous. We can infer from this that the men in France have also harrowed "clods" of ground by shelling and fighting over them. This "harrowing", however, serves no useful purpose other than to "harrow" or worry those at home, who scan the newspaper casualty lists and wait for the fateful knock of the telegraph boy. Therefore, Hardy is implying here that the farmer's work is of more benefit to the community: he grows crops to provide food and doesn't cause any worry to his loved-ones in the process.

The farmer's "slow silent walk", enhanced by Hardy's use of alliteration and sibilance, suggests a lack of speed and noise, which seem wholly appropriate to the farmer's work, but through which Hardy is again able to imply a contrast between this sedate scene and the noisy haste of war. The speed with which he describes their movement could also said to be reminiscent of a funeral procession, which again calls death and war to the reader's mind.

The old, stumbling horse demonstrates an implied hardship for the farmer, compared - metaphorically in the reader's imagination - with the charging steeds of the cavalry in battle. The army commandeered many horses at the beginning of the war and cavalry officers took their mounts with them when they left to join their units, leaving only the older animals behind for farm work. Hardy implies a resentment towards this circumstance, suggesting obliquely that farming is just as important as fighting.

The farmer and his horse are half-asleep which again demonstrates the slow pace at which everything moves in the countryside, compared to in the war, but this also shows us that man and beast have performed this task for so long that they don't need to be especially alert: it is almost like a habit for them; and one which will continue unabated. Also this sleepiness carries a suggestion of how hard the farmer has to work each day, which can again be obliquely compared to the lack of sleep experienced by the men in the trenches. Hardy's use of the word "stalk" to describe the movement of the farmer and his horse could also be seen as another comparison with the fighting soldiers. This word is not really appropriate to the actions of the farmer ploughing a field, but here Hardy perhaps wants to portray all men as hunters and protectors of their land - just like the soldiers.

The second verse starts with the repetition of the word "Only", which has the same effect as it did at the beginning of the poem. Here, Hardy is suggesting that the fire represents more than "thin smoke without flame", since it also calls to his mind the massive fire and destruction of the Western Front, which he implicitly contrasts with the necessary fire created by the farmer, who is burning the grass that he has cleared from the field before ploughing. There are, however, no flames here, so this domestic fire is less destructive than the imagined fires of war: this means that nature's cycle can continue, because nothing is being destroyed.

Hardy's allusion to the falling dynasties refers us back to the title of the poem, in which nations are destroyed by war, but also to the situation where rulers may topple in the face of defeat. These events, however, have no effect on the countryside routine, which rotates year in, year out, regardless of the world's events.

In the third verse, the words "yonder", "maid" and "wight" are all archaic terms, reinforcing the suggestion that this scene had originated much earlier than the First World War. A "wight" is an archaic reference to any person or man, but is also a poetic or literary term for a spirit or ghost. Therefore, Hardy may be suggesting here that the maid's companion is dead - possibly having died in battle - or even that the maid is a ghost too, exemplifying the fact that, through the generations of country folk, nothing changes. This suggestion is enhanced by his description of the couple as "whispering by", which gives them a ghostly intonation. There is something surreal and unearthly about this couple, who would seem unable to disturb the ebb and flow of country life: perhaps because they don't really exist. Hardy ends the poem by explaining that "war's annals" or records will have faded into nothing, before the story of the ghostly couple's love dies.

The whole point behind this piece is, essentially, that the basics of life - from Hardy's perspective - will continue, regardless of the war, which like all wars, is transient and, changes nothing of any real importance - in his view.

Hardy was renowned throughout the conflict for his support of Britain's involvement and was a member of the government-run Secret War Propaganda Bureau, as well as joining the "Fight for Right Movement". The manifesto of this latter organisation said: "The spirit of the Movement is essentially the spirit of Faith: Faith in the good of man: Faith, therefore, in ourselves, Faith in the righteousness of our Cause, Faith in the ultimate triumph of Right; but with this Faith the understanding that Right will only win through the purification, the efforts and the sacrifices of men and women who mean to make it prevail." (Excerpt taken from the "Fight for Right Movement" pamphlet at the Imperial War Museum). Hardy also believed that those who worked on the home front were providing just as much of a service as those who were fighting in the trenches, whether directly or indirectly and one of his main concerns appears to have been for the perpetuation of the "English" way of life. In this, he was joined by others, such as Edward Thomas, whose poem As the Team's Head Brass warrants some comparison with Hardy's piece. Both poems depict very similar scenes, which could be said to be archetypally English in nature. However, Thomas's piece is much more pessimistic in tone than Hardy's, the narrator giving the impression that everything is being done for the very last time. Edward Thomas, like Hardy, was deeply troubled about the future of his beloved country and, when war was declared, although he was officially too old to enlist, he joined the Artists' Rifles in July 1915, believing - after much deliberation - that his duty was to fight for the essence - the very soil - of England. He feared that the war would result in the loss of a way of life that he cherished no less than Hardy and Thomas was prepared to die to protect that ideal, which he did on Easter Monday, 9th April, 1917.

Hardy's language in this poem is archaic, reflecting his rural theme. His rhyme is simple (abab), which usually allows the reader to focus on the meaning of the words within the poem. However, this piece falls short, because Hardy is trying to say too much with too little: his meaning is so well masked that at first glance, the poem really reads as a mere description of a rural scene, which makes it less relevant within its First World War context. Hardy's poem was supposed to stir the nation, which after the costly Battle of Loos in the autumn of 1915, was beginning to wonder about the war. However, it may well have failed in its purpose since its message is not really strong enough and doesn't bear comparison with much of what was being written at elsewhere at the time by poets such as Grenfell, Sorley and Gibson. In addition, the battles of Verdun and, more influentially, the Somme, which followed in 1916, probably put paid to any romanticised notions of the war and nature being seen as one, making this perspective not only outdated, but also somewhat macabre.

RUPERT BROOKE

Although represented in most First World War poetry anthologies, Rupert Brooke is sometimes seen as old-fashioned or outdated and not truly representative of the soldier poets, and to a certain extent, this is true. However, it should be remembered that his *1914 Sonnets*, from which the three poems given here are taken, were completed by January 1915 - very early in the war. Brooke's poems are very similar to others which were being composed at that time and they reflect the feelings of many of his generation who, to a great extent, were already 'lost' before the war even began and only appeared to find themselves when the conflict gave them a purpose and brought a new meaning and significance to their often tragically short lives.

BIOGRAPHICAL DETAILS

Born on 3rd August 1887, Rupert Chawner Brooke was the middle of the three sons of William Parker Brooke, a Classics master at Rugby School, and his wife Mary. Rupert was an extremely handsome young man, who shone both academically and on the sports field, making him universally popular. His time at Cambridge University was marred by unsuccessful love affairs, upon which he always embarked full of romantic hopes, and upon their failure, suffered abject depression. Brooke travelled a great deal between 1910 and 1914, returning to England only a few weeks before the First World War began. Among his friends and acquaintances, he counted Arthur and Violet Asquith (children of the Prime Minister), E. M. Forster, Virginia Woolf, Wilfrid Wilson Gibson and Winston Churchill. As First Lord of the Admiralty, it was Churchill and his secretary, the prominent literary figure, Edward Marsh, who arranged Brooke's commission into the Royal Naval Division. He sailed for Gallipoli on 28th February 1915, but died en-route as the result of an infected mosquito bite, on 23rd April - St George's Day. Before leaving England, Brooke had already completed his *1914 Sonnets*, which would immortalise him as the quintessential representative of 'the lost generation'.

PEACE

This sonnet begins by drawing our attention to the fact that Brooke feels that the youth of England is perfectly suited to the challenge that lies ahead. He thanks God for allowing his generation the opportunity to serve their country in this fashion. His sense that England's youth has been slumbering shows that he may have felt his life had little purpose before the war. This was a commonly held concept amongst the upper class young men of the day whose pursuits could now be said to be "idle". The war, it would seem, gave them a purpose.

He goes on, in the next two lines, to demonstrate the keen athletic powers of these eminently suitable young men, who will turn away from the idle pursuits of their youth, and embrace a better, cleaner future. This shows his sense that the assured victory (which most people saw as a foregone conclusion) will ensure the future of his nation. He seems to imply that the country will be made clean or strong, by victory, suggesting that he perceives that pre-war England lacked these qualities, and that it is the duty of his generation to return the nation to a former glory.

This is re-iterated by his suggestion that these men will be glad to leave behind the old world which has become tired and careless. They will also happily turn their backs on those who have not had the honour to enlist and serve their country. The final line of this stanza, which refers to the love as being empty could be a reflection of his failed pre-war love affairs, which in the grand scheme of things he now perceives as insignificant, although at the time their failure had made him extremely depressed. This shows how his priorities have now changed.

The second stanza refers to the magnitude of war and death: nothing is important, or for that matter even exists - not illness or grief - only death. However, death is described more in terms of a long peaceful sleep, rather than the end of life. This is a not the violent, horrifying death of Wilfred Owen's *Dulce Et Decorum Est*; this instead is the picture of a glorious death: bringing release. He believes that in death the heart will find happiness, which demonstrates that, to him, life had, perhaps, become a source of unhappiness. He admits that there may be pain to be endured before the final release of death, but even that will eventually end. The pain to which he refers, however, might be a reference to the grief which those who are left behind may feel. In this case, he seems to understand that this sense of loss will not last forever and will eventually be relieved.

This poem, like many of Brooke's, shows the poet's idea that the war has given England's youth the opportunity to sacrifice itself for the greater good of their country, and that such a sacrifice is the only noble and just course of action for a young man to take. Such nationalist pride was quite common in the early days, and even years, of the First World War. Brooke does not speak of bullets or bayonets, in fact his image of death is quite serene - like a man simply falling asleep.

He sees death as an enemy, but also as a friend, implying that to sacrifice himself in this way, although it would remove him from his loved-ones, would also grant him the ultimate fulfilment of his life. This also suggests that, to him, death - as a friend - provides a means of escape, either from his own existence, or from a world in which he possibly feels that, without the honour of either a noble death, or a victory, he would have no future.

THE DEAD

Like Brooke's other 1914 Sonnets, this poem again emphasises the honour of dying for one's country. Even those who were poor (not in a monetary sense, but in the sense of having a worthless or empty life), have been enriched by death - given gifts rarer, and more valuable, than gold. The gifts they have been given are the knowledge that their sacrifice has not been in vain and that they have served their country. He uses the word "us", emphasising that he felt his own pre-war existence had little purpose.

Unlike in his other poems, though, Brooke points out that these sacrifices, although worthwhile, are not without cost. These men, he says have given up their youth and their future - a career, old age and the opportunity to have children - or to have "a life". He implies, however, that what they have done - the sacrifice they have made - has earned them a place in history - their immortality.

In the second stanza, he reiterates this by saying that these deaths have enabled the earth to effectively, be reborn. Honour, Holiness and Nobleness exist again in the world. These have been earned by the sacrifice of a generation - but he insists that this is what they were born for - this was their heritage. It is almost as though he were saying that they were put on earth, at this moment in history, specifically to right the wrongs of previous generations and return the earth to its former glory. The war has given young men, he states, the opportunity to prove themselves worthy.

Again, this sentiment was fairly common at the beginning of the First World War. Many young men believed that it was their duty to protect their loved ones, their king and their country from the enemy. Brooke's language in his poems turned this sense of national pride into a serene crusade to bring goodness back to the earth again.

THE SOLDIER

This is Brooke's most famous and frequently quoted poem. It is unashamedly patriotic - he mentions the words 'England' or 'English' six times in just fourteen lines of verse. Simply put, this sonnet demonstrates that Brooke feels that, whatever happens to him - wherever he ends up - he will always be proud to have been born an Englishman.

Again, as in his other sonnets, he paints a picture of English serenity. He believes that it is his nationality which has made him the person that he is and his strong patriotic feelings shine through, above all else in this poem.

Even death,he believes, cannot remove that sense of pride from him and his passing will not be in vain if, at home in England people are, once again happy and at peace. He feels that by his death he will have given back to England everything, and more, that it gave to him. The happiness and security earned by his sacrifice will buy his eternal peace.

This beautiful poem evokes the idealistic image of a perfect England in a 'golden' age, such as many believe existed immediately prior to the First World War.

This poem has also come in for some criticism, over the years. Many feel that in *The Soldier*, Brooke places too much importance on his own sacrifices. Among those who believed this were Edward Thomas and Charles Hamilton Sorley, who, in their poems, placed more importance on the general sacrifices being made by so many, and on the loss of a way of life which the war would bring about.

Such criticisms may carry some merit, but should not detract from the fact that Brooke's 1914 Sonnets struck a chord at the time, with many who felt that to fight and die for one's country was justifiable. It became one of the most popular poems of the war, selling over 300,000 copies during the ensuing ten years. Its popularity only waned when the more realistic war memoirs began to be published.

HERBERT ASQUITH

The poem given here may seem archetypal of Herbert Asquith's class and upbringing and this is true. It is also representative of much of the early war poetry. However, Asquith's viewpoint changed as the war progressed and, despite the fact that his father was the Prime Minister, by late 1916, he was writing much harsher and more critical verse.

BIOGRAPHICAL DETAILS

As the second son of Herbert Henry Asquith and his first wife, Helen Kelsall Melland, Herbert Asquith and his siblings enjoyed a fairly privileged upbringing. Born on 11th March 1881, Herbert - like his father and brothers - attended Winchester College, before studying law at Balliol College, Oxford. In 1910, he married Lady Cynthia Charteris, with whom he had three sons: John, Michael and Simon. During the First World War, he served in the Royal Artillery, reaching the rank of Captain. His older brother, Raymond, however was killed in action in September 1916. After the war, Herbert returned to his pre-war profession as a lawyer. He died in 1947, at the age of 66.

THE VOLUNTEER

This poem was first written in 1912, then was amended at the beginning of the first world war, possibly to reflect that conflict. It appeared on its own, published in pamphlet form in 1915, then in a volume entitled The Volunteer and Other Poems in 1916, published by Sidgwick and Jackson, being one of twenty-two poems of various tone, some of which are much less pro-war than this particular piece. For example, in The Sunset, Asquith refers to death being the only victor in war - rather than emperors - and comments that the dead sentries buried underground will look up and ridicule the living.

Given Asquith's background and the fact that, at the time of writing this piece, the poet's father was the Prime Minister, he was hardly likely to write an anti-war poem at this stage of the conflict, especially given that it was actually composed initially before the war even began, but when the conflict was uppermost in many minds. However, it must also be said that, this piece is also perfectly in tune with many other poems that were being written at the time, by other, less politically involved poets.

The title of the poem is meant to encourage - rather than goad - others to enlist or 'volunteer', in common with the man who is the subject of the poem. Asquith's tone implies that the life which the army has to offer such volunteers is so much more rewarding and exciting than their roles in civilian life, which he portrays as drab.

The poem opens with a description of a dead soldier, although Asquith describes him as a "clerk", because that had been his job in civilian life. This, it would seem, is not a particularly young man, as he had been working as a clerk for "half his life", which suggests he is at least in his late twenties or early thirties, depending upon how long he had spent at school. (Asquith himself was thirty-three years old at the beginning of the war, so may have been writing about a man of similar age). Asquith's use of the word "spent" to describe the passing of this man's career, suggests that the man has been used up or exhausted by his years of civilian experience, which are also referred to as "toil". In this way, Asquith provides a rather dim view of the clerk's past, which he enhances with the use of the word "grey" to describe the city in which the man had worked. Asquith continues with this dreary account of the clerk's previous life, telling us that the man had assumed, before the war, that his future would hold no excitement, but would continue to "drift away", implying that he was achieving little in his prior occupation. He describes the man's participation in life as somewhat half-hearted, suggesting that, if life were a "tournament", the pre-war clerk would not have broken his lance - or done much by way of excitement, honour or courage. This reference to medieval jousting contrasts with the battle in which the clerk would have just died, which would not have featured any of the pomp and finery involving in knightly jousts.

Next, the reader is transported into the realms of fiction and romance, reminded that the clerk, in life, might well have enjoyed reading such literature, although his "bright eyes" as described here, only serve to remind us that he can no longer see anything and that they have lost their brightness, because he is dead. Nonetheless, in his imagination, the clerk had seen the "legions" of ancient armies, presumably French (or maybe Roman) as their ensigns are "gleaming eagles", as well as ranks of horses charing by. Asquith's description of the skies above these horses as "phantom" serves two purposes: it reminds us that this is really an imagined scene, given ghostly qualities; but it also gives the event a dark, ethereal aspect, harding back to his earlier description of the man's past as being "grey". He reiterates this account of drag greyness, through contrast, reminding the reader of the bright colours involved in medieval tournaments: the "oriflamme" being the Knight's standard, which would generally have been coloured scarlet. This contrast makes the dull tedium of the man's previous life even more stark. This section of the poem also serves to introduce the notion, continued into verse two, that although the man may have had a drab existence before, his time was spent dreaming of better and more honourable occupations than "toiling at ledgers".

Continuing with the clerk's daydreams of heroics, Asquith tells us that the man now feels "satisfied". He has passed from the "twilight" of his dreary civilian life, through the glory and heroism of his dreams and into the "halls of dawn", which may be a reference to the beginning of a new life, or may refer to Valhalla - the place in Norse mythology where those killed in battle travelled to after death. This was perceived as a giant hall: a place of great beauty and light and certainly an enormous contrast with the dark "twilight" of the moments immediately prior to death. Asquith tells us that the clerk's "lance is broken", which immediately gives him the air of one who has fought a brave and noble battle, but who does not see death as a defeat. This, Asquith goes on to quantify further, by explaining that the man feels "content" with the moment in which he died: that very moment in which he felt both life and death at the same time, gave him a "high" fulfilment.

Asquith then points out that the clerk feels so satisfied with the manner of his own demise, that he requires no thanks or other form of compensation: the realisation of his dreams and a noble death are all the reward he requires. Indeed, despite being dead, the man has no need for a "hearse", or any other funeral trappings, to take him away from the battlefield. He is happy instead to lie there on the French fields with the dead of earlier English battles. Asquith's mention of Agincourt is not unusual for literature written at the beginning of the First World War.

Comparisons were often made between the 15th Century battle fought by France and England in which the vastly outnumbered English forces defeated the French on their own soil, and the way in which the British Expeditionary Force were trying to fight off the German advances through Belgium and Northern France in 1914. This likening between two generations of heroic warriors was quite common in early First World War poetry, especially given Shakespeare's stirring St Crispin's Day speech from his play Henry V (the battle of Agincourt was fought on 25th October 1415 - St Crispin's Day):

"And Crispin Crispian shall ne'er go by,
From this day to the ending of the world,
But we in it shall be remembered -
We few, we happy few, we band of brothers;
For he to-day that sheds his blood with me
Shall be my brother; be he ne'er so vile,
This day shall gentle his condition:
And gentlemen in England now a-bed
Shall think themselves accursed they were not here,
And hold their manhood cheap whiles any speaks
That fought with us upon Saint Crispin's Day."

It is easy to see from this speech why many recruiting poets felt that references to Agincourt were appropriate for their cause in the early stages of the First World War.

The theme of this poem is that only by fighting and, if necessary, dying can men hope to find fulfilment and contentment and any form of satisfaction. Although this may seem an unrealistic and short-sighted perspective by today's standards, at the time this was not an unusual stance at all. Many poets - both combatant, like Asquith, and non-combatant, held the same or similar viewpoints and it was only after the Battle of the Somme that the general mood changed, although some altered their perspective earlier than this, based on their personal experiences.

Asquith's language in this poem is intentionally archaic, reminding the reader of England's history and former glories and, therefore, what it was that many volunteers perceived they were fighting for. However, as a shortcoming, the rhyme pattern is a little contrived and awkward, making this poem much less attractive and detracting from the overall effectiveness of the piece.

JULIAN GRENFELL

Despite the fact that Grenfell is only really known, within this genre, for writing this one poem given here, it can still be found in the pages of most anthologies. This may be due to the fact that the poem, together with Grenfell's statements that he enjoyed war have encouraged some to think of him as a 'happy warrior'. Alternatively, it might be because, rather poignantly, the poem was first published in The Times on the same day as the announcement of his death.

BIOGRAPHICAL DETAILS

Born on 30th March 1888, Julian Grenfell was the oldest of the five children of MP, William Henry Grenfell, who was made First Baron Desborough in 1905. Julian's mother, Ethel, was better known as Ettie and was a renowned society hostess who had a string of male admirers. In spite of the supposed advantages of his birth, Julian had a troubled childhood, outwardly happy, yet constantly striving to please his domineering mother. His education took place at Summerfields Preparatory School, then Eton and finally Balliol College, Oxford. He fell in love with Lady Victoria Marjorie Manners, although his mother rejected his choice, refusing to admit her to the family home at Taplow. In 1909, Julian wrote a series of essays which criticised the standards and morals of English Society, to which his family reacted badly, causing them to snub both Julian and his opinions. At this point in his life, Julian sank into a long and deep depression. In 1910, as had long been anticipated by his family, Julian was commissioned into the Royal Dragoons and was sent to India and then South Africa. As war looked inevitable in the summer of 1914, Julian's regiment were recalled to England and by October, he was in the Ypres Salient, where he served with gallantry, being awarded the Distinguished Service Order the following month. On May 13th 1915, a shell exploded close to him, a splinter becoming lodged in his skull and, although initially no-one thought his injuries serious, his parents were called to his bedside in Boulogne, where he died on 26th May. His younger brother Gerald, known as 'Billy' was also killed in action on 30th July 1915.

INTO BATTLE

This nature poem is, essentially, a celebration of life, the joy of fighting, and the honour of death, seen, by Grenfell, as a satisfactory fulfilment of man's existence.

This sense of joy is shown in the opening stanza, where the glory of a spring day is described. This can be contrasted with the later poems of, for example, Wilfred Owen, who even in his descriptions of this season in *Spring Offensive*, talks of cold winds which prepare the men for battle.

Grenfell's language, on the other hand, in the first six lines of this poem, is gentle and cheery. The final two lines of the second stanza remind us of the war - changing the emphasis of the poem. It is Grenfell's belief that those who refuse to fight might as well be dead; and those who die fighting are the better for it: their lives are enriched and made more valuable by the manner of their death.

He re-iterates this in the third verse. He states here that men get their physical strength from nature - the sun, the earth, the winds all empower men and through the earth man is reborn. Death is not seen as the end, but as the conclusion of this coming-together between man and nature. In Owen's *Spring Offensive*, by contrast, men have turned their back on nature like an old friend or lover from the past. In Into Battle there is no futility - dying is a means to gain greatness and satisfaction.

Man is not merely linked with the earth. In the fourth stanza, Grenfell states man's connection with the stars and the heavens. His choice of these three constellations is interesting: the ancient Egyptians believed that the Dog Star (Sirius), being so bright, was responsible for the summer heat; Orion, the hunter, famed for slaying wild animals, pursued the Seven Sisters (Pleiades) and upon his death, was placed as a constellation behind them, to continue the chase evermore. These constellations all represent strength - even the Seven Sisters, although pursued, are never caught.

Grenfell returns to earth in the following verse, this time to the trees. His trees are friendly - a guiding hand showing the men the way through the valley. Owen's valley, on the other hand, is full of unyielding brambles clutching and clinging to the advancing troops; his men are like unmoving trees - a much more sinister and threatening image of nature than the one painted by Grenfell.

Man's ability to blend and communicate with the earth is not limited to inanimate natural objects. In the sixth and seventh stanzas men and birds are linked. The kestrel and owl offer friendly warnings and endow men with their speed and good hunting senses. The blackbird, on the other hand, wisely bids man to enjoy his final hours - to seize the day - the singing is a metaphor for living; Grenfell is saying that if this battle is the last action you do on earth, fight well, for you may not get another chance.

The attitude of men in the hours of fear and boredom waiting for battle, when they tended to believe the worst, are contrasted with the noble courage of horses. It should be remembered that, as well as enjoying riding and hunting before the war, Grenfell was in the Royal Dragoons. He spent his First World War in the trenches, but his time in South Africa and India would have been spent on horseback.

In the ninth verse, the battle finally begins. To him it is a heated moment of joy, during which nothing else matters. His description of being taken by the throat and made blind could be an allusion to the poison gas which the Germans had employed for the first time only a few days before this poem was written.

The final two verses deal with the glory of death. The dying man doesn't much care about the manner of his death, whether it be by lead (bullet), or steel (bayonet). The battle is, again, likened to nature - this time the noise is described as being like thunder. The sounds of death coming from No Man's Land, which many would later describe as screams or cries, are compared by Grenfell with singing - thus giving the whole experience a musical and mystical quality. Finally he evinces the safety and sanctuary of death, which will wrap the dead in soft wings. The feeling this line evokes is one of purity and sanctity in death.

This poem was very popular at the time of its publication. Like Brook's *1914 Sonnets*, it promotes a gentle and heroic image of war. This was not untypical of much of the poetry being written at this time. Its publication, coming on the day of the announcement of Grenfell's death, made it even more poignant, as the author was now deemed to have made a noble sacrifice himself which, in the eyes of the public, further served to justify the content of his poem.

Hindsight is a wonderful tool with which we may look back and possibly deride this poem as unrealistic and a glorification of war. This would be unfair. Grenfell wrote what he felt. As with Rupert Brooke, who can say whether his tone would have changed had he lived longer.

JOHN MCCRAE

The poem which Jon Stallworthy has selected here, was not John McCrae's only composition during the war, although it is now his most well-known and, together with Laurence Binyon's *Fall the Fallen*, is one of the most frequently quoted poems of the First World War. Many poets were writing in similar tones to those displayed here in the earliest months of the conflict. Most of them, however, changed their minds and opinions during the course of the war and their poetry reflects this. McCrae, on the other hand, wrote later verses, which contain much the same message as the one shown here.

BIOGRAPHICAL DETAILS

John McCrae was born on November 30th 1872 in Ontario, Canada and, despite ill health, studied hard to become a doctor. In 1899, however, when Britain became involved in the Boer War, McCrae put all of that to one side, enlisted in the Royal Canadian Artillery and set sail for South Africa. By the time he returned to Canada, he had risen to the rank of Major and gained praise for his leadership qualities. In 1902 he returned to medicine and within six years had been appointed Physician to the Royal Alexandra Hospital for Infectious Diseases in Montreal. When the First World War began, McCrae offered his services to the military without hesitation and was appointed Brigade Surgeon, with the rank of Major. In October 1914, he sailed from Canada and spent several months training in England before arriving in France in February 1915. He served throughout the conflict and was promoted to the rank of Lieutenant-Colonel. On January 24th 1918, he was appointed Consultant Physician to the First British Army. This appointment, however, preceded his death from pneumonia by just four days.

IN FLANDERS FIELDS

This poem, originally entitled *We Shall Not Sleep*, has a simple message: that the sacrifices being made by so many should not be in vain, and that those who follow should continue to pursue the cause for which these men have died.

John McCrae has written this poem from the perspective of the dead, addressing the living. He speaks of all the things that the dead miss or will no longer be able to enjoy, and then pleads with the living, urging them to keep faith with the dead, in order that they may rest peacefully.

In the first verse, McCrae describes his whereabouts, making it clear that he is writing from the perspective of a fallen soldier, but also that the war continues around him, regardless of the flowers that grow, and the birds that sing. War, and therefore death, pay no attention to nature, and the killing goes on.

The second stanza expands on the first, but the tone is more remorseful. Here he expresses sorrow at the passing of unfulfilled lives and regret at lost opportunities. Finally, in the third verse, comes the appeal to the living, that they should continue to fight for the cause so that the dead may finally rest.

The theme of this poem is fairly clear: that the dead deserve not to go unnoticed, and that the living have a continuing responsibility to carry on the fight. This latter sentiment has, over time, been diluted and re-interpreted as a plea that the living should not forget those who have died. It seems clear, however, that McCrae's intention was to demonstrate that the survivors should carry on with the physical fight against the enemy. One of the reasons for this loss of meaning over the years, is that this third verse has often been omitted altogether. In the period following the end of the First World War, thoughts turned naturally towards peace and forgiveness and it was not necessarily prudent to remind the public of previous hostilities. What was considered decent patriotic sentiment in war-time, was not required reading when thoughts of peace and reconciliation were paramount.

McCrae's use of language in this poem is also interesting. He contrasts the larks singing with the overpowering cacophony of the guns; the crosses represent death, yet he stipulates that the dead are not yet even asleep, since they will not be allowed to rest until the fighting is finished. He gives these nameless dead appealing characteristics to make us feel even more sympathy for them - he points out that all of them have, in life, been loved by someone and have given love in return. His reference to the dawn and the sunset implies birth and death, which are natural enough in the normal course of events, but in this instance, life has been snatched from these men before they have even had the opportunity to experience it to the full. The mentioning of dawn and/or sunset is frequently used by poets, such as Wilfred Owen in *Anthem for Doomed Youth*, Siegfried Sassoon in *Attack* and, probably most famously of all, Laurence Binyon's *For The Fallen*.

The tone of *In Flanders Fields* is fairly typical of the time during which it was written (May 1915). Julian Grenfell's *Into Battle* was written at the end of that April, while Rupert Brooke's *1914 Sonnets* were completed early in 1915 and published that June. There are some obvious similarities between these poets, as in, for example, their belief in the justness of the cause for which they were fighting. They all perceive, although possibly for different reasons, that to fight the war to its conclusion is the right and proper course of action. McCrae's assertion that the dead can only find true peace if others follow them, demonstrates a call to arms. This is possibly because he and his family had retained strong links with Britain and he felt, and had demonstrated, both in the First World War, and previously in the Boer War, that his loyalties lay with The Empire and all that it stood for.

The main difference between these poets is their perception of death. Brooke and Grenfell perceive death through battle as glorious - a worthy and fitting end, which makes both the dead and the earth enriched. This sentiment is echoed by Charles Hamilton Sorley in *All The Hills and Vales Along*. McCrae, on the other hand, sees death as a source of regret and sorrow - there is no glory in McCrae's poem, only the assertion that the dead should be allowed to rest peacefully, which they will do once the fighting is over.

Unlike many later poets, such as Owen and Sassoon, McCrae does not attach any sentiment of waste or futility to these deaths, unless those who are left behind do nothing. Whilst his message is very different from that of Sassoon, for example, these two poets share a loyalty towards the victims of the war. The difference between them is in their ideal solution: Sassoon wanted (and indeed tried) to end the fighting because he believed that Britain's war aims were unclear and that the lives of so many men were being needlessly wasted. McCrae, on the other hand, while regretting the losses, urges others to avenge them, by continuing the fight on their behalf.

McCrae's belief that the living should avenge and mourn the dead could also be contrasted with the attitude of Charles Hamilton Sorley in his poem *When You See Millions of the Mouthless Dead*. Sorley maintains in this poem, that there is little point in mourning the dead. They have been claimed by death and as such cannot hear your words, see your tears or respond to your grief. Both poems were written early in 1915 but the difference in their content is so marked that the reader could easily believe Charles Hamilton Sorley was writing much later in the war.

In Flanders Fields captured the imagination of millions of people who were just beginning, like McCrae, to understand the awful human cost of the First World War. His statement that these men should not go forgotten to their graves, coupled with a sense of empowering their survivors to continue the fight in their name, was at that time a stirring declaration. Whilst it is easy to look back with hindsight and the eyes of the 21st century and criticise such an imperialistic point of view, to do so would be unreasonable. The writing of poets such as McCrae, Brooke, Grenfell etc., must be judged, more fairly, on the basis of their lives and the world in which they lived.

CHARLES HAMILTON SORLEY

Charles Sorley presents us with an unusual image of the war, considering the time during which his poems were written. At the time he was composing the two pieces given in this anthology, most poets were writing patriotic, stirring verse either encouraging young men to enlist and fight for King and Country, or inspiring them with tales of honour, duty and the thrills of battle. If the poems chosen by Jon Stallworthy are to be seen as representative, then Sorley's impressions were clearly very different.

BIOGRAPHICAL DETAILS

Born on May 19th, 1895 in Aberdeen, Charles Hamilton Sorley was the son of a university lecturer. Both Charles and his twin brother attended King's College Choir School before Charles won a scholarship to Marlborough College, where he first began writing poetry. In 1913, he won a second scholarship, this time to University College, Oxford, but decided that prior to taking up his place, he would go travelling. Thus, when war was declared in August 1914, Charles Sorley was in Germany and found himself under arrest. He was imprisoned for eight hours, before being released and ordered to leave the country. On August 26th he enlisted in the 7th Battalion of the Suffolk Regiment. He arrived in France the following May and by August had been promoted to the rank of Captain. He was shot in the head and killed instantly on October 13th 1915 and, as his body was never found, is commemorated on the Loos Memorial to the Missing at Dud Corner Cemetery.

'ALL THE HILLS AND VALES ALONG...'

This poem is, in some cases called *Route March*, but it would seem that Sorley himself left it untitled, so it has adopted its first line as a title.

Written shortly after the outbreak of the First World War, this poem could be interpreted as a celebration of death in the sense that re-joining with the earth should be man's ultimate ambition. Its rhyming couplets and jaunty style give it the air of a happy marching song, which contrasts well with the content. Sorley's use of language reinforces this - the subject matter is death, but he uses the word glad or gladness seven times during the poem, and the words joyful and merry also appear on several occasions. This is a poem about the ranks, not the officers: the private soldiers would have sung on the march up to the front; the officers would not.

The first verse sets the tone for the rest of the poem - the men should be glad to give their lives back to the earth, which will be happy to receive them. In the second stanza, Sorley urges the men to consider what lies ahead. He implies that the manner and length of their lives are unimportant compared to the manner of their deaths. He compares this with Christ and Barabbas. Barabbas was the condemned prisoner who was chosen by the Jews to be released, thus sending Christ to die on the cross. The implication here is that death is indiscriminate: the best, most worthy will not necessarily be the ones to survive; but if all men go gladly to their death, the earth will be able to store up all their happiness, as though it were goodness, and this will in turn replenish the earth. This reiterates the first line of this stanza, where he suggests the men should forget about past sins - for in death all will be treated equally.

In the third verse, Sorley talks of the earth only knowing death and not tears, meaning that the earth will not mourn those who will die. In fact, he says, it was the earth that with easy pleasure grew the hemlock with which the Greek philosopher Socrates was killed. This joyous, unlamenting earth, in fact, he says, continued to blossom at the foot of Christ's cross. It will, therefore, continue to flourish when you, the soldier, are dead.

In the final verse, there is an air of celebration where Sorley seems to believe that the earth is laughing and echoing the sounds of the men. This echo, Sorley implies, will continue, even when the singing and marching have all stopped. The final, rousing, section urges the men on to die happily.

This poem is not patriotic: nowhere does it mention the country from which these soldiers come. This was fairly unusual for poetry written at this time, which tended to be full of patriotism, but there is evidence that during his stay in Germany, Sorley had witnessed some German soldiers singing. This, together with hearing the British soldiers' marching songs, may have prompted the writing of this poem.

Sorley makes no mention of his own death: this is not a poem which talks about sacrifice or waste. The men are not dying for King or Country, nor for their fellow man, but for their love of the "earth"; of nature. Unlike in Julian Grenfell's *Into Battle*, the men will not be enlarged by death, but the earth will; there is no joy in Sorley's battle, just the sure inevitability of death.

To Sorley, though, death is not the end. Twice during the poem he says that the men are only sleeping; he talks of the earth storing their gladness, which implies that it will be there for them to return to later. There is a sense that, to Sorley, death is seen as a fresh beginning; a reawakening.

'WHEN YOU SEE MILLIONS OF THE MOUTHLESS DEAD...'

This untitled poem, was among those found in Sorley's kitbag after his death. Many critics recognise it in, an awareness and talent which, had he lived, could have rivalled that of Wilfred Owen. This could be said to be true of the form and language, particularly given this poem's nightmarish quality. Sorley's sonnet, however, urges us not to praise or mourn the dead, while Owen extols their virtues, particularly when compared to those who mourn them. Owen often uses bitter recrimination as in, for example, *Apologia Pro Poemate Meo* in which he states his opinion that the dead are infinitely more worthy than those whom they have left behind.

Another interesting point which immediately strikes the reader in Sorley's sonnet is the quantity of dead people he envisages. Bearing in mind that this poem was written some time before October 1915, Sorley is showing remarkable foresight and accuracy in his prediction that there will be millions of dead.

There is a shadowy, ethereal quality to Sorley's sonnet: the pale soldiers which march through your dreams lead us into the poet's idea of how one should mourn the dead. This is given in the form of a list of instructions.

Sorley informs us that we need not promise to remember them. He says there is no point in praising them, or crying over them. Neither should we honour them. The reason for all of this is that, being dead, they are deaf, blind and indeed mute - hence "mouthless" - so they can neither appreciate, understand or respond to our sentiments.

He then urges us to appreciate that, although our loved-ones may be dead, many other, equally deserving, men have died before. The dead are no longer exclusively ours to mourn and we should not think of them in this way, or imagine that we are able to recognise them among all the countless others. Death has taken possession of them.

As well as being compared to some of Wilfred Owen's work, many have also seen this sonnet as a response to Rupert Brooke's *The Soldier*. Sorley had been critical of some of Brooke's work, paying particular attention to his obsession with his own sacrifice, and sentimental attitude. As in *All the Hills and Vales Along*, there is no use of the first person in this poem: Sorley talks about the war and death as though they affect others, not himself.

Another parallel could be drawn between this poem and Laurence Binyon's *For The Fallen*. This poem, part of which is read out every year at Remembrance Day services, was first published in September 1914, so it is not unreasonable to suppose that Sorley might have read it. Binyon asserts that we will (and indeed should) remember the dead on a daily basis, and also that their youth is eternal. Sorley, on the other hand, is more blunt: remembering the dead is pointless - they cannot appreciate it, and they are not eternally young, they are dead.

There is no trace of sentimentality in this sonnet, which looks quite harshly at the reality of death through war, making, unlike Brooke and Binyon, no allowance for patriotism or emotion.

A. E. HOUSMAN

In most anthologies, the editor will choose to present poems from very different sources. In the case of First World War poetry, this will always include an element of non-combatants, sometimes in the form of those who were too old to enlist. This is the case with the work of A E Housman and he, like Kipling and Thomas Hardy, for example, due to their literary stature, are often included to give an 'elder statesman' perspective of the conflict.

BIOGRAPHICAL DETAILS

Alfred Edward Housman was born near Bromsgrove in Worcestershire on 26th March 1959, the son of a country solicitor and oldest of seven children. He attended King Edward's School in Bromsgrove and then St John's College, Oxford. He failed to pass his degree in Classics, however, and found work at the Patent Office in London. While there, he also published several academic articles, enhancing his reputation as a scholar to the point where in 1892, he was awarded the Professorship of Latin at University College London. From there, in 1911, he became Senior Professor of Latin at Trinity College, Cambridge. The literary work for which he is now most famous, A Shropshire Lad, was published at his own expense in 1896. The tone of the poems contained in this book, which idealised country life, made them a great success, especially amongst many of the soldier poets, who perceived it as their duty to protect and defend the English way of life. For Housman, his main interest remain Classics and especially Latin, while poetry was always treated as more of a hobby. Housman died in 1936 at the age of 77.

EPITAPH ON AN ARMY OF MERCENARIES

This poem was published in The Times in 1917, three years after the First Battle of Ypres, leading many to erroneously assume that it was written at around that time. However, Housman wrote this piece in the immediate aftermath of the First Battle of Ypres, in late 1914, which fact makes perfect sense, given the title of the poem. The British Expeditionary Force (BEF), which initially went to war in August 1914, consisted of regular, paid, professional soldiers, leading Germany, which had a much larger army of conscripts to refer to the British as an army of "mercenaries", for the simple reason that the men were being paid. This was an enormous injustice to a professional body of men, but this was also a mind game, designed to belittle and undermine the confidence of the men in the BEF. This army, commanded by Sir John French, contained approximately 100,000 men, making it by far the smallest of all the major European powers, the first men landing in France on 7th August 1914. The tiny BEF, however, managed to hold up the advancing German forces, who were attempting to reach the French capital in the autumn of 1914, as part of the Schlieffen Plan. This delay led the German Kaiser, Wilhelm II, to comment on his irritation at "Sir John French's contemptible little army". Whether this was meant as another actual insult, or to imply that the BEF was contemptibly small, is unclear. Either way, the Regulars took the name to their hearts and delighted in being referred to as "the old contemptibles" from then on - even if only to spite the Germans!

The fact that this poem is called an "epitaph", or memorial, is a clue to the fact that more than half of the 100,000 men of the original BEF were listed as casualties after the First Battle of Ypres, which ended in mid-November 1914, after just over five weeks of fierce fighting. These were losses which the British Army could not afford, but the battle had also cost the German army over 100,000 casualties, and had halted their advance, leading to stalemate. The title of the poem is, therefore, ironic: at least in part, since Housman implies that the men for whom he is writing the "epitaph" were most certainly not "an army of mercenaries". That he wrote this in the immediate aftermath of the near obliteration of that supposed "army of mercenaries" should also be obvious. There would be no point in writing such a poem three years after the event, when many other battles had taken place, and the army concerned had long-since been replaced by one of volunteers and conscripts. Therefore, it can be seen, simply from the six words of the title (and a little bit of historical research or knowledge) that this is a poem of a very specific time and place.

Housman is being intentionally ironic in some of his statements in this poem. Elsewhere, however, such as in the opening, he makes accurate comments, that in the early days of the conflict, it had felt as though the sky was falling in upon the world. This is really a metaphorical commentary on the situation in those early weeks, when the British Army, which had a reputation for being proud and indomitable, had been forced to retreat from Mons. News of this, when received in England, was greeted with dismay and disappointment, even though the government still tried to portray the manner of the retreat as a "victory". Housman goes on to describe this time as "The hour when earth's foundations fled", denoting the impact that this situation had upon the civilian population and the devastating nature of the news. The poet refers, once again, to the notion of the soldiers as "mercenaries", saying that this was their "calling", although this is purely ironic, since what he really means is that they did their soldierly duty, despite the fact that the Germans might choose to insult them by referring to them as "mercenaries". He acknowledges that they are paid for their services, but also that they have paid a high price themselves, since they are dead.

Some have perceived, in this final line of the first verse, a Biblical reference to Romans, Chapter 6, Verse 23, which states that "the wages of sin is death" and, although this may well be the case, it should also be remembered that Housman was an Atheist and had been for over forty years by the time he wrote this poem. The remainder of the Biblical quotation reads: "but the gift of God is eternal life through Jesus Christ our Lord", so Housman's meaning here is almost certainly satirical and may not even be Biblical at all, but merely based upon a saying, which was widely used, without there necessarily being any religious implication. Housman may also have been making this comment as a criticism of those who wanted to bring religion into the war, seeking either to justify or condemn the conflict, in God's name.

In the second verse, Housman returns initially to less ironic tones, praising the strength and bravery of the soldiers who "held the sky suspended" with their shoulders, thus giving the men a Godlike status. He goes on to say that, because the army held its ground, or "stood" still, the very "foundations" of the earth are kept secure. Again, this almost deifies the efforts of the men, making them seem capable of superhuman feats. In this way, Housman shows his true feelings of pride in the actions of the British Army, as well as explaining the importance of their deeds. Next, he once again makes a religious reference, suggesting that God has "abandoned" the people and the lands that the British Army is defending. This is probably a reference to the people of Belgium, who Housman may well have perceived as having been abandoned by God, being as many of them had become refugees. His own non-belief could, again, have made him angry towards those who brought the role of the church into the conflict in a positive light, and he perceives that the army are, in fact, the only defenders of those whom God has left to fend for themselves. In return for this sacrifice, however, he asserts that the men are not asking for payment - as "mercenaries" would - but instead they take the "sum of things". In other words, they'll accept their lot. They are professional soldiers, who know the risks involved in their jobs and if that means making the "ultimate sacrifice" for their country, then that will be their "sum of things" and their "pay".

Housman, like many in his position - namely an elder statesman of literature and a non-combatant - writes in praise and gratitude for those who do a job that is not required of him. Perhaps it is this knowledge, of his own lack of involvement, that makes his gratitude all the more poignant. Here, however, there is also an undertone of anger towards those who would dare to call the men of the British Army "mercenaries", but also at those who threw religion into the melting pot. As the war progressed, and the BEF was permeated, beyond recognition, by more and more volunteers and, eventually, conscripts, the ethos of the New Army may have been a little different. However, the regular army battalions always tried to maintain the same traditions, even when territorials and new recruits had replaced those who had fallen in the early battles. Housman's use of a simple rhyme scheme and easy metre in this poem help him to communicate his message, without any complication or confusion on the part of the reader.

HUGH MacDIARMID

Another unusual poem, which was written as a direct response to Housman's earlier piece.

BIOGRAPHICAL DETAILS

Born in August 1892, Christopher Murray Grieve, whose pseudonym was Hugh MacDiarmid, grew up in the Scottish town of Langholm in Dumfries and Galloway, where his father was a postman. Before the First World War, he worked as a journalist and during the conflict, he served with the Royal Army Medical Corps in Salonica, Greece and France. He returned to Scotland in 1918, suffering from cerebral malaria. After the war, he moved to Montrose and, although still working as a journalist, he began to take more of an interest in poetry and literature. He continue to pursue all three for the rest of his life. MacDiarmid was always politically active and became a founder member of the National Party of Scotland in 1928. His reputation increased and he is now recognised as the greatest Scottish literary influence of the twentieth century. MacDiarmid died in 1978 at the age of 86.

ANOTHER EPITAPH ON AN ARMY OF MERCENARIES

I have not written a conventional analysis of this poem for the very simple reason that I have been studying and writing about First World War literature for over thirty years and this particular poem has always made me angry. Indeed, why Jon Stallworthy has done it any justice by including it in his anthology is, frankly, beyond my comprehension. This has nothing to do with it being a "bad" poem, although it is (in my opinion), but has everything to do with its content which is bigoted, contemptuous and denegrates the men of the BEF in particular and the 1914-1918 war in general - which I, for one, will not condone, by wasting my time in analysing it. Besides which, no student or teacher should require a full-blown line by line analysis of this piece as the poem itself is really quite easy to understand: it is a blatant insult towards the men who fought in the First World War, specifically the BEF, whom A E Housman had praised in his earlier poem of similar title (written in 1914). According to MacDiarmid these men were "professional murderers" who did nothing to save "anything worth any man's pride" - in fact according to him, they didn't even know what that was.

This man, who apparently holds himself above those "professional murderers" served in the Royal Army Medical Corps during the war and was, therefore, not called upon to kill in the name of his country. However, showing true gallantry, when it came to his convictions, he also waited until A E Housman was only months away from death, before publishing his response to the older, and better, man's poem, presumably to prevent the more learned gentleman from having any right to reply. If he had any moral courage, he would have come forward with this opinion earlier and submitted himself to Housman's renowned capacity for sarcasm and cutting riposte.

If you carry out a search for this poem on the internet, you will find several discussion threads relating to it, its meaning and the poet, some of which become rather heated. Other critics of this piece have highlighted the fact that, as MacDiarmid was a communist and Stalinist, he was (presumably) not averse to "murder" for the right cause or ideology, but evidently his scruples only applied to "murder" in the cause of war, making his perspective somewhat distorted. Others have chosen to take an alternative viewpoint, even arguing that *Housman* should be the poet to be criticised for calling the soldiers mercenaries in the first place, whereas MacDiarmid's final two lines of poetry make a "telling and emotional point very effectively", which thought is somewhat disturbing and shows a lack of understanding of the concept of irony in Housman's piece.

Nonetheless, while I will not analyse this piece, as a matter of principle, what I will say is that, in my opinion, what remains are six lines of verse, poorly written and meanly expressed, by a man who lacked moral courage and appreciation for what others had sacrificed on his behalf. Naturally, Hugh MacDiarmid was as entitled to his opinion as I am to mine. My point, however, is that, if those supposedly "professional murderers" hadn't been prepared to take "impious risks" and die, he might not have had the freedom to express his opinions with such impunity. He didn't have to be grateful, he didn't have to fawn at their feet in supplication. If he didn't agree with what had been done he could have taken up his argument with the politicians who started the war in the first place, not insult and deride the brave men who fought and died in it. If he couldn't do this and he didn't want to be counted among those who, like Housmen, Binyon, Chesterton, Kipling, Nesbit and many others, felt beholden: he just had to be quiet.

CARL SANDBURG

An American poet who did not see action in a European theatre of war, Sandburg gives here a viewpoint of conflicts from generations past and present, from the perspective of nature.

BIOGRAPHICAL DETAILS

Born on January 6th 1878, Carl Sandburg was the son of Swedish immigrants. His father, August, was a railway worker and, with seven children, of whom Carl was the second oldest, the family was very poor. Carl left school at the age of 13 and went out to work at various jobs, to bring extra money into the household. He served during the Spanish-American war and, upon his return, enrolled at Lombard College in his hometown, Galesburg, Illinois. Sandburg attended Lombard for four years, but left without obtaining a degree in 1903. In 1908 he married Lilian Steichen and they had three daughters. Sandburg had already begun writing and had produced two volumes of poetry. However, the need for a regular income made him turn to journalism and he worked on the Chicago Daily News for man years. Real recognition of his poetry was slow to materialise, but in 1914 he published a volume entitled Chicago Poems, which met with great acclaim. Over the following years, Sandburg continue to write poetry, as well as novels and children's stories, together with a two volume biography of Abraham Lincoln. This brought financial success, enabling the family to move to Flat Rock, North Carolina, where Sandburg died on July 22nd 1967.

GRASS

This poem was first published in 1918, in a volume entitled Cornhuskers, for which Carl Sandburg was awarded the first of his two Pulitzer Prizes. It has an unusual, free form in three stanzas, using very basic and simple language, which allows the message to be more easily understood. The essential message here is that humans forget about war too easily, allowing nature – or more specifically, the grass – to cover up their crimes.

The poem is narrated by the grass itself, which Sandburg has personified, making it seem rather fed up and disdainful that mankind keeps repeating the same mistakes, never learning from the lessons of the past. He mentions several historical battles: Austerlitz and Waterloo are both Napoleonic, extremely costly and influential battles; Gettysburg was a major event in the American Civil War. These battles all sealed the fate of the participants, one way or the other. However, nothing was learned as a result of these battles and men went on to repeat their mistakes at Verdun and Ypres – both of which were calamitous and utterly pointless. In this sense, Sandburg seems to imply that not only does man repeat his mistakes, but he actually makes them worse and more serious as time progresses.

Sandburg intentionally uses harsh language here such as 'pile' and 'shovel' when referring to what should be done with the bodies. He does this to prove his point, that if mankind is going to forget so quickly, he cannot really care about the dead, and there is little point in pretending otherwise. This issue is further reiterated by the impatient tone of the personified grass, which seems to just want to be allowed to 'work', presumably because it knows that, before long, some foolish man will come along and make another war.

Within a few years – maybe two, maybe ten – people will have forgotten this place, and the heroes who died here, and this notion seems to make the grass even more angry and impatient than before. The final two lines strike some as being resigned or impassive, but their detachment from the rest of the poem's irony strikes me with sadness. The circuitous inevitability of man's necessity to fight cannot be helped or heeded – it will happen just as surely as day follows night.

ROBERT FROST

Frost's poem here provides one of his customary descriptions of the natural world, this time coupled with the destruction of the war.

BIOGRAPHICAL DETAILS

Robert Lee Frost was born on March 26th 1874 in San Francisco. His mother, Isabelle and father, William were both teachers and William also worked as a journalist on the San Francisco Evening Bulletin. William's untimely death in 1885, at the age of 35, left the family in extreme financial difficulties. Isabelle decided to move the family to New England, where William had been born and where his relations continued to reside. Thus she, Robert and his younger sister, Jeanie settled in Lawrence, Massachusetts. Robert began writing poetry and performed well at school, both academically and on the sports field. In 1894 his first poem was published and a year later, at the age of 21, he married his sweetheart, Elinor Miriam White. During the course of their marriage, they had six children, although two of them died in infancy. In 1911, the family travelled to England and it was here that Frost wrote many of his best poems, as well as becoming friends with other poets, such as Ezra Pound and Edward Thomas. When the First World War began, the Frosts moved back to America and bought a farm in New Hampshire. Literary success followed, including a Pulitzer Prize in 1923 - the first of four such awards. Although Frost's popularity continue to rise, this success was not mirrored in his personal life, as two more of his children died and also his wife, Elinor. Frost lived on until 29th January 1963.

RANGE FINDING

This poem was first published in 1916, in a volume of Frost's work entitled Mountain Interval. Frost and his young family had been living in England until early 1915, becoming especially good friends with the English poet, Edward Thomas and, it would seem, had picked up on his feelings that the war was causing a great many changes to the natural world, most of which were unwelcome.

The title of this poem refers to the practice, usually undertaken by the artillery, of measuring the distance required to hit a specified target. Quite often, the gunners would under- or over-estimate in their firing and the settings of the gun would need to be adjusted before firing again. Sometimes this action refers to the infantry, who would use snipers to pick out specific targets within their 'range'. In the case of this poem, however, Frost does not make it clear to which type of soldier he is referring and I believe it is probably both, as he speaks of the 'battle', which suggests artillery and a 'passing bullet', implying infantry.

The poem opens with a description of a torn cobweb, which the spider has created, like a 'diamond', presumably both in shape and appearance, as it may be covered in dew and have a shiny, diamond-like resemblance. This 'battle' or bombardment has also destroyed a flower, which had been growing beside a bird's nest on the ground. The bomb, or bullet did all this damage before causing any human casualties and yet the natural world still appears to carry on as before: the flower is still 'bent double' and the mother bird still feeds her young in the nest. Meanwhile, a butterfly which had been wanting to rest on the flower, has to change its direction to accommodate the fallen bloom, although it still manages to find somewhere to stop.

In the second verse, Frost goes on to explain that during the night, when presumably things were quieter, spiders have created a series of webs between the stems of the mullein plants, which are now covered with the morning dew. Suddenly, however, a 'passing bullet' shakes the droplets of water from the webs, the movement of which fools the spider into thinking that she must have trapped a fly. She scurries out to find her prey, but of course, discovers nothing and so, goes away again.

In this sonnet, Frost's language is quite simple and straightforward, which is intentionally done, so as not to detract from his message, which is that mankind is disrupting nature – or at least trying to. Man's need to fight causes nature to adapt itself, rather than the other way around and one senses that Frost feels that this is wrong and that it upsets the balance of the natural world.

WALLACE STEVENS

Jon Stallworthy rounds off this initial selection of American poets with a piece by Wallace Stevens.

BIOGRAPHICAL DETAILS

Wallace Stevens was born on October 2nd 1879 in Pennsylvania. After attending Harvard University and the New York Law School, he was called to the Bar in 1904. He worked as a lawyer in New York City until 1916, whereupon he moved to Connecticut and took up a position at the Hartford Accident and Indemnity Co. In 1909, he had married Elsie Viola Kachel and their daughter, Holly, was born in 1924. His fame as a poet came late in life and although he initially had some of his work published in 1914, his first book of verse was not printed until 1923. He never gave up his job in order to write full-time, preferring to compose his poems in the evenings, after work. Wallace Stevens died in August 1955 at the age of 75.

THE DEATH OF A SOLDIER

Although there is no precise date of composition for this poem, it was first published in 1923 in Stevens's volume of poetry entitled *Harmonium*. According to James Longenbach (Joseph H Gilmore Professor of English at Rochester University), Stevens wrote this poem with one particular soldier in mind – namely Eugene Lemercier, a French soldier who was killed in April 1915. Lemercier had written many letters to his mother while he was serving at the front and, following his death, these were gathered together and published under the title *Lettres d'un Soldat*. Stevens used this same title for a sequence of poems, of which *The Death of a Soldier* is the eleventh.

The essence of this poem is the inevitability of death, but not the death that comes with old age, for the person dying here is a 'soldier'. So here, the inevitability of death is within the context of war. Stevens likens this to the season of autumn which is a common metaphor in First World War literature and falling, dying leaves can often be seen as the epitome of death in war. Men, however, are not immortal; there can be no comparisons with Jesus, who rose from the dead, because man is not a 'three-days personage'. For man, death is the final end, resulting in no 'memorial', or remembrance, because he – or at least the manner of his death - will all too soon be forgotten.

In the final verse, Stevens implies that even when the wind stops blowing and the leaves – or men – stop falling, the clouds will still continue to cross the sky in whichever direction they choose. In a way, this makes no sense, as without the wind, the clouds would become stationary. However, Stevens's point here seems to be that nature has a will of its own, independent of mankind, which will pursue its own direction, regardless of what mankind does

GUILLAUME APOLLINAIRE

Apollinaire was an influential figure in early twentieth century literature and art, as well as a participant in the conflict.

BIOGRAPHICAL DETAILS

Born in Rome on August 26th 1880, Apollinaire was a larger-than-life character, whose real name was Wilhelm Albert Vladimir Apollinaris Kostrowitzky. His mother was Polish but the identity of his father remains a mystery. He was bought up in Paris and the South of France and later adopted the name by which he is now known. He found work at a Parisian bank, but his main interest lay in the arts and he soon found himself in the company of artists such as Pablo Picasso, Marc Chagall and Eric Satie. In addition, as an art critic, he is credited with creating the word 'Surrealism' as representative of the early 20th Century art movement, whereby reality is distorted, such as the works of Salvador Dali or René Magritte. In 1911, Apollinaire was arrested and questioned regarding the theft of Leonardo da Vinci's Mona Lisa, although he was released a week later, without charge. When the First World War began, Apollinaire enlisted in the French infantry and served on the Western Front. He was badly wounded in 1916 and did not serve in the army again. Apollinaire died on 9th November 1918 of the Spanish influenza which was, at that time, sweeping across Europe.

CALLIGRAM, 15 MAY 1915

A book entitled *Calligrammes* by Apollinaire was published in late 1918, shortly after his death and he is credited for the creation of this form of visual poetry, in which the words are made into shapes which represent their meaning. In this instance, there are two rhyming couplets, which set the scene, in which the poet describes his own position, 'under a willow tree', with shells whining overhead, beneath a blue-black sky. This description, although probably quite literal, also serves to introduce the somewhat exotic, even romantic, depiction of an 'evening star' which follows.

The image - and words - beneath the star represent a cannon and this final section personifies the shells and they, like the stars, are made to seem like a beautiful woman. In both language, shape and form, there are elements of the surreal in this poem, which could easily be fitted with Apollinaire's background and perceptions.

BENJAMIN PERET

Although young at the outbreak of war, Péret served in the French army and went on to become an influential and revolutionary influence in the surrealist movement.

BIOGRAPHICAL DETAILS

Péret was born on July 4th 1899 in the Western French town of Rezé. Throughout his life his had a strongly rebellious streak and it is believed that he enlisted at the beginning of the First World War - in spite of his youth - in order to avoid being arrested. He served for the duration of the conflict and, afterwards, became involved in the new Surrealist movement. Later in the 1920s, he joined the Communist Party, before leaving France for Brazil with his wife, the singer, Elsie Houston. He later returned to Europe and fought in the Spanish Civil War. Always politically active - if not volatile - Péret's attitude was steadfastly revolutionary and remained so until his death, in Paris on September 18th 1959.

LITTLE SONG OF THE MAIMED

Benjamin Péret's surrealist background is easily visible in this somewhat alarming poem. With no rhyme or regular form, the poem makes for difficult reading in every sense. It is, essentially, a diatribe against the treatment and conditions meted out to maimed soldiers. Verdun was the site of a battle which lasted through most of 1916, in which the German intention was to cripple the French army. Conditions for both sides were diabolical and by its termination, there were nearly one million casualties. For many French people, the cost of this battle, despite the town's historical and strategic significance, was too great. Péret's message here appears to be an angry outburst at the authorities, who presumably believed that the award of a Croix de Guerre would in some way compensate for the loss of a leg. His suggestion that the rats ate his leg could be taken literally in that if a limb were blown off, it would not be unusual for rats to devour the remains. Alternatively - and more probably - Péret might be referring to the enemy, metaphorically, as having taken his leg and he, in return, consuming (or killing) them.

W. B. YEATS

As a major poetic force in Irish literature, Yeats has a deserved place in many anthologies: whether that place should be amongst the poets of the First World War is another matter. Stallworthy's choice of these poems goes to show that there were other political forces at work during the First World War - most notably the ongoing arguments over Home Rule in Ireland - and that these had a great bearing on the opinions of many Irish people towards the conflict and their own country's involvement.

BIOGRAPHICAL DETAILS

William Butler Yeats was born on June 13th 1865 in County Dublin, Ireland. His father, John was a lawyer-turned-artist, while his mother, Susan, came from a wealthy family in County Sligo. Yeats attended schools in London and Dublin and began writing at an early age. In addition he developed a lifelong interest in spiritualism and the occult. As both he and his poetry matured, he met many other literary figures of the day, including Katharine Tynan, Oscar Wilde and George Bernard Shaw. In 1916, at the age of fifty-one, he married Georgie Hyde-Lees, who was his junior by twenty-seven years. Despite the age-gap and Yeat's' infidelities, theirs was considered a successful marriage, which resulted in the births of two children. In 1923, Yeats was awarded the Nobel Prize for Literature and during that decade he was twice commissioned to serve on the newly formed Irish Senate. In 1936, he edited the Oxford Book of Modern Verse, which has become famous - or infamous - for the editor's exclusion of any poetry by Wilfred Owen. Yeats died in 1939 in Menton in the South of France and, although he was initially buried there, at the end of the Second World War, his body was moved to County Sligo.

ON BEING ASKED FOR A WAR POEM

Possibly written as early as 1915, this short poem provides a criticism of the genre of war poetry as a whole, which even at that stage of the conflict, was prolific. It is clear to see from these few short lines that Yeats believed that there was no place for poetry within the politics of the day - however much one might disagree with the politicians. While others may have sought to use their poetic voice to influence the statesmen, Yeats seems to have believed that this course was ineffectual and, therefore, unworthy of a true poet. Instead, he avers that a man should be content with entertaining young girls and old men, and not interfere with other matters, in which he can have no real control.

Upon reading this piece, it becomes easier to see why Yeats chose to exclude the works of Wilfred Owen from his edition of the Oxford Book of Modern Verse, published in 1936. However, this argument of non-intervention in political issues fails utterly when one reads two other poems, written by Yeats in 1916. Easter 1916 and Sixteen Dead Men are both written about the Easter Rising in Dublin which took place in April 1916. In this poems, it would seem that Yeats' political reticence has been cast aside, in favour of his 'poet's mouth'.

Yeats' reasons for effectively declining to write a conventional 'Great' war poem (although one could argue that he actually acceded, by writing this piece), may have had more to do with his own feelings about Ireland's involvement in what many perceived to be an English conflict, than his own beliefs on poetry and politics. One could also contend that he might have hoped to silence other poets, of whose war poetry, he seems to have harboured a fairly low opinion.

EASTER 1916

Written in September 1916, this poem describes the poet's reaction to the Easter Rising which had taken place in Dublin in April of that year. In an earlier piece entitled September 1913, Yeats had written about the Dublin Lockout, and some suppose that this piece is a continuation of his earlier commentary on the changes and upheavals in early 20th Century Ireland.

Easter 1916 opens with Yeats describing his own occasional meetings with some of the revolutionaries. In his verse, he derides these other men, seeming to believe himself above them and even contemplating the jokes which he may later make at their expense. He and his own friends, he asserts, merely live among such people, rather than really sharing in their existences and beliefs. Much of this somewhat superior attitude may derive from Yeats' comparatively aristocratic upbringing - his father having been a lawyer and portrait painter, while his mother came from a wealthy mill-owning family. The first verse ends, however, with a 'change' as Yeats acknowledges that from these somehow 'inferior' beings a 'terrible beauty' has been created.

The second verse goes on to describe some unnamed individuals and their roles prior to the uprising. One of these - the 'man who kept a school' - is probably Patrick Pearse, another may be identified as John MacBride, who had married Maud Gonne in 1903. Gonne had been the great love of Yeats' life and, although she had not returned his feelings, his affection for her remained constant for many years. His description of MacBride as a 'drunken... lout', guilty of a 'most bitter wrong' may allude to MacBride's ill-treatment of his wife, which had angered and distressed Yeats at the time. Even MacBride, however, seems to be forgiven for his past sins, as he has 'resigned' his former ways to partake in the revolution. Again, therefore, this verse ends on a note of 'change'.

In the third verse there is a different tone. Gone is the first-person narrative, to be replaced by a description of the changes which take place in nature. Yeats alludes throughout to 'stone', which is surely the most unchanging of all natural elements, and this may reflect the stony determination of the revolutionaries, to achieve their aims, regardless of the personal consequences. Thus, the 'stone' seems to be in the 'midst' of everything - both natural and human.

The fourth verse reverts back to a narrative form and opens with a reference to the fact that too much suffering may harden the heart, which is presumably Yeats' interpretation of the revolutionaries' attitudes. He then goes on to wonder how many must die and be mourned before it will be deemed 'enough', and whether these deaths have been 'needless'. Yeats' allusion to England keeping 'faith' is a reference to the Nationalist's belief that if they supported Britain during the First World War, Home Rule would be granted at the end of the conflict. As such, Yeats seems to be questioning here, whether the revolutionaries should have waited to see if this would be the case, before entering into a costly internal conflict. He goes on to commemorate some of the leaders of the revolution by name, including John MacBride. He asserts that the memory of them, as well as of the nationalist movement - represented by the colour green - would be 'changed' forever by the actions of the Easter Rising.

It is really quite difficult to deduce from this poem, whether Yeats supported the revolutionaries, or not. He certainly seems to have been commemorating their loss and the date of the conflict itself has some bearing on the poem. It began on 24th April 1916. This poem has four verses (the fourth month), two of which have twenty-four lines and two of which have sixteen. However, his message is still unclear. One may presume that, while he might have supported their aims, he did not advocate the means which they had chosen to employ. As a result of the fighting between the revolutionaries and the British Army, over 500 people were killed and 2500 wounded, most of whom were civilians. The abiding themes throughout this poem are of 'change' which leaves in its wake a 'terrible beauty'. Perhaps the horrific human cost was deemed by Yeats to be too great a price to pay for the 'beauty' of freedom and independence.

SIXTEEN DEAD MEN

Sixteen Dead Men, like *Easter 1916*, is a poem based around the events of the Easter Rising in April 1916. The main ring-leaders amongst the Revolutionaries, were executed in May 1916 and, although there is some confusion as to whether there were fifteen or sixteen of them, this poem is undoubtedly about their plight.

The opening of this poem refers to the fact that, prior to the executions, the revolution had not been popular among the general population, mainly due to the high number of civilian casualties. Yeats refers to the sixteen men as continuing to 'loiter' among the living, stirring up trouble, as though they are still alive, when in fact he is really alluding to their memory, which fuelled the flames of the nationalist movement.

The second verse refers to the nationalists who urged their fellow Irishmen to support the British in the First World War and bide their time until Germany was defeated and Home Rule granted. However, Yeats argues that these reasonings carry little weight now that Pearse (Patrick Pearse, one of the main ring-leaders) and MacDonagh (Thomas MacDonagh - another leader of the revolutionaries) are both dead.

Yeats finally goes on to surmise that the revolutionaries will no longer listen to their earthly comrades, being as they will have found new friends with whom to converse. 'Lord Edward' [FitzGerald] and [Theobald] 'Wolfe Tone' were Irish Revolutionaries from an earlier time. Both men had played actives roles in the Irish Rebellion of 1798 and died as a result of their participation, in both cases, at the hands of their British enemies. Yeats assumes that the newer revolutionaries will find more in common with their long-dead counterparts than with the living, who talk of 'give and take'.

In this poem, Yeats seems to show more support, sympathy and understanding for the revolutionaries than in Easter 1916, although by the time he write the latter poem, the leaders mentioned here had been dead for five months. This may demonstrate Yeats' own confusion as to his feelings and reactions towards the rebellion and its leaders and this poem certainly seems less clouded by his own personal animosity towards John MacBride, who is not mentioned here.

AN IRISH AIRMAN FORESEES HIS DEATH

This is probably Yeats' best known poem, within this genre and is often his only inclusion within anthologies of First World War poetry. Despite his pre-occupation with the troubles in Ireland, Yeats did feel some of the effects of the European conflict. His particular friend and co-founder of the Irish Literary Theatre, Lady Augusta Gregory, lost her only child, Major Robert Gregory, in January 1918 and this poem is written in his memory.

The poem begins with the pilot's definite assumption that he is going to die and goes on to point out that he is not fighting because of any particular feelings of either love or hated towards friends or enemies. As narrator of this young man's short life, Yeats refers to Gregory's home with fondness, but also with the certainty that no single death can really affect his countrymen. He claims that he did not choose to fight because he was forced to, nor out of loyalty to his country, or because it was the popular thing to do. Instead, it would seem that Gregory chose to fight out of the sheer 'delight' of flying.

When required to 'balance' or weigh the unlived portion of his life and the years which have gone before, Gregory - at least according to Yeats - seems to have believed that it was all a 'waste', when compared with his chosen manner of death.

The language and tone here begin in a fairly positive theme and this continues until the final four lines, when the poem becomes more thoughtful and philosophical. This is not a glorification of war or death, but an expression of the joy which this particular young man found in flying. Yeats may, however, have had a secondary motive in writing this piece. Lady Gregory had already lost her husband in 1890 and Major John Gregory was her only child. Yeats may have felt that to write about him dying thus - contented and fulfilled - might provide his dear friend with a little solace in her mourning.

REPRISALS

Like *An Irish Airman Foresees His Death*, *Reprisals* was written about - or in this case, to - Major John Gregory, the only child of Yeats' friend Lady Augusta Gregory, who was killed in action in January 1918.

Reprisals opens with the commentary that Gregory, as its subject, was something of a hero, having shot down 'nineteen' enemy planes - at least according to Yeats. As such, the poet asserts, his death might be referred to as 'good' - namely a death in which the victim has at least achieved something noteworthy prior to his demise. However, this idea is tempered by the poets assertion that neither the living nor the dead can really refer to their lives, or their deaths in a positive way anymore.

Yeats then refers to a conversation in which Gregory seems to have alluded to the final year of his life as 'exciting'. He then, however, seems to urge the young man to remember that, while he may have joyous memories of battle, not everyone has the advantage of such a positive outlook and that if he could rise from his grave in Italy and return to his native Kiltartan Cross, he might find some there who were beginning to doubt the 'cause' for which he had been fighting.

The following reference to the soldiers at home, 'murdering' Gregory's tenants may relate to the Black and Tan forces who served under the Royal Irish Constabulary in the early 1920s. These men were often targeted by the IRA and deaths frequently resulted in 'reprisals' against civilians. These revenge attacks were often brutal and unpredictable. The Gregory family owned land in County Galway and it is to the local inhabitants of this area that Yeats is referring. Many towns, villages and farms were burned-out by the Black and Tans, thus leaving the 'new-married women' with nowhere to live and nurse their young babies, yet the law and parliament remained impotent. (The Black and Tans were disbanded in 1922).

The poem closes with a change in tone. Gregory is no longer seen as the heroic young fighter-pilot, but rather as just another of the 'cheated dead'. Here it is as though Yeats is angry with Gregory for having put his own desires and feelings before those of his tenants and countrymen. While Gregory may now rest among the dead, others are left to fight and die, defending his country. The notion that he and others have been 'cheated' in death may refer to the fact that despite the British promises of Home Rule in return for Irishmen fighting in the First World War, this was slow in coming and the resultant occupation and violence seemed a poor reward for their loyalty.

Yeats' tone and language in this poem are unmistakably angry and reflect the
idea that, although he and many others were willing to perceive Germany as the
enemy during the Great War, they did so with one aim in mind - to gain their
freedom and independence from British rule. The Irish soldiers who returned
from the conflict found, almost universally, that they were treated with disdain
by their countrymen for having wasted their time fighting alongside the British.
It would seem from this poem that those who died were held in equal contempt,
for having wasted their deaths.

SIEGFRIED SASSOON

One of the best known and, justifiably, most often-read of the war poets, Sassoon is a man of difficult character, whom one cannot help but admire in spite of - or maybe because of - his many faults. He was a man who made the First World War his own personal conflict, for the very simple reason that the First World War made him the man he was. He took his feelings of guilt and anger to the grave, leaving us with a wealth of poetry, which unlike the works of any other poet in this genre, truly evoke the impact which the war had on the men who fought it.

BIOGRAPHICAL DETAILS

Born on September 8th 1886 at Matfield in Kent, Siegfried Loraine Sassoon was the second of the three sons of Alfred and Theresa. Alfred Sassoon came from a family of wealthy Jewish bankers, but had been disowned by his family upon his marriage to Theresa, who did not share his faith. When Siegfried was five years old, his parents separated and his father died four years later. Following his education at Marlborough and Clare College, Cambridge, Sassoon returned to Kent and took up the life of a country squire. He also began writing poetry and, in March 1914 he moved to London in order to mingle better within the literary circles of the capital. Immediate war was declared, Sassoon, a keen horseman, enlisted as a Trooper in the Sussex Yeomanry. However, a bad fall left him with a broken arm and, once healed, he decided to transfer into the Royal Welch Fusiliers. He sailed for France in November 1915, where met Robert Graves, with whom he became great friends. In June 1916, he was awarded the Military Cross for retrieving wounded men from No Man's Land. HIs recklessness throughout this time earned him the nickname of 'Mad Jack'. In April 1917,

Sassoon was wounded in the shoulder and sent back to England. It was while recuperating from this wound that he, under the influence of pacifists such as Bertrand Russell, wrote his famous Declaration against the war. The result of the publication of this document was that Sassoon was sent to Craiglockhart Military Hospital in Edinburgh, where he famously met fellow poet, Wilfred Owen. Eventually Sassoon was overwhelmed by his feelings of guilt and decided that he must return to active duty. He returned to France - via Palestine - and by July 1918, he was back on the Western Front. It was here that he was shot in the head - an injury which ended his participation in the conflict. After the war, Sassoon found it difficult to settle and, after several unsatisfactory homosexual affairs, he married Hester Gatty in December 1933. Their only child, George, was born three years later. Eventually, Sassoon and Hester separated and he lived on alone at Heytesbury House in Wiltshire. In 1957, Sassoon was received into the Roman Catholic Church. He died on September 1st 1967 and is buried at St Andrew's Church in Mells, Somerset.

THEY

This poem was, according to *Seigfried Sassoon: The War Poems* (edited by Rupert Hart-Davis), written on October 31st 1916. At that time Sassoon was in England, recovering from Trench Fever - a relatively serious, but common illness. He spent some of his leave staying in London, at the home of Robbie Ross, an art critic and - most famously - loyal friend to Oscar Wilde. Max Egremont, Sassoon's most recent biographer, states that on this particular evening, Ross, who was angry about the jingoism that persisted in the country, read aloud some extracts from a sermon by the Bishop of London, in which he claimed that the fighting soldiers would have their souls cleansed by their participation in the war. Unable to sleep, this sermon milled around in Sassoon's head and during the night, he got up and wrote down this poem.

Like many of his poems, this is quite simple and opens with a direct speech in which the reader is subliminally encouraged to imagine a cassocked Bishop, standing in his pulpit, preaching to the congregation before him. We are made to believe that the Bishop has a full knowledge and understanding of the war, with his righteous moralising. He tells us that the soldiers will, of course, be different when they return from the war (note: 'when', not 'if'), because they will have done their duty, defended their country and defeated the enemy. There is an underlying arrogance in this statement, however, in that the Bishop does not doubt victory, or that the men will return. These words, when read now, seem to demonstrate a complete lack of understanding on the Bishop's part, but at the time of its composition, there were many who continued to believe in this type of message. In the poem, that is where the satire comes in. Sassoon repeats these platitudes, quite openly and without a hint of irony, for the sole purpose of dismantling them more effectively in the second verse.

When the speech changes, at the beginning of the second stanza, we are now presented with the reality of the war. The more colloquial language demonstrates that the 'boys' are ranking soldiers, rather than officers and the use of this tone adds, intentionally, to the realism of the piece. The list of unappealing consequences of serving in the war is intended to shock and is assisted by the use of real names, which personalises the whole poem. In this way, Sassoon presumably hoped that, since most people would probably know a soldier named either 'George', 'Bill', 'Jim' or 'Bert', they might pay more attention to his message, rather than the Bishop's. He rounds off the poem with one of his customary knock-out lines, in which he suggests a very unsympathetic response from the Bishop. In this way, he is almost defying the public to support the church - suggesting that if all the horrors of war are known to them, surely the church should be able to come up with a more satisfactory response.

They, although one of Sassoon's earliest satires, remains one of his best. At the time, although some found it a difficult read, it was remarkable well received. Sassoon believed that the publication of this piece marked the first time that the word 'syphilitic' had appeared in a poem. In fact, the *Cambridge Magazine*, in their publication of the poem, on January 20th 1917, removed the offending word. Sassoon's intention here - as in much of his poetry - was to shock the public out of its complacency and into an acceptance of the harsh reality of war. He achieves this by his use of simple rhyme patterns and verse forms, together with everyday, uncomplicated language and, of course, his trademark, cutting irony.

THE HERO

This poem was written in August 1916. The title is, of course, ironic, in that Jack is not the perceived idea of a hero in the conventional and accepted sense of the time. The first verse deals with the mother's pride when she is told of the heroic nature of her son's death. Despite her obvious grief, she receives great comfort from the knowledge that he died a hero.

In the second stanza, this sentiment is contrasted with the officer's relief at having done his duty, and told the woman of her son's death. He is glad, however, to be able to leave the grieving woman behind.

The third verse reveals the truth: Jack had not died a hero's death. Instead, he had panicked and tried to get himself sent home. The image portrayed of Jack here is of a man who found the war and constant threat of death impossible to cope with and had finally died a needless, unremarkable death.

The language of the final stanza is much more realistic and harsh than the first two, as we learn that Jack was blown to pieces. The description of Jack's fear, and his brutal death, leave nothing to the imagination and this helps to emphasise the differences between the gentle sanctity of the family home and the horrors of the trenches.

The mother's reaction provides the officer with some justification for his falsehood, although his insecurity in his chosen standpoint is obvious from the description of his demeanour. It could be argued that the Brother Officer has, like Jack, shown a cowardly side to his nature - choosing not to tell the old lady the truth and therefore forcing her to live a lie, provides him with an easier solution than being honest with her, and having to deal with the consequences of her shame as well as her grief.

The poem appears, on the surface at least, to sympathise with the mother; but one should always remember Sassoon's capacity for satire. He found the false pride of civilians distasteful; their lack of understanding of the realities faced by the soldiers was a constant thorn in his side. He, therefore, sympathises with her as much for her delusion as for her loss.

The fact that the officer lies not only protects the mother, but also Jack's memory, so it could be argued that Sassoon sympathises, at least in part, with Jack. The representation of Jack seems harsh and unforgiving, but this could, again, be Sassoon's use of irony. Jack's actions should not make him any less worthy of remembrance than those who went blindly into battle, displaying little or no fear. In the end Sassoon points out that his death has gone unnoticed, by everyone except his mother. This would be the accepted reaction of the public to the death of the coward but Sassoon seems to be asking - why should it only be his mother who grieves for him? Is he any less deserving of their thoughts, just because he seems to have lost his nerve? He could also be suggesting that those at home have no right to judge the conduct of a soldier at the front, given their meagre understanding of conditions there.

At the same time as he wrote *The Hero*, Sassoon also penned *The One-Legged Man*, which tells of a soldier's relief at being out of the war. He describes how, in coming home, this young man now has the opportunity to live a full life, admire the countryside, find a wife and settle down. In the final line, we learn of the sacrifice which the man has had to make for this peace of mind - he has had a leg amputated. Sassoon, at this time, was vehemently opposed to the glorification of the war and the idea of the "supreme sacrifice", whether it be through death or permanent disfigurement.

It is also possible to compare Sassoon's character, Jack, with Hibbert in *Journey's End* by R. C. Sherriff. Like Jack, Hibbert tries to get sent home and panics at the prospect of being made to continue to fight. Stanhope's reaction as the senior officer is initially harsh, but once he has got Hibbert to see that there is no way out, other than court martial, and death, he empathises with him and lets him know these feelings of fear and foreboding are common - in fact he suffers from them himself. Although he does not like Hibbert as a person, Stanhope's understanding, like Sassoon's demonstrates that many officers could sympathise with those soldiers who found the horrors of war impossible to tolerate.

THE REAR-GUARD

On April 16th 1917, Sassoon received a bullet wound to his shoulder. A few days earlier, he and his Company Commander, Major Kirkby were told to report to Battalion Headquarters to receive order for the attack in which Sassoon was to be wounded. This meant a journey through the underground tunnels of the well-fortified Hindenburg line. While searching through the dark tunnels, Kirkby had mistaken a dead German for a sleeping soldier and had attempted to rouse him in order to ask for directions. Once Sassoon had been wounded and sent back down the line he was evacuated back to England and sent to Denmark Hill Hospital in London, where he wrote The Rear-Guard. The poem is written in the third person, suggesting that Sassoon is describing this event, factually, as it happened to someone else. In Sassoon's autobiography, Siegfried's Journey, he makes no mention of this specific event, although he does in his diaries as well as giving a vivid description of the tunnels themselves. He also gives a full account of this episode in his fictionalised autobiography, Memoirs of an Infantry Officer. In this description, he is moving along the tunnel by himself. There is no mention of Major Kirkby (or Leake, as his character is known in this book). It is Sassoon (Sherston) who touches the dead body and curses its lack of response, before realising that the man at his feet is dead. This fictionalised account, written more than a decade after the event, borrows much of the poem's atmosphere and language.

The poem opens with a vivid description of someone attempting to find their way along a dark tunnel. These three lines achieve their succinct realism by the use of metaphor and personification, so that the reader immediately knows that this is a dark, unpleasant place, presumably with a rank smell and littered with debris, since the man is forced to grope his way slowly and requires a 'torch' in order to see. In addition, Sassoon gives these lines a more haunting feel by his description of the torch as 'prying'.

In the second verse, Sassoon goes into more detail regarding the content of the tunnel. He describes a list of worthless waste, which will become more significant to the reader in the next verse, when we discover that there are also dead bodies present, showing how insignificant these have become. There is also a sense of remoteness created in this stanza as the man is the tunnel is clearly cut off from the battle above him, but equally he does not seem to belong in the tunnel either. Sassoon's description of 'the rosy gloom of battle' serves several purposes. Firstly it provides a good contrast with the 'prying torch' of the first verse, but it also reminds the reader that other events are taking place on the surface. The fact that these are described as 'rosy' is ironic, since a battle would not normally be referred to in this way. However, this simply reinforces the isolation and haunting atmosphere of the tunnel.

The third verse brings us to the main point of this narrative. Sassoon describes the soldier tripping over a body - which he assumes is sleeping - on the floor. He tries to rouse the corpse, ordering the dead man to guide him to headquarters. It is only after he has kicked the dead man and still received no response, that he shines his torch upon the dead man's face. Although this event did not actually happen to Sassoon, his description here is life-like and vivid. Nowhere in any of the prose accounts does it state that Major Kirkby kicked the corpse, which he had mistaken for a sleeping soldier, but Sassoon's accounts of that time reveal that he, unlike Kirkby, was exhausted, having not slept for several days. It is possible, therefore, that he is imposing his own imagined reaction to being in this situation. His use of the phrase ' "God blast your neck!" ' is interesting as, although he does not mention it here, his prose accounts state that the dead man had been wounded in the neck. Once his torch light has established the man's death, the descriptions become even more graphic, which helps the reader to imagine this horrific scene.

In the final verse, the soldier moves on, still struggling to find his way. Eventually he comes upon a stairway, at the top of which he daylight - or at least twilight. Even as he prepares to mount the steps, however, the light pouring into the dark tunnel reminds him that some of the 'creatures' there are still alive. Finally, he climbs the steps into the welcome 'air' on the surface. Sassoon's description of the light as 'dawn's ghost' helps us to place this poem to a more particular time of day. Dawn would be the customary time for a battle to commence, but here the poet refers to the 'ghost' of dawn, suggesting that this is the time of day which is left behind when the dawn has died - namely daytime. However, by the end of this verse, he is even more precise, as he tells us that it is now 'twilight' - a time of day often used by poets to suggest death, or finality, which in this instance, Sassoon turns around to suggest release and freedom. The realisation that there are men in the tunnels who are still alive, is not that surprising, as these underground areas were often used as headquarters, as well as giving the men somewhere to sleep, cook and eat. This was especially true of the very well constructed German tunnels, of which the ones on the Hindenburg line were a fine example.

There were two drafts of this poem, the first of which was written in Sassoon's diary. Although he rewrote the final poem only hours after completing the first draft, he made several changes, most of which served to tone down the horrors of the underground scene and the dead body. He also added the final line, which is absent in the first draft, but which helps to round off the poem. In addition, he makes no mention in either draft of the fact that the body which Major Kirkby disturbed was actually that of a German soldier, although there is a clue in the title of the poem, in that the Germans had abandoned these tunnels, leaving their dead behind as a macabre 'rear-guard'. One could argue, perhaps, that Sassoon omitted this fact in order to make his poem more acceptable, or even popular. However, such platitudes are not really in Sassoon's style and it is much more likely that, to him, the nationality of the soldier did not matter. The point was that, regardless of who he was, or where he was from, this man had been abandoned and forgotten - a permanent inhabitant of 'hell'.

THE GENERAL

Like most of Sassoon's poetry, *The General* has its foundations in reality. In her biography of the poet, Jean Moorcroft Wilson states that, in this instance, the reality may have occurred in April 1917 when Sassoon was serving with the 2nd Battalion of the Royal Welch Fusiliers. During the course of a march up to the front lines at Arras, the men passed their Corps Commander. Sassoon had a low opinion of incompetent senior officers and that is the message reflected here. The poem was written later in the same month, after Sassoon had been wounded in the shoulder.

The opening of the poem, as direct speech, immediately draws the reader into the scene and we can easily imagine the General smiling benevolently as the troops pass him by. In fact, one of the men even comments to his friend upon how 'cheery' the General is. However, Sassoon immediately curtails this jollity, by pointing out that most of the soldiers have since died, including both 'Harry' and 'Jack'.

Sassoon's language and personalisation of the characters in this poem is uncompromising and intended to shock the reader. In this way, he makes his opinion of the General and his staff officers very clear. The language, both in direct speech and narrative, is colloquial, allowing the reader to more easily and readily see the perspective of the men, rather than the General. Sassoon also manages to shock the reader by using a simple rhyming pattern, which seems to end neatly at the end of line six, but to which he then adds a jarring seventh line, which disturbs the metre of the poem.

Many poets held the same, or similar, views to those which Sassoon demonstrates here and their poems on this subject make for interesting comparisons. These include Alan P Herbert's *After the Battle*, in which he describes the mens' feelings upon receiving somewhat over-zealous and insensitive congratulations from a General at the end of a costly battle. In this instance the General shows no understanding of the emotional toll which the battle has taken on the men: an attitude which angers Herbert. In fact, he goes a stage further in another poem, which is untitled, but which is attributed to him by Lyn MacDonald in her book *Somme*. In this poem, Herbert goes to the extent of naming the General (Major General C D Shute), and deriding him for criticising the poor state of hygiene in the trenches. This is a humorous verse, but one suspects that behind it lurks a serious message.

GLORY OF WOMEN

This poem was written some time between July and November 1917, while Sassoon was a Craiglockhart Military Hospital in Edinburgh. In July of that year, Sassoon had written his Declaration against the continuation of the war, in the hope of a court-martial, which he anticipated would be publicly humiliating for the authorities. Instead of taking this action, he was ordered to report to a medical board, which decided that he must be suffering from shell-shock and dispatched him to the care of Dr W. H. R. Rivers at Craiglockhart.

Although Sassoon liked this poem himself, it is not generally considered to represent the poet at his best. He makes great use of irony, even to the extent that the poem takes the form of a sonnet - a type of poem which is predominantly reserved for verses about love. The title is an irony in itself, since the poem has nothing to do with the 'glory' of women - in fact it is quite the opposite and without the irony, would surely have to be entitled 'Shame of Women' instead.

The reader could assume that Sassoon is speaking from personal experience here - although he does make rather a lot of sweeping generalisations - but one should also bear in mind that Sassoon found women habitually difficult to get on with. He had been in England for several months by the time he went to Craiglockhart and had become increasingly angered by the continued jingoism which he experienced. These two aspects of his life at that time, essentially, made women an easy and obvious target.

The first eleven lines of the sonnet are concerned with British women, presumably the wives, lovers or girlfriends of serving soldiers. Sassoon asserts that these women seem to delight in the war, enjoying the heroism of the men and believing firmly in their bravery. The women refuse to acknowledge the unpalatable side of war, so wounds must be in a 'mentionable place' and there is no such thing as cowardice - or even fear - no matter how horrific the war might become. Although Sassoon mentions death as a possible outcome, he enhances his low opinion of female callousness, by stating that the only effect this will have is that they will 'mourn' the loss, suggesting that other than that, they will feel nothing and that once their period of mourning is over, they will return to normal.

Lines ten and eleven bring a change of tone, however, as Sassoon's language become much harsher when he is describing the war, rather than the womens' misguided perceptions. In the final three lines, the poet turns everything around and addresses himself to a 'German mother' who sits by a fire, making socks for her son who, unbeknown to her, is already dead. These three lines force the reader to recall the poet's earlier statement that the young British women have been making shells - which have, presumably, been used to kill German soldiers - just like the woman's son. In this way, Sassoon may be trying to get women to see that they could be said to be partly responsible for that mother's loss. He shows much more sympathy towards the German mother than he does for the British women. This may be because the mother does not seem to be seeking any 'glory' for her son - or herself - or it might be an allusion to the fact that Sassoon, in common with many other soldiers, did not hold the German soldiers personally responsible for the war - that was a blame which he levelled firmly at the door of politicians and jingoistic civilians.

EVERYONE SANG

This poem was written in April 1919, shortly after Sassoon had taken up the position of Literary Editor of the Daily Herald, which was at that time, the only daily Socialist newspaper in Britain. (It would go on to become The Sun on 15th September 1964). Sassoon had taken up this position for several reasons: firstly financial; secondly, he wanted a fresh start, having just left the army; thirdly, the politics of the newspaper suited him at the time and, finally, he anticipated making the literary page the finest in Fleet Street.

Everyone Sang is often included in anthologies of First World War poetry and, there is nothing wrong with this, provided that the poem is properly interpreted. Sasson did not write this as a 'war' poem, but as a 'peace celebration'. According to his autobiography, *Siegfried's Journey*, the poem was written one evening, when Sassoon had been feeling lethargic and 'depressed'. He found that the words came into his head 'from nowhere' and he wrote the poem down quickly before going to bed. The next morning, he decided that he liked what he had written and sent copies to some of his literary friends for their opinion. It met with almost universal approval - the only noted critic at the time being Robert Graves, who commented acidly that everyone 'did not include me'.

The problem with this poem lies in the fact that many analysts and editors assume that Sassoon is celebrating the end of the war. This is not really the case, as in *Siegfried's Journey* he says that the 'singing' to which he refers in the poem is the 'Social Revolution' which he hoped and believed would come about. Some others, possibly including Graves, misinterpreted the message behind the poem and it quickly became categorised as relating to the armistice celebrations. Sassoon's initial pleasure at the composition and its popularity, waned over the years, probably due to these misunderstandings and the constant requirement of explaining what he had really meant.

The poem opens with the suggestion that 'Everyone' has suddenly begun to sing. Bearing in mind that this poem is about social revolution, we may assume that this is a reference to a raised political awareness and voice, among the working classes. Sassoon goes on to tell us that the singing - or striving for social equality - offers 'freedom' to those who have previously been confined. This freedom will allow them to rise about their current situation and seek a better life for themselves. In his reference to the people as 'birds' who 'wing wildly' he draws the reader's attention to this idea of freedom, by the use of alliteration. The orchard is 'white' because there are blossoms on the trees, which tells us that it is spring - a common poetic device to signify a new beginning.

In the second verse, the singing comes to more of a crescendo, with the implication that there has been some unspoken agreement that 'everyone' is hoping for the same outcome in their future. Just the anticipation of this new life and freedom is enough to make the poet tearful. He is even able to forget the 'horror', which is his only real reference to the war. Sassoon saw this new beginning - which for him started with his job at the Daily Herald - as an opportunity to put the hell and horrors of the war behind him and that is what is reflected here.

Suddenly, at the end of the poem, 'everyone' is transformed into a 'bird', which is poetically representative of freedom. The fact that the 'song was wordless' may be an implication that the message of hope is so implicit that no words of explanation should be required. His suggestion that 'the singing will never be done' is probably a reference to the fact that, having found their voice, the people will have gained a new strength and will never again be the 'prisoned birds' of the first verse.

It seems a shame that, through the misinterpretations of others, Sassoon's pleasure in this poem waned. In fact, a recording of it, made by the poet in later life, is so monotone that he really sounds rather fed-up with the idea of having to recite it, although this may, at least in part, be due to the fact that he disliked giving recitals anyway. It would seem that even when he did try to leave the war behind and look forward to a brighter future, there was always going to be something to drag him back to Hell.

EDWARD THOMAS

Unusually, Edward Thomas had written all of his poems before he went to fight in France. This gives his poetry a more lyrical, pastoral air than many of the other soldier-poets.

BIOGRAPHICAL DETAILS

Edward Thomas was born in London on March 3rd 1878 and grew up there. However, as his parents were originally from Wales, the family spent many holidays there and this was how Thomas developed his love of the countryside, which is so evident in his poetry. He attended various schools but at the age of fifteen was enrolled at St Paul's in Hammersmith. While he was there he met his future wife Helen Noble, who was the daughter of one of his mentors. In 1898, he began his degree at Lincoln College, Oxford, although he returned to visit Helen during the holidays. Helen became pregnant and the couple were quickly married in June 1899. Their son Merfyn was born seven months later, followed by a daughter, Bronwen in 1902 and finally Myfanwy in 1910. When Thomas graduated in 1901, he took the unusual step to become a full-time writer, which resulted in the family living in a precarious financial position, especially as he also struggled with ill-health and depression. In 1912 Thomas met Eleanor Farjeon, who fell in love with him, but kept this a secret, knowing that he was really devoted to Helen and remained instead a close friend to the whole family. The following year, Thomas also began a friendship with the American poet Robert Frost, who was living in England at the time, and contemplated returning to America with Frost shortly after the First World War began. Unsure whether or not to enlist, Thomas wrestled with his conscience for many months before eventually deciding to join up in July 1915. He embarked for France on January

29th 1917, having already completed all 144 of his poems. He was killed in a shell-blast on Easter Monday - April 9th - 1917 and is buried at Agny Military Cemetery in the Pas de Calais.

IN MEMORIAM (EASTER 1915)

This poem was written on April 6th 1915, just a few months before Edward Thomas decided to enlist in the Artist's Rifles, which he did in July, at the age of 37. Thomas had spent months deliberating over what he should do: he had a wife and three young children, who were dependent upon him; but he also felt a sense of duty and responsibility towards his country. Eventually, he decided to enlist, believing that he was defending the very essence of England and Englishness - not just a way of life, but the actual soil of the nation.

In Memoriam (Easter 1915) reflects Thomas's perception of the ordinary things that either have already been or will be lost, and that can never be recaptured, which perspective typified the experiences of many during the First World War. Originally, this poem had no title and the manuscript bore just the date upon which it was written. The title by which the poem is now known was evidently added by an editor at a later date. Whether this was done posthumously, bearing in mind that Edward Thomas was killed on Easter Monday 1917, is not known, but it would seem an appropriate tribute to the poet.

The poem opens with what appears to be a simple description of a woodland scene. However, Edward Thomas's language is deceptive: the "flowers" are suggestive of beauty, but are also reminiscent of funerals; the fact that they have been "left thick" reminds the reader not only of a graveyard scene, but also of the knowledge that the woodland is untended, since the young men who might have done this job, have gone off to war. These flowers have not grown naturally, but have been "left", which implies something outside of the natural order: they are discarded and, because they are neglected, they will die, which reminds us of the men dying on the battlefields, their bodies lying "thick" upon the ground. Thomas's use of the word "nightfall" introduces a sombre, melancholy tone of darkness, which contrasts with the floral opening to the poem, making us realise his true meaning. Flowers usually have a natural association with birth or new beginnings, which a poet would normally connect with dawn. However Thomas wants to create the opposite effect, introducing the gloom of "nightfall" to suggest an ending, rather than a beginning of things. The flowers remind Thomas of the men who are "far from home" - both literally and metaphorically, so here we are led to believe that he is speaking of those who are away from home, serving in France or Flanders, as well as those who are dead and are, therefore, even further from home. The mention of Eastertide is noteworthy, as it is a time of great religious significance, being the fifty days between Easter Sunday and Pentecost Sunday. Ordinarily, this would have been a time of celebration, but during an event as catastrophic as the First World War, it is easy to imagine the conventions of religion being tested. This imagery also provides another contrast between the traditional Easter and Pentecostal celebrations, against the mournful sadness associated with the war.

Edward Thomas goes on to remind the reader that the men who are "far from home" will not walk in the woods "with their sweethearts" again; nor will they gather up the flowers that will continue to grow there, because they will not be returning from the war (or, one may possibly infer that, if they do return, such things will have much less significance for them). This idea reinforces Thomas's view that everything, right down to the basic fundamentals of life, was changing; it was for these things that Thomas was going to fight. His use of the word "gathered" for the picking of the flowers, also brings to mind the harvest, which is another rural and religious celebration, as well as the idea of the men gathering the women into their arms, which - because the men will not be returning - will remain forever empty.

Thomas paints a soft, romantic image of rural England in spring, obliquely contrasting this with the reality of the noise, death and destruction of the battles of the First World War, which, following a pause through the winter of 1914-15, had just begun again with the Battle of Neuve-Chapelle in March. As an older man (he was 37 when he wrote this poem), Thomas was probably also struck by the notion that the younger generation would miss out on the simple pleasures of youth and courtship that he and his wife, Helen had enjoyed and that many young women would be left grieving for lost opportunities.

The language employed in this poem, although evidently simple, is also deliberate. So, for example, Thomas has rhymed "wood" with "should"; the first word creating an air of certainty, the second leaving the reader in doubt. The "wood" is a reference to something that will remain steadfast, regardless of the war; the word "should" reminds us of the intransigence of mankind - that his future is less certain. In addition, the phrasing of the last few words of the poem is deliberately awkward. It would be more normal and flowing to say "and will never do again". However, by delaying the word "never" for as long as is grammatically possible, Thomas not only raises the hopes of his reader, only to dash them, but also creates a more jarring tone to the final words, forcing the reader to contemplate his meaning more closely, rather than taking it for granted.

The poem has a tone of sad reflection and mourning, not only for those who have died and for the everyday activities which they enjoyed, but also for a way of life which Thomas felt was threatened by the war and which he believed could not survive the destruction that the war would inevitably bring to England's shores, fields and woods. Although Thomas may not have entitled this poem himself as "In Memoriam", it is most certainly intended as a lament for the men, women and way of life of a generation that did not realise it was about to become lost.

THE CHERRY TREES

This poem was written in the late spring or early summer of 1916, possibly as a recollection of the sights which Edward Thomas might well have witnessed on one of his many solitary walks that he used to take in the countryside around his home at Steep, near Petersfield in Hampshire. Thomas, at the time of writing, had recently been granted leave from Hare Hall, at Gidea Park in Essex, where he had been acting as a map-reading instructor. During this time, Thomas was making the difficult decision as to whether to remain at Hare Hall in safety, or to apply for a Commission and seek a posting overseas. He eventually chose the latter and, by November 1916, he had undergone his training and been transferred to 244 Siege Battery, Royal Garrison Artillery, as a Second Lieutenant.

Poems such as this seem to represent the poet's attempts to come to terms with the cost of war: both from a personal perspective and looking at the cost to the natural world. This was a theme to which Edward Thomas frequently returned, as can be seen in other poems, such as *In Memoriam (Easter 1915)* and anthologists, like Jon Stallworthy, often place these two poems side by side, assuming that they were written at similar times, despite the many months that elapsed between their compositions, showing the seriousness with which Edward Thomas treated this topic.

In this poem, Thomas writes of simple "Cherry Trees" which are so heavily laden with blossom that their branches "bend over". This gives us a metaphor for new life springing up, as well as the image of bounty - almost to the point of surfeit - leaving us to wonder whether the trees will be able to support all the fruit that will follow in the wake of the blossom, or whether the weight will be too much and will break the boughs. As such, this could be taken as an analogy for the destruction of the war: perhaps Edward Thomas is questioning whether the country, represented by the trees, can take the weight of the losses it is having to bear, or whether it will also break under the strain. The blossom, or "petals" are being dropped by the trees onto an "old road", implying that the trees have no use for the blossom, but also that the "old road" won't either, since it is barren, or infertile land, on which nothing can grow, making this a hopeless scene. This notion is reinforced by the statement that "all that passed" along the road "are dead", by which we may assume that soldiers have marched to war along this route, but have since died. We may, perhaps, infer that the men of a local village have all volunteered together, or maybe that the village has witnessed the passing of a regular BEF unit at the beginning of the war, which has since perished. Bearing in mind that this poem was written in the late spring or early summer of 1916, it pre-dates the Battle of the Somme, which saw the demise of so many volunteer "Pals" battalions, so although either of these situations is possible, the latter is, perhaps, more likely.

The "petals" that have fallen from the tree cover the grass "as for a wedding", creating an image of flowers that have been scattered, traditionally, at the feet of a bride and groom. This scene is one of great happiness and hope for the future, which Thomas enhances further, describing the day as an "early May morn", thereby reminding the reader not only that there might still be such weddings happening somewhere in the countryside, but also of the changing seasons. However, he immediately dashes this sense of hopefulness, pointing out that "there is none to wed", presumably because - as he has already told us - "all that passed are dead".

This, like Thomas's earlier poem In Memoriam (Easter 1915), is a sad and mournful reflection, detailing the loss, not only of life, but also of a way of life. The men who would have walked down this road on their wedding day, are now dead; the women, therefore, have no-one to marry, so their lives are materially altered; their expectations lowered. Additionally, future generations must also be affected, because the young men have died, so they will not marry and have children, which metaphor is represented by the blossom being discarded, or abandoned by the tree and falling onto a barren road where nothing can grow. Finally, the rural landscape is altered, as there is no-one left to tend the land, depicted by the imagery of the bent and potentially broken trees.

Thomas's language is deliberately melancholy. Although he writes of blossom and weddings, he does not want the reader to harbour any feelings of optimism, so he couples cheerful words with cleverly placed pessimistic ones. For example, he rhymes "shedding" with "wedding", the latter being a positive event, bringing hope for the future, new life and cheerfulness; the former being a metaphor for discarding or abandoning something which is no longer required. In this instance, the thing being discarded is the blossom, which Thomas had used to represent new life and growth. So, these contradictory terms, juxtaposed in their rhymes, reinforce the message that all hope for the future is now lost. Thomas then goes on to repeat this exact process, rhyming "dead" with "wed", to the same effect.

The image created here is one of a rural idyll, gone awry, but not through natural causes. Man has made the petals fall, and the boughs bend, the roads barren and the women unwedded. As such, this makes Thomas's sadness all the more profound, as one senses that he feels something could (and should) have been done to prevent this situation; this end. If the causes had been natural, he might have found it easier to accept and had less grounds for his melancholy. As it is, his regrets are more earnest, perhaps, because he feels - at least in part - responsible.

RAIN

This is a complex and complicated poem which requires some fairly detailed understanding of the poet's background and his sensibilities, as well as the concept that someone who is suffering from depression - as Thomas frequently did - does not see things from the same perspective as others might. Depression takes many forms: Winston Churchill used to call his a "black dog", which seems a bizarre, even slightly friendly description for something that is so consuming and destructive. To those who have never been depressed, it often seems as though the sufferer has simply given up and cannot be bothered to 'get a grip'. This is not the case: they are not capable of taking control. It would appear that Thomas displayed the typical symptoms of depression throughout most of his adult life, some of which are reflected in this poem.

In the late summer of 1911, Edward Thomas had written a prose account of his feelings while lying in the dark, listening to the rain. This account can be found in his book The Icknield Way, which was published in 1913. In this passage, Thomas creates a dull and depressing atmosphere of a rain storm: not as something which cleanses and refreshes, as storms often do, but as something which destroys everything, including both "life and death". The account is very dark, showing not only the extreme stress that Thomas was under at the time he wrote it, but also the effect which the weather, especially when prolonged and unremitting, can have of someone of his sensibilities. He speaks of himself as being overwhelmed by the enormity of the rain, which absorbs or "swallows" everything in its wake, making him feel "little" and "forgotten", as though he were "never alive". He ends the piece acknowledging the "full truth of the words

I used to love... in the days before the rain: 'Blessed are the dead that the rain rains on.'" So, although the rain he is describing is destructive, he can still recall a time when it served a different, and better, purpose, making his rain, possibly symbolic: a metaphor for anything that consumes completely and wantonly.

This passage and the knowledge of it, provide invaluable background information when examining Thomas's poem, *Rain* and, indeed, it is hard to see how one can hope to fully appreciate the poem without knowing of the prose account. *Rain* was written very early in 1916, while Thomas was still at Hare Hall, Gidea Park, in Essex, where he worked as a map reading instructor, having been promoted to the rank of Lance-Corporal in November 1915. Throughout his life, Thomas had been plagued by frequent and worsening bouts of depression and would often take himself off into the countryside - sometimes for days on end - to avoid being confined by family life. He was, nonetheless, devoted to his wife, Helen, whose love for him remained constant, despite their many trials.

Rain is clearly a poem written by a depressed person, made obvious by the fact that Thomas writes about himself as though he were dead and wishes that state upon himself. He refers to his life as a "solitude" and to his state as "solitary"; comments that he realises he is going to die, which might be more easily understood if he were writing this while lying in a trench or a dugout with shells screaming overhead, rather than in a hut in Essex, before Thomas had decided to apply for a posting overseas. There is also desolation as he can hear "nothing but the wild rain" and even his position, although safe in reality, is "bleak", showing that he can see no future for himself. He anticipates that when he is dead, he won't be able to hear the rain, or to thank it for cleansing him. Many poets saw the rain as having cleansing powers and here, Thomas seems to believe that it has the properties to remove all of his impurities and return him to the innocence of birth, when he was "born into this solitude". He seems to feel as though no-one shares or understands the depths of his despair or loneliness.

Next, Thomas repeats the line from his prose account of the rain storm, written five years earlier: "Blessed are the dead that the rain rains upon", which was a popular West Country superstition, meaning that if it rained on a coffin at a funeral, then the soul of the departed had arrived safely in Heaven. However, not being dead yet, Thomas hopes - prays even - that no-one whom he "once... loved" is either dying or lying in the same predicament as himself: feeling sympathetic, yet "helpless" towards both the living and those who will die, in other words, apathetic. The "broken reeds", which represent those who are waiting to die, have ceased to exist in their previous form: they don't wave in the breeze like they should, but are just "still and stiff", which again, Thomas says, is how he feels. So, not only is he like the "cold water", floating without purpose or feeling among the "broken reeds" - or the men waiting to die - but he is also a "broken reed" himself, since he anticipates his own death.

All his love is gone, he says, except his love for death, because that is the only love which the "wild rain" has not "dissolved". At the end of the poem, Thomas seems to imply that a love of death is the only "perfect" love, which can never "disappoint" and it could be interpreted that not only does he love death, but it loves him back. This final couplet may be a reference to Shakespeare's Sonnet Number 116, in which he states the firmness and strength of love, which can, if strong enough, withstand any "tempests and is never shaken", even if that tempest be the passage of time or beauty; a change in circumstances or even the infidelity of one or other of the parties. Shakespeare goes on to say that, if he be proved wrong in his assertions about love, then "I never writ, nor no man ever loved.", so heartfelt are his feelings on the subject of the strength of true love. Thomas, however, seems prepared to argue this point, to a degree at least, since his strongest love is not for a woman, but for death, in which he finds nothing to "disappoint", even when he looks for approval to the "tempests", which Shakespeare had urged him could only strengthen human love. In finding this approbation from the "tempests", or the worst that life has to offer, we must assume that the love of death makes Thomas, somehow, more complete than any other love he has experienced.

Although we do not know exactly what form of depression Edward Thomas suffered from, we do know, from various biographies, that it manifested itself in self-doubt, feelings of insecurity, the need for periods of solitude, mood changes, restlessness and violent outbursts. This poem reads as though, when writing, Thomas was in a dark place, where he could see no value to his existence. He perceives himself as either already dead, or useless and no better than a "broken reed". He also assumes himself to be unloved: "Like me who have no love", since this description may apply not only to the love he feels, but also to the love he thinks he receives. By extension, this must also mean that he believes that the only thing that does love him is death. This assumption is blatantly untrue and unfair, as Helen's love for him, though frequently tested, never faltered, and she remained loyal and true to him, even after his death. The thought process, however, is typical of someone in the depths of depression, who cannot see any reason why anyone should love them, making death seem like rather an attractive alternative.

The desolation in this poem is consuming and I have rarely read anything so depressing within this genre. The poet's numb acceptance of death does not mask his feelings of pity for those who might be "dying tonight", although he qualifies this, as he only seems concerned for people that he had once loved, making this quite a selfish pity. This propensity for putting everything that is positive into the past and dwelling only on the negative may smack a little of self-pity, especially when one bears in mind that he was writing in complete safety. If the piece had been written in peacetime, one's interpretation would be entirely different and one could assess the poem purely from the perspective of the poet's depression. However, although the depression must be accommodated, the poem still feels a little self-indulgent, considering the hell that others were going through at the time.

Thomas looks at everything in this poem only from his own viewpoint: "I shall die"; "washing me cleaner than I have been/ Since I was born"; "here I pray that none whom once I loved"; "like me who have no love", etc. This suggests self absorption, wallowing in his own experiences, which at this point, didn't really amount to anything very significant, compared with those of many of his fellow countrymen. It could be argued, therefore, that the poem reveals another thought process: we might question whether this period marked the beginning of Thomas's doubts about his own role in the conflict. Was he wondering whether he should be doing more and what might be the consequences of such a decision? The loneliness of the one not participating fully in the war may be a mark of his "solitude". Is his "helplessness" caused by the fact that he knows his death, of which he feels assured, will ultimately make no difference and that he will become just another sacrifice? It is worth remembering that, although Thomas was devoted to Helen and their children, his love for his country may well have been the guiding force behind the decision as to whether to risk everything overseas, or stay safely in Essex. Nonetheless, even this abiding love of country was not the "perfect" love he, perhaps, craved: it had proved disappointing. He possibly sensed that his love was very one-sided; that England did not love her soldiers as she might have done; that those at home, for whom sacrifices were being made, did not always appreciate the hardships of those who fought. When he had enlisted in July 1915, Thomas had described his feelings and reasons for fighting, as follows:

"It seemed to me that either I had never loved England, or I had loved it foolishly, aesthetically, like a slave, not having realised that it was not mine, unless I were willing and prepared to die rather than leave it."

Perhaps, as he began to contemplate applying for a commission and a posting overseas, or at least questioning his role in the conflict, the idea of leaving and dying for his country was beginning to become a reality. It is also possible that in *Rain* he is asking himself some of these profound questions: is his love for his country that perfect love, or does it disappoint? Is it unrequited, or is it returned as fully as it is given? If it disappoints, then the only thing really left for him is death, since to live on, "helpless" and "broken" by his shattered dreams, would be so much worse.

AS THE TEAM'S HEAD-BRASS

The title of this poem, and its first line refer to a team of horses, ploughing a field and the glint created by the sun catching their bridles as they turn back and forth. This team of horses could also be an allusion to the horses at the front, who would have pulled artillery and supply carts through the muddy battlefields.

The narrator notices a couple disappear into the woods in the distance. The first two lines of this poem are symbolic of continuing life: the horses ploughing the field denote the beginning of another year of growth; the lovers going into the woods, presumably for some clandestine affair, demonstrate nature's rebirth. It could be noted, however, that the lovers mentioned are not necessarily people: Edward Thomas often referred to animals and birds as "making love", thus giving them an almost human quality.

The narrator tells us that he is sitting in the branches of an elm tree, which has fallen across the furrows in a section of the field that has already been ploughed. This fallen tree could be a reference to the fallen soldiers in France, who lie in barren fields, just like this one being ploughed. From here he watches the remainder of the ploughing. Charlock is a weed of the mustard family with bright yellow flowers: therefore the field appears to be turning from yellow to brown as it is ploughed, just as the plants, trees and flowers in France have been destroyed. The choice of yellow as a colour provides an internal rhyme pattern with the words "fallen" and "fallow" from the previous two lines.

Each time the horses approach him, as they plough monotonously up and down the field, the narrator fears that he will be run-down, but the ploughman pauses sufficiently each time to exchange a few words, before turning the horses and working his way back up the field. It is as though, by sitting on the dead tree, the narrator (and the reader) fear that he has some affinity with the fallen.

Initially the two men talk about the weather, but then their conversation turns towards the war. The ploughman scrapes the blade of his plough as he turns the horses back towards the woods. This also reminds the reader of the blades being used to kill the soldiers at the Front.

The narrator learns that the elm was felled by a heavy snowstorm. This serves as a reminder of the many soldiers who must have died during the cold winters, as though they too have been "felled" by the weather. He asks the ploughman when the tree will be removed and is informed that this will not occur until after the war has finished. Again, there could be said to be a similarity between the tree and the dead soldiers, who will not have proper graves (or in many cases will not have a grave at all) until the war is over. Many dead soldiers were left in No Man's Land and have no known grave, or remained there until the fighting had died down sufficiently for their bodies to be recovered. This conversation between the two men is broken by a gap of ten minutes every time the ploughman turns to plough another length of the field.

The ploughman enquires whether the narrator has served in the war. When he receives a negative answer, he suggests that the man might be avoiding service. The narrator replies that he would happily go if only he knew that he would definitely be coming back. He says that he feels he would not mind losing an arm, but to lose a leg would be a different matter altogether. It is quite likely that Thomas, himself, felt this way - for him the prospect of no longer being able to enjoy his long walks in the countryside would have made life seem intolerable. Death, on the other hand, would be more favourable, since he would no longer want for, or worry about, anything.

The narrator asks whether many men from the surrounding area have gone to the front and died. The ploughman informs him that one of his work-mates had been killed the previous March. In fact, he informs us, the man was killed on the very night of the blizzard which felled the elm tree. This again reiterates the similarity between the fallen tree and the dead soldiers. The ploughman believes that if his mate had not gone to the front and been killed, the tree would by now have been removed. This indicates that, for those not directly affected by death, life carries on much as before.

However, if the tree had been removed, he should not have been able to sit there and have this conversation. In fact, he says, everything would be different without the war. The ploughman believes that, in that case, the world would be a better place. He then decides that, provided everyone could come back alive, everything might be alright. The word "might" is important here since it demonstrates the doubt in the ploughman's mind, that their world will ever be "alright" again.

As the plough turns one last time, the lovers leave the wood, reminding us once more that, for some, life is continuing. The narrator watches the plough work its way through the field. The churning of the mud, once more, brings to mind the muddy battlefields: the uneven tread of the horses and the ploughman call to mind the stumbling and dying soldiers.

This poem continually uses imagery of light and dark: the brass glints in the sunlight; the yellow charlock also represents the sun, light and life which are being cut down by the plough. The woods speak of darkness, since we cannot know what happens in there. The earth also symbolises the dark, in both its colour, its reminiscence of the battlefields and the image of the earth as a grave.

In addition, we are constantly reminded of the images of birth (or life) and death. The very ploughing of the field itself represents the potential birth of new crops, while also bringing about the death of the weeds. The weeds themselves embody plants which serve no purpose - they are deemed useless. This could be equated with the idea that those dying in the war, are being cut down for no reason - their deaths serving no useful purpose. The lovers entering the woods, whether they are human lovers or not, epitomise the suggestion that life goes on as before, and that for some, it will continue to do so, with or without the war.

This poem represents two sides of nature: the death and destruction of war on one side; the continuity of life and the strength of nature itself on the other.

Towards the end of the poem, the ploughman introduces a note of optimism that all might be well; this is short-lived since the narrator feels that everything is being done for the last time. The language used at the end of the poem is down-beat: "crumble", "topple over" and "stumbling", all of which denote finality. As the Team's Head-Brass was written while Thomas was trying to decide whether or not to apply for a commission and go overseas to serve, and as such, it reflects his uncertainty about the future.

During his time as a map-reading instructor, he had found himself with less and less time to enjoy his walks in the countryside, which may have led him to reflect on how his life would change should he find himself physically maimed and unable to pursue this activity again. He also worried about the future for his family, should the worst happen. Thomas looked upon his role in the family very traditionally and feared for Helen and his children's security should he not return.

Edward Thomas found it difficult to compare his war-time persona and responsibilities with his peace-time ones and possibly had difficulty contemplating the future in the knowledge that his old world and values would probably have disappeared for ever. Even if he survived, so many others would be dead, that his beloved England, and a way of life he had come to depend upon, might never recover.

The conversational tone of this poem could be compared and contrasted with other poems, such as *Comrades: An Episode* by Robert Nichols, or *They* by Siegfried Sassoon. Both Nichols and Thomas use conversation as a means of telling a story and creating a scene, whereas Sassoon is more likely to use it to demonstrate the personality of someone involved. He also uses speech as a way of reinforcing irony with directly-spoken sarcasm.

Unlike Nichols, however, Thomas's conversation is not between soldiers, but civilians.*Comrades: An Episode* is set in a trench and in No Man's Land, and deals with the relationships between soldiers serving at the front. Conversely, *As the Team's Head-Brass* uses rural England as its location, and deals, fundamentally with the relationship between man and nature. This reflects the poet's concern for his native country by creating a scene which he fears will soon cease to exist.

IVOR GURNEY

Perhaps better known as a composer of music, Gurney is, nonetheless, a notable poet, whose works have until recently, been much ignored.

BIOGRAPHICAL DETAILS

Ivor Gurney was born on August 28th 1890 in Gloucester. His father, David, was a tailor and owned his own shop, where Ivor's mother, Florence also worked. Ivor was one of four children: Winifred, Ronald and Dorothy being his siblings. They were a down-to-earth, working-class family, who found Ivor's artistic temperament difficult to understand. His was educated at King's School and joined the Cathedral Choir at the age of twelve. In 1911, he was awarded a scholarship to the Royal College of Music and, later, in order to escape from London at the weekends, he took a job as organist at Christ Church in High Wycombe. There, he was befriended by the churchwarden, Edward Chapman and his family, with whom he lodged. When war broke out in August, Ivor immediately tried to enlist, but was rejected due to his poor eyesight. Eventually, however, he was accepted into the Gloucester Regiment. His mental instabilities, which were at this stage little more than eccentricities, were already apparent, but he found the strict regimes of army life suited him. After training, he arrived in France on May 26th 1916.

Although Gurney is well known as a poet, his real talent lay in musical composition, and while in the trenches, he wrote prolifically - music, poems and letters. He was wounded in the arm in April 1917 and then that September, he was gassed and sent back to England. His mental problems re-surfaced and eventually he was invalided out of the army, having suffered a complete breakdown. The next few years were very difficult as Ivor struggled to stay in work and faced the rejection of his family. The Chapmans remained loyal throughout, but in 1922, Ivor's brother, Ronald arranged to have him committed and certified insane. Ivor escaped from Barnwood House - a private asylum near Gloucester - so it was decided that he should be transferred to Dartford in Kent, in the hope that removing him from his beloved Gloucestershire would lessen his desire for freedom. From then on, Ivor's mental health deteriorated and he died on December 26th 1937 from tuberculosis. He was a man of rare and often unappreciated talent, with a great sense of fun. A self-effacing character who was always quick to praise others, offer encouragement and show affection - even when he received little in return.

TO HIS LOVE

There is some confusion over the subject of this poem. Some anthologists maintain that it describes the aftermath of the 'death' of F. W. Harvey, a close friend of Ivor Gurney. Harvey was reported as "missing, believed killed" in August 1916, although this was, in fact, inaccurate as he had been captured by the Germans and remained their prisoner until the end of the war. Although it is not clear when Gurney wrote this poem, it did not appear in print until 1919 when his second volume of poetry War Embers was published. By this time, he would have been aware that Harvey was still alive, so the subject is not necessarily him, but may have been another friend, or even from Gurney's imagination.

The first two words sum up the depth and finality of Gurney's feelings. His friend is dead and he obviously deeply regrets his passing. He goes on to tell us that he can see no future as all the plans they made are of no value now. He remembers walks they used to take in the hills, but with the realisation that they will not do so again. Others, represented by the sheep, will carry on as before, able to ignore his pain at the loss of so dear a friend.

Next, he appears to discuss his feelings with another acquaintance who had been equally familiar with their friend's appearance. In doing so, he reminds us once again, that everything has changed. The dead man would be unrecognisable now, even to his greatest friends, although he seems to imply here that they should remember him as he was, rather than concentrating on what he has become.

Even though no amount of remembrance can alter the fact that his friend is dead, Gurney is proud of the fact that he died with honour and wants to commemorate this by covering his grave with a carpet of violets, reminiscent of his beloved Gloucestershire countryside. This gives the impression that there will be some kind of memorial or funeral service, which, of course, cannot be. The final verse begins in an almost panic-stricken tone, as though Gurney himself has suddenly realised that the dead will remain unburied. He wants the body hidden from sight, covered with flowers which will shield the living from the memory of the man's wounds, and remind them of happier times. By referring to his body as a 'thing', Gurney is not necessarily just being imprecise, but he is reminding us that not all bodies, whether those of friends or enemies, were recognisable after death. The colour of the 'thing' and its wetness suggest that the wounds are fresh, and yet it would seem he is unable to identify exactly what it is he is looking at. He is also reminding us how difficult it will be for him to forget these hideous sights and this contrasts with his earlier happy memories of his friend while he was still alive. It is the end of this poem which makes some anthologists believe he could not have been writing about F. W. Harvey as he would not have seen a body or its wounds. This does not, however, prevent him from imagining such things.

To His Love is a poem of remembrance - both of the life of a dead friend, and of home and more hopeful days. The "Love" of the title is not necessarily a homo-erotic reference, but is more likely to concern his feelings for the English countryside which the dead man can no longer enjoy. This poem celebrates human friendships, but also points out how difficult it is to witness the horrors of war and remain untouched by them.

Another poet who shared Ivor Gurney's love of the English countryside was Edward Thomas. He demonstrated this in many of his poems. In The Cherry Trees and In Memoriam (Easter 1915), Thomas speaks of various elements of country life, particularly those surrounding the changing seasons and flowers, which the dead will no longer be able to experience. All of Thomas' poems were written before his departure for France, which accounts for the more pastoral air to his work. This is a tone which Gurney includes within To His Love, while providing a greater contrast between this and the horror of the war.

BALLAD OF THE THREE SPECTRES

This poem was probably written in February 1917. It was certainly included in a letter which Ivor Gurney sent to his friend Marion Scott which was dated the 15th of that month. The letter also contained a Preface for Gurney's collection of poems which would be entitled Severn and the Somme, which was published later that year.

The poem opens with an image of the narrator being accosted by the "three spectres" of the title. He is knee-deep in "mud and water", giving the impression of him being frozen to the bone. The reader, therefore, wonders whether the poet is imagining the appearance of these ghouls partly because he is so cold that he can no longer even think clearly. The winter of 1916-1917, when this poem was written, was the coldest of the whole war, so it is not unreasonable to surmise that a soldier might start to hallucinate after several months in such extreme conditions. Gurney describes these ghostly visions as mocking and ridiculing him directly, rather than anyone else, which may suggest that he felt the implications of the predictions that would follow applied to him alone, and no-one else. The allusion to the ghosts "walking abreast" implies that these are the spirits of fallen soldiers, who would have a much greater understanding of the situation in which a ranking soldier finds himself than a new recruit, or even another serving soldier, since they have died already and can now look back and see everything with a greater degree of comprehension.

The first of the "three spectres" then speaks, although he seems to direct this speech more to his fellow ghouls than directly to Gurney. This ghost suggests that the poet is a courageous soldier, showing no fear, even of the spirits that haunt the dark. Some critics have suggested at a hint of irony or cynicism in these words, but personally, I do not see this. He goes on to suggest that the soldier will be lucky and be injured, but only with a "Blighty" wound - namely one which guarantees repatriation to a hospital in England, but which doesn't cause any lasting damage. The ghoul assumes that this will give great cheer to the soldier, in spite of his injury, because he will get some respite from the war and the fears and worries of being in the trenches.

The second of the ghosts then replies and, again, is talking to his fellow "spectres" rather than to the poet. He comments that he doesn't believe the soldier has such a "lucky" face as his "comrade" had suggested. The use of the word "comrade" here reinforces the idea that the ghosts are former soldiers. This ghoul, however, doesn't have such a promising fate in mind for the poet: indeed, he believes that the soldier will die, not directly in battle; not quickly by a bullet or bomb, but by being frozen to death. Again, this suggestion helps to strengthen the idea that the extreme cold is having an adverse effect on the poet. He cannot imagine even a gory or bloodthirsty death for himself, but instead a lingering and useless one. In addition, the ghost notes that the last place the poet will see before dying would be "Picardie" (a region in France), rather than his beloved Gloucestershire. This notion would also have depressing connotations for Gurney, since his heart belonged very much to his home county.

In the fourth verse, Gurney points out that, although the first two ghosts have spoken of fearful futures for him, he is much more concerned about the malicious predictions of the third spectre, who suggests that he will keep on living throughout the entire war, only to perish right at the very end. This would appear to be Gurney's worst nightmare: to be forced to live on through the horrors of the war and then, just as peace and freedom seem to be within reach, to have them snatched away. This ghoul, however, may not be implying the poet's actual death at the end of the "war's last dawning", as he may be suggesting that to live afterwards, knowing and understanding all that has gone before is actually a far worse fate - an "agony", in fact. For a ghost, who is, by definition, already dead, to imply that life after the war would be far more fearsome than death during it, is a profound statement indeed.

In the final verse, Gurney reveals the conclusion of these ghostly predictions: the first two spectres, he declares, are "liars", which statements he reinforces by pointing out that he has not been wounded, or killed. Indeed, we may assume that he is somewhere behind the lines, training perhaps, as he is "sloping arms" (where the soldiers are ordered to place their rifles on their left shoulder at a sloped angle supported by their left arm). The counting, "one-two-three", would have been the commands issued by a sergeant-major according to which the soldiers would have carried out the drill. Gurney seems to assume that , because he has survived thus far, the first two ghosts cannot have been speaking the truth about his future. However, he believes he now has to wait until the very end of the war to find out whether there was any truth in the prediction of the third ghost. This assumption on the part of the poet, presumes that he would not die or be wounded with a "Blighty" in between times, which options Gurney seems to have ruled out.

Gurney's language in this poem is simple. Although written in 1917, he roots the piece in the Somme, telling us that he is near Ovillers (which is actually Ovillers La Boiselle), a town lying to one side of the main Albert to Bapaume road. This was the site of heavy fighting during the battle of the Somme in 1916, resulting in many casualties. Later, Gurney also mentions Picardie, the region of France in which the Somme is situated. He clearly wants his reader to be fully aware of the importance of that dreaded battleground. He uses a simple "abab" rhyme scheme, so as not to detract from his message, that to live through the war may be worse than injury or death. He also makes significant use of internal rhymes, such as "three jeering fleering" and then links this with "unfearing" a few lines later. There is plenty of direct speech and some colloquial language, although these do not detract from the meaning of the poem or make it difficult to read, as can sometimes be the case. There is also an obvious link between this poem and Shakespeare's Macbeth in that these "three spectres" are immediately reminiscent of the three witches who predict Macbeth's fate.

Gurney's own future would be haunted - not only by the war, but also by his own psychological difficulties and, it could be argued that he lived his life after the war in an increasing "agony" of hopelessness of intolerable confinement, some of which he perhaps foresaw. In this poem his message is that to survive the war may not bring the release that some might assume, since to do so, one would first have to live through it. In the option provided by the first ghost, there is an element of "luck", but there is also a vague hint at cowardice, or at least that those who escape with a "Blighty" have evaded the worst. With the second ghost's prediction, there is an element of uselessness: that death is not glorious, glamorous or heroic, but that it is likely to achieve nothing whatsoever and to be absolutely pointless. Despite the despondency surrounding these two options, however, they are seen as preferable to survival: the waiting and not knowing; the endless anticipation followed by the "agony" of either dying or living and knowing that life could never be the same again. Whichever way he turned, the alternatives presented offer a bleak future to Gurney, but one which was actually not far from his own reality, since here was a man, who in years to come would beg to be allowed to die.

THE SILENT ONE

This poem was probably written between 1922 and 1925 and was found in a dated notebook labelled "Best Poems", which were written after Ivor Gurney had been admitted to a mental institution in the autumn of 1922. It is unclear, however, whether the poem was written at Barnwood House in Gloucester, or at the City of London Mental Hospital at Dartford in Kent, where Gurney was transferred in December 1922, following several escapes from the former institution. Many of Gurney's post-war "war poems", such as this, address his feelings towards those with whom he served and the memories of a time which, for him, was more appealing than the enforced incarceration which stretched ahead.

The title leads seamlessly into the poem itself, but is worth taking a moment to consider, since 'the silent one", although obviously dead, is also a reminder of the noise and destruction that had surrounded the poet during the war. This makes silence and, by extension death, seem quite an attractive prospect. "The silent one" had "died on the wires", or the barbed wire which would have skirted the trenches, offering protection from attacking troops, but also a barrier through which it frequently proved impossible to penetrate. Men would often get caught up trying to break through the thick entanglements and would become an easy target for machine gunners and snipers. Gurney recalls here that there had actually been two dead men on the wire, but he only focuses on one, remembering his style of speech - a "chatter" - which had a heavy Buckinghamshire accent. That county is right in the middle of central/southern England, which Gurney may be using as representative of the fact that this man was typical of the "average" soldier: there had not been anything especially different or outstanding about him; he was a normal, simple man from the middle parts of England. His "chatter" is now "silent" and all of the loveliness and charm that Gurney had associated with him, is lost.

The poet goes on to point out that, despite the dead man's evident simplicity and country appeal, he had also been courageous. He had confronted the barbed wire, although it had still been intact and impenetrable, the artillery having clearly failed in its task of breaking through the enemy's defences. Gurney describes how the dead man had simply "stepped over" the wire, as though it were nothing more than a minor inconvenience, but goes on to explain that he believes these actions denote him as having been a "fool" - albeit a "noble" one. This label of foolishness may have been earned as a result of Gurney's disbelief that the man would blindly follow orders to go through the wire, despite knowing that such an action would result in his own death. However, the addition of the word "noble" and the knowledge of that way in which the man had just "stepped over" the wire, implies more admiration than this description might suggest. Gurney was renowned not only for his wry sense of humour, but also for his admiration of those with whom he served. So while he may have thought the dead man foolish, he also seems to have admired his actions. Gurney explains further that the dead man was a non-commissioned officer (NCO), having earned his "stripes" (this would make the man either a corporal or a sergeant: the former having two stripes, the latter, three). He would, therefore, have had a position of some responsibility and the fact that Gurney - a private - still respected this superior NCO, shows that the senior man had done his job well. Nonetheless, despite his courage and nobility, the man's foolishness - or perhaps we could say bravado - has led to the end of his own life. Gurney describes this event very simply; having led us to this point, and without any emotion or overstatement - the man's life just "ended". This over-simplicity, coupled with the silence of the dead man contrasts with the noise and furore of battle, but perfectly encapsulates the fact that death is final.

Gurney then makes a comparison between the dead NCO and himself. He thinks of himself as "weak" and "hungry", both of which may be taken literally, or these may be seen as metaphors for someone who is delicate and, perhaps, unappealing and who yearns, with great eagerness to stay within the relative security of the "line" - or the trenches - rather than battle in the open danger of No Man's Land. Gurney recalls lying beneath the "unbroken" barbed wire, shying away from the danger and remaining there "unshaken", as though the wire had offered him some feeling of security against the battle that raged above him. This sense of invulnerability had been broken by the interruption of an officer, who had suggested that Gurney might "crawl through" a gap in the wire. The poet describes the accent of the officer in much less complimentary tones than that of the NCO who had died on the wire. The officer's pronunciation, although polite, is described as "finicking" or fussy, rather over-particular, and giving the impression that he is not a countryman like the NCO - or indeed Gurney himself. We are given the idea that this was a "gentleman" officer, well educated probably, but lacking in common sense, since he had suggested Gurney should sacrifice his life when others had clearly failed in this same objective. Gurney's low opinion of the officer is made very clear by the tone he adopts here and the contrast between this and his earlier description of the NCO, for whom Gurney would seem to have had a great deal more admiration.

Nothing in this place had been safe, it would appear; even the "darkness" had formed a target to be "shot at". This suggests an irrationality: that unable to see clearly, men were firing wildly at anything in the dimness. It is small wonder, then, that, unable to perceive any hole in the wire himself, Gurney had "politely" declined the officer's suggestion. Naturally, if Gurney had really disobeyed an order such as this, he might have found himself on a charge, but this poem is written retrospectively, with some poetic licence. Gurney anticipates that if he had followed the officer's order, he would soon have been dead: there would have been no alternative, given the ferocity of the firing that surrounded him. Having reached the decision to do nothing, Gurney had remained beneath the wire, listening to the "bullets whizzing" overhead. He recalls thinking of music, which is hardly surprising, given that Gurney was a composer, but may seem strange in such circumstances. The "music" here may be a therapeutic remedy to the noisy disturbance of battle, but is also a contrast with the silence of the dead NCO, who is the subject of the poem. Gurney had also sworn profusely, but not blasphemously, presumably because swearing had helped him to overcome the natural fear of the situation in which he found himself. He probably felt, however (somewhat tongue in cheek), that he ought to remain "polite to God" so as to ensure His protection. Gurney would seem to have felt as though he were withdrawing into himself, hiding from his fear and the war; then trying to overcome this and face it all again, before retreating once more. Finally, he had tried to mentally face "the screen" not only of the literal barbed wire fence that blocked his way, but also of his own fear of the battle's wrath.

This closing description is very apt and thought-provoking, bringing to mind the waves of fear and attempted bravado that must have been the experience for many soldiers in such a situation. There would have been an expectation of behaviour and bravery - not only from others, such as officers and NCOs but also from oneself. In Gurney's case, this would have been coupled with his own deep psychological problems, which pre-existed the war, but which actually found some temporary relief during the conflict, due to the regimented "normality" of his life in the army. We can see in this and Gurney's other late poems, a sort of regret for the passing of those day during which he had discovered comradeship and a sense of shared responsibility.

It is also noticeable in *The Silent One*, that Gurney shows a marked degree of respect for the NCO, but has little regard for officers, who are represented here as pompous, reckless and rather stupid. One senses that he would not show nearly as much regret if the man lying dead on the wire had been the "finicking" officer, rather than the "lovely" Buckinghamshire NCO. Gurney, generally, had more time for the lower ranks than he did for the officers and, looking back, as he was when he wrote this poem, with the benefit of at least four year's hindsight, his perspective does not seem to have altered. Many of his earlier poems such as First Time In, refer to the comradeship of the simple soldiers who fought bravely and sought no more than a warm place to rest and their songs of home to cheer them. There are no officers here: indeed Gurney rarely mentions them in his early pieces. His later poems, such as The Bohemians or War Books are more critical of the "establishment" and its view of the conflict, which Gurney sees as being at odds with the realities of the slogging infantrymen.

Gurney's style of writing, once he was incarcerated, became much more distinctive and individual, making this poem more difficult to compare with others. One could, however, look at poems which offer descriptions of battle or trench scenes and the feelings of the men participating, such as *Break of Day in the Trenches* by Isaac Rosenberg, *Insensibility* by Wilfred Owen or *The Hero* by Siegfried Sassoon. However, because Gurney's poem was written retrospectively, his language is somewhat softer and there is less bitterness and irony than in many other pieces - although that is also a reflection of the poet's nature. Gurney was an extremely quiet and gentle man, despite the fact that his illness could make him prone to bouts of violence, which were outside of his control. He shows this empathetic side of his personality in his poetry, demonstrating an understanding for the suffering of others that never wavers.

ISAAC ROSENBERG

Often ignored by anthologists, Isaac Rosenberg features heavily in Jon Stallworthy's collection. Three of the poems given are standard and may be found in several other anthologies, but the first two are more obscure and serve to demonstrate Rosenberg's feelings upon and about the outbreak of the war.

BIOGRAPHICAL DETAILS

Isaac Rosenberg was born on November 25th 1890 in Bristol. His twin brother died at birth and Isaac was never physically strong himself. His parents had only emigrated from their native Lithuania three years earlier and eventually the family settled into the Jewish community in the East End of London. Isaac was always artistic, but the family's limited finances forced him to leave school at the age of fourteen and find work as an engraver's apprentice. In 1911, however, his fortune changed and some wealthy Jewish benefactors paid his tuition fees at The Slade School of Art. The following year, as he continued to study, Isaac also began writing poetry and sent some of his early work to Laurence Binyon, who encouraged him to continue writing. In June 1914, having completed his studies at The Slade, Rosenberg decided to move to South Africa, where his older sister, Minnie, lived. He remained there until May 1915 when he returned to England. Initially, he tried to enlist in the Royal Army Medical Corps, but his physical condition was too poor, so he joined a Regiment of 'Bantams', set up specifically for men who were under 5'3" tall. Rosenberg served throughout the war as a private soldier and found it difficult to mix with the other men. He also suffered from ill-health, by despite this, in nearly two years of active service, he was only granted one spell of leave. In March 1918, the German Army launched its Spring Offensive, in which it hoped to destroy the Allied forces before American troops could arrive in great numbers. Rosenberg began this battle in the Reserve trenches, but the Germans advanced so quickly, that he was soon in the front line and was killed in the early hours of April 1st 1918..

ON RECEIVING NEWS OF THE WAR

This poem was written in the autumn of 1914 at Cape Town, South Africa, where Isaac Rosenberg was staying with his sister, Minnie who had recently married civil servant William Horvitch and moved there. Although there was a nine year age-gap between these two siblings, we may assume they were quite close and, when Minnie had her first son in 1922, she named him Isaac. Rosenberg's health had never been good and the decision to visit South Africa had mainly been made in the hope that the warmer climate would lead to some improvement. He also hoped to pursue his artistic career, which had not taken off quite as well as he had hoped, following the completion of his studies at the Slade School of Art in London. Having only left England in June 1914, however, the declaration of war, which everyone at first assumed would be over within a few months, did not immediately strike Rosenberg as a reason to return home. Nonetheless, that did not prevent this poet with an artist's perspective from writing about his view of the forthcoming conflict.

The title tells us that the poem is a reaction, as though Rosenberg has literally just heard about the outbreak of the war and has felt the need to sit down and write this as an immediate response, possibly because at such a distance from home, he may have believed there was little else he could do. His natural aversion to killing and diminutive stature (Rosenberg was less than 5'3" tall) would not have made him think immediately of enlisting anyway. Rosenberg's reaction, therefore, might well have been to turn to the arts that he so enjoyed and cherished in order to express his feelings about the war and what it might mean for the future.

The poem opens with a strange and seemingly inappropriate reference to "snow", although it should be noted that when the war was declared in early August, it would have been winter in South Africa. While there may not have been any actual snow on the ground in Cape Town, Rosenberg is using his memories of winter weather in England, which is currently absent from his life, as a representation for the war. So "snow", "ice" and "frost" all become illustrations of death and destruction, as well as depicting the difference between the current warm conditions in Europe and the cold harshness that war symbolises. These winter references, with their natural allusions to whiteness may also have been metaphors for the innocence that would be lost on the field of battle.

This becomes clearer in the second verse where Rosenberg points out that the world or "land" will know this coldness of winter, even at a time of year that would traditionally to him have been the height of summer because it understands the changing seasons that come and go and will acclimatise. Equally the world and nature will adapt accordingly to the frostiness of war. Men, however, he says, will not understand what is happening, because, we must assume, they don't fully comprehend why they are fighting. Rosenberg's seeming confusion here over the seasons and man's evident lack of understanding demonstrates his sense of isolation at the time, when other poets were relatively clear about why men were going to fight and would only later become disaffected as to their purpose. Due to his distance from home, Rosenberg may have lacked the connection and, therefore, probably failed to grasp something that was being made obvious to those in Europe.

In the third verse, Rosenberg makes it clear that if anyone will bear the responsibility for the war and its consequences, it must be the old. He speaks of them as "malign", implying an evil nature, but also says that they offer a "kiss", which suggests deception in their actions. By this we could infer that Rosenberg is describing politicians or statesmen, rather than the older generation as a whole, since the former groups would have more power and influence as well as more capacity and opportunity to deceive by saying one thing, but doing another. His suggestion that their actions will turn "our lives to mould" is rather thought-provoking and his language is emotive as it suggests a rotting of the nation as a whole, but also of individuals. Taken with the benefit of hindsight, as we can, this passage in fact becomes rather prophetic, as so many men would die and rot in No Man's Land during the course of the war and Rosenberg would later write of this "strange decay" to great effect in his poem *Dead Man's Dump*.

This evident ability to look into the future continues into the next verse, where Rosenberg describes the physical consequences of the war in Biblical terms, saying that the destruction will affect God himself. The "red fangs" and bloodshed are apt descriptions of the devastation of battle, all of which will make God "mourn" for the "children" or men, who will die as a result. The imagery here is potent and powerful: the "red fangs" creating the impression that war is a wild beast that cannot be tamed or sated. This verse creates the impression that no good will come of the conflict, although Rosenberg then seemingly contradicts this supposition in the final verse, implying that through the "crimson curse" that is the war itself, the earth - indeed the "universe" - will be returned to its former "pristine bloom".

This is a lyrical, although somewhat confusing and contradictory poem, which probably reflects the poet's difficulty in relating to events which seemed to remote from where he was at the time. Additionally, it may indicate a sense of contrition that Rosenberg could not participate in these events in any way from where he was, and that mankind, of which is was, of course, a part, had brought about its own ruin. This outlook, coupled with passing the "blame" onto previous generations can be seen in the work of other early war poets, such as Rupert Brooke. In his sonnet *Peace*, for example, Brooke states his belief that his generation has been "matched" with this particular time in history and awarded the task of returning to its former glory, a "world grown old and cold and weary". Julian Grenfell also agrees in part with Rosenberg's philosophy, stating in his poem *Into Battle*, that by fighting men shall have "increase", and in return, as though in gratitude, the earth will grant them "warmth", "speed" and "rest".

Another poet who, like Rosenberg, was not in England when war broke out, was Wilfred Owen, who wrote in his poem entitled *1914*, how the "Winter of the world" was closing in. Owen was actually in the relatively hot climate of southern France in August 1914 (remaining in that country until September of the following year) and it can be seen from this poem that his outlook was not too dissimilar to that of Isaac Rosenberg, although Owen seems to have perceived at the time that some of the greatest losses would come, in his opinion, in the worlds of art and literature. Owen also sees the coming war as a scourge, represented by the "wild winter", which will bring about a "new" spring, although the cost of this regeneration, he states, will be "blood for seed". Perhaps the distance from home had quite an effect on both of these poets since, although some of their views can be seen to be echoed in the words of the other early poets, they lack the enthusiasm, jingoism and even patriotism of much of the 1914 war poetry. Both Rosenberg and Owen see instead a wider perspective of the eventual cost of the war, but at the same time, do not feel personally touched by or related to it.

Owen would eventually become more disillusioned in his writing about the conflict, losing his philosophical tone, and gaining instead anger and bitterness. These emotions, however, failed to consume Rosenberg who, as a private soldier, rather than an officer, glumly and resignedly accepted his lot within the army, realising it was not within his power to change the views of other with his poetry. Instead he moved on to effectively state the obvious and create masterpieces such as *Dead Man's Dump* and *Break of Day in the Trenches* which, through his artist's eye provide some of the most brutal, harrowing and poignant descriptions of trench warfare that have ever been written or read.

AUGUST 1914

This poem was written in 1916, almost certainly after June, since that was the month in which Rosenberg first went to France and, according to Dominic Hibberd and John Onions in their anthology *The Winter of the World*, this poem was composed there, rather than in England. Rosenberg was serving near Bethune with the King's Own Royal Lancaster Regiment, although he did not settle well into either routine army life, or the manner of existence which soldiers faced in the trenches. Unlike many other soldier-poets, Rosenberg wrote a lot of his poems while actually in the trenches (the manuscripts show some staining and tearing to corroborate this) and some of his poems can, therefore be seen to have a greater degree of immediacy and intimacy than the works of other poets, who wrote at a greater distance from the conflict itself.

The title of the poem belies the date of its composition. This is really, therefore, a retrospective piece, in which the poet is looking back to the beginning of the war and wondering, perhaps, if it has been worth all the pain and loss; what has been achieved or gained and whether this will continue into the future.

The poem opens with a question in which Rosenberg, essentially, wonders what has been damaged by the war. He creates an atmosphere of finality and lasting destruction here by the use of the imagery of the "fire" which will have "burnt" away so many aspects of life. From this we may easily assume that there will be no return, as these "burnt" relics of life will not be able to rise up and live - or even exist - again: they are gone for ever. Next, Rosenberg makes suggestions as to exactly what it is within a person's life that will be "burnt". Firstly, he proposes the "granary" or store of affection or love that is kept closest to one's heart. In other words, the memories and thoughts of loved ones which one holds dearest, Rosenberg believes and questions, might have to be sacrificed at the expense of the war. Additionally, he asks whether another cost to those who fight will be the people and things they will "miss". This "much", which sums up the enormity of the loss involved, may be the lost experiences, opportunities, loved-ones and hopes for the future. What Rosenberg doesn't make clear, however, is whether these losses and final burnings are brought about by death, or simply by participating in the conflict. Does he, perhaps, see it as sufficiently damaging to a person, that they should just take part in the war?

In the second verse, Rosenberg imagines the three stages of a man's life, giving them descriptions in the form of nouns, rather than the more usual adjectives. "Iron" could be representative of toil and hard work, and especially, perhaps, of youthful exertions; "honey" could be said to be indicative of love, or life's sweeter rewards, such as personal happiness. Finally, "gold", naturally represents a more financial benefit, but being as Rosenberg has placed this at the end of his three stages of life, then "gold" could also be said to be the final rest and peace earned after years of hard "iron" toil. Rosenberg goes on to say, however, that both the "gold" and the "honey" are "gone". This implies that all hopes for the future, in terms of love, rewards, happiness, rest and peace, have been consumed by the war. There is also, within these lines, the implication of the sacrificing of the benefits of old age, or as Rupert Brooke phrased it, in his sonnet, *The Dead*:

"These laid the world away; poured out the red
Sweet wine of youth; gave up the years to be
Of work and joy, and that unhoped serene,
That men call age…"

The difference between the two poets is that Brooke seems to welcome - even relish - the prospect of "immortality", while Rosenberg sees it as a final sacrifice, leaving men with nothing in their lives but the "hard and cold"

Reverting back to his description of their lives as "iron", Rosenberg expands on this, explaining that this youthful work - or war as it has now become - spreads like "molten" metal, permeating everything in their lives, so that nothing remains untouched by its hardness. We can also infer from this that when this "molten" iron, or the heat and fury of the "iron" battle is over, it will harden men: even those who survive will no longer be the same people as they were before. Rosenberg reiterates this image of destruction in the final two lines. Here he may be implying that the men who are destroyed by the war (whether dead or alive) are like a damaged gap in the ordinary lives of others who remain untouched by the conflict: the war-wrecked are like a "broken tooth" on an otherwise beautiful face - the face, again, being representative of those who remain "serene" (as Brooke would have it). At the same time, however, this final sentence could be taken slightly differently, the imagery being possibly representative of the landscape. So, the "burnt space" may be No Man's Land and the "broken tooth" could be the damaged surroundings of trees and houses. It is worth noting that within a few miles of the devastated trenches, the land would still have been "fair" and "ripe", and as untouched by the war as someone sitting safely at home in England. Given the human content of the previous sections of this poem, however, the former explanation seems more likely, although the imagery of the latter should not be ignored, since Rosenberg could have written this piece in a trench and may have used the sights that surrounded him as metaphors for the harm that was being done to mankind.

This is another of Rosenberg's lyrical poems, full of emotive imagery, which makes it clear that this piece was written in close proximity to the conflict. With his artist's eye, Rosenberg had a unique capacity to see his surroundings from a different perspective to that employed by many of the other soldier-poets. The imagery of the "burnt... fire" of life in verse one, coupled with that of the closing sentence, is powerful and thought-provoking. The reader is immediately made to realise, through Rosenberg's use of language, the cost of the war, to the youth of society and their sorrow at missing out on whatever their future might have held. The fact that, given the title of the poem, this piece is written retrospectively implies that Rosenberg may be suggesting that two years of war have achieved nothing and that he can foresee no improvement for the future.

Other poems which could be compared to *August 1914* include Edmund Blunden's *The Zonnebeke Road*, in which the poet also examines man's relationship with the war, as well as the way in which even the natural world seems to have turned against mankind. There is no hope here and life has nothing left to offer, except a certain "disdain" for death, which is not surprising, given that the life he describes is so distressing, making death seem a challenging alternative. The main difference between the two poems would have to be Rosenberg's economy: he manages to convey similar emotions and messages, using infinitely fewer words. Other poems worthy of consideration in conjunction with *August 1914*, albeit for different reasons, are Rupert Brooke's *1914 Sonnets*, such as *The Dead* and *The Soldier* and other early war poems, like Herbert Asquith's *The Volunteer*. These offer useful comparisons with Rosenberg's piece in that the early poems show how the war was originally perceived, in terms of its cost to the men who fought, which can be contrasted with the later perception of a ranking soldier, like Rosenberg, rather than one of the officer poets like Brooke and Asquith, or even other later works by Siegfried Sassoon or Wilfred Owen, for example. The early officer poets speak of bravery, glory and honour, giving their poems a somewhat old-fashioned air. Indeed, Asquith's *The Volunteer* contains language which is both romantic and archaic, reminding the reader of England's former glories. Sassoon and Owen wrote in a different tone again. Their poetry that touched upon the effects of the war on men was much more embittered, as can be seen in Owen's *Dulce et Decorum Est* or Sassoon's *Glory of Women*. Their anger is almost universally directed at civilians, or sometimes senior officers, as can be seen in Sassoon's *The General* or *Base Details*. Even where Sassoon, for example, is less vociferous and more reflective, as in *The Death-Bed*, the perspective can be seen to be very different from that expressed by Rosenberg, who seems more personally involved and affected, rather than looking on at the suffering around him. We sense that, because he is an unhappy, ranking soldier, he feels the pain and loss belong more directly to him.

BREAK OF DAY IN THE TRENCHES

The title of this poem automatically inspires hope in the reader: the break of day representing a new beginning and new hope. Even in the trenches, one is inclined to believe, it might have been possible to wake up feeling thus, even if only because, momentarily, one had forgotten the war.

The first line, however, immediately lowers the spirits. Light is beginning to break through as dawn approaches, but this event is not heralded with any degree of optimism. The word 'crumbling' used here has more than one connotation: it could suggest the literal crumbling of the parapet, which would be the soldier's view as he look towards the dawn; alternatively it could be used to demonstrate the disintegration of the mens' lives and their world. You could also argue that 'crumbling' being quite a gloomy word suggests that the coming dawn is not a cheerful event, but merely marks the beginning of another monotonous day; that the days merge together - no one being better or more worthwhile than the previous.

This sense of timelessness continues into the next line; the language here serving to reiterate the feelings of boredom and monotony. Giving the word 'Time' a capital letter brings to mind Old Father Time and evokes an image of an old man representing the passing years. The mention of a druid represents an ancient religious group renowned for, amongst other things, performing human sacrifices, usually at dawn. This could be interpreted as a suggestion that the soldiers are themselves being sacrificed, and will, therefore, not experience the full passage of time, as their lives will have been wasted. It should also be remembered that dawn was a frequently chosen time of day for launching attacks, on the basis of taking advantage of half-light, and catching the enemy unawares before he had fully woken up. For this reason, companies in the front line trenches would "stand-to" at dawn, before breakfast, and await any potential enemy attacks. This probably enhanced the association between sacrifice and that particular time of day.

In the third line, the poet seems to imply that everything around him is dead, except the live thing which has just leaped over his hand. Then, however, he informs us that this 'live thing' is a rat. Traditionally associated with death and disease, this rat is mocking and triumphant as though it believes that it has conquered the men.

Suddenly, in line five, an element of natural beauty is introduced, contrasting greatly with the perceived ugliness of the rat, and the darkness and monotony of the first two lines. However, this beauty is tempered by the reminder that the poppy has come from the parapet, which we already associate with crumbling disintegration. Without in the least admiring its beauty, he sticks the poppy behind his ear, just like a pencil or a cigarette. This demonstrates that the poppy has little significance, compared to the rat.

The poet seems to find the rat oddly amusing, but suggests that his fellow soldiers would shoot the vermin if they understood, as he in fact does, that the rat does not care where he gets his food from; he is not their loyal companion: he is selfish and concerned only for his own survival. The description of the rat's nature as 'cosmopolitan' demonstrates this, as he believes that the whole world is his to enjoy, the war being, to him, just a means of acquiring food. Despite the rat's sub-human nature, the way he is described in this poem also allows him an almost human quality. It could be interpreted that Rosenberg's humanising of the rat demonstrates that to him, the men are like rats, concerned only with their own survival and killing, when required to ensure the same.

He tells us that the rat will, of course, cross from one trench to another, with no perception of 'enemy' or 'friend', but purely to feast on whatever is most readily available. The rat can cross No Man's Land without fear - unlike the men and, therefore, this journey is perceived as something pleasant, whereas it is something which the men fear. Again, the rat is triumphant - this ability to cross over No Man's Land unimpeded places the rat above the men. Although it is not unheard of, it is fairly unusual to refer to No Man's Land as 'green'. Possibly this colour is being used ironically, or to represent that things outside the trench are living normally, like the poppy. It also provides an excellent internal rhyme with the words before and after: 'sleeping green between'. The fact that this area is described as sleeping is also interesting. There are, we learn later, dead bodies lying in No Man's Land, so perhaps Rosenberg, like many other poets, perceives the dead as merely sleeping. Or possibly, he is implying that, at least while no battle rages, the land itself may sleep.

The poet imagines the wry, almost gloating, smile of the rat as he scuttles past dead bodies en route, yet he describes these bodies not in terms of death or decay, but using strong, vivid language reminding us of the mens' best physical qualities when they were alive. These dead men, he asserts, have not been so fortunate as the rat. It is interesting to note that he doesn't compare the dead men's misfortune with himself but with the rat. This makes the reader question whether he feels that the rat is better off than all of them - both the living and the dead; or whether he feels that he may as well be dead himself.

Now the tone and language change and the dead men are no longer allowed the physical qualities he previously gave them. He claims that they have been murdered on a whim. The fact that he describes the dead as being bound to their murderers implies that the guilty party is the person - or institution - paying them. In this case that would either be the army or the politicians. The image of death he creates here is more gritty and realistic. Describing their resting place as the very centre of the earth suggests that the land itself has been wounded or cut open, an image which is reiterated in the description of the ravaged fields in which they now lie.

He then enquires, presumably of the rat, whether he can perceive fear in the eyes of the dead. It is worth noting that he says 'our eyes', not 'their eyes' which, again, suggests that he associates himself more with the dead than the living. The shells and guns are described as 'shrieking' while the sky is a 'still' heaven. Perhaps he is ironically suggesting that the earth now is more like Hell than Heaven. It seems that he is now mocking the rat, challenging it to find a symptom of fear in the mens' eyes - where he knows that there will be no demonstration of feeling whatsoever. The fact that these are 'our' eyes, however, suggests that he is also beyond fear.

Suddenly we are returned to the image of the poppy, but again, not to admire its beauty. Having their roots in the veins of the men could be a comparison with the colour of the flower and blood; or he could be implying that as the mens' bodies rot into the soil, the poppies 'feed' on them - just like the rat. Again, he returns to an image of death: the poppies keep dying - just like the men, in a seemingly endless cycle.

The poet believes, quite falsely of course, that the poppy behind his ear is safe. He forgets that in picking the flower, he has killed it. This affords the poppy the same arbitrary sense of impending death as the men. Also the flower is now bound to its murderer as were the men. Being behind the poet's ear is by no means safe, but does imply that their deaths, or lives, are linked. It is as though he feels the poppy gives him a sense of security. The poppy, he says, is white with dust, which could be a reference to the words used in a funeral service: 'ashes to ashes, dust to dust'. This might confirm that he knows that the flower and (by connection) the poet himself, are already dead - or as good as.

This is a bleak poem, devoid of hope for the future. The poet does not mention any other people, except the dead; in fact the only other living thing is the rat. The poppy, once picked, is dead. It is as though, thus surrounded by death, Rosenberg feels drawn towards that state himself. Both the rat and the poppies are deemed to be feeding off the dead men, thus giving them a element of triumph and superiority.

There is a feeling of monotony in this poem: time does not appear to move on; there is no progress, other than that of the rat. This could be said to be reminiscent of Wilfred Owen's *Exposure*, which relates the tedious and pointless waste that epitomises the lives of the soldiers; as though those who are still alive should be unfavourably compared with the dead. Another poem which warrants some comparison with *Break of Day in the Trenches* is Siegfried Sassoon's *Prelude: The Troops*. The vocabulary and language used in these two poems is quite similar. For example, both mention the dawn as a dreary, gloomy time of day: for Rosenberg it 'crumbles', while for Sassoon it is dull and grey - neither of these descriptions give the reader any feeling of the usual optimism associated with daybreak. Both poets suggest that the men are being murdered - this is strong language which leaves no doubt as to an author's viewpoint, or the feeling that a great proportion of blame should be attached to those deemed responsible. In both poems, there is a reference to green grass, but in neither case is this used to represent hope or life, but is more a reminder that such thoughts and aspirations have been abandoned. These two poems also share an allusion to dust: Rosenberg appears to hint at a funeral service, while Sassoon refers to entire armies of men who have become dust.

Rosenberg's poem was written in the summer of 1916, while Sassoon's appears to have been produced towards the end of 1917, and like much of his work, makes his anti-war, anti-establishment viewpoint very clear. Both poems share a similar message: that the war is a gargantuan waste and completely futile; both point a finger of blame; and both, without upholding the war in any virtuous manner, praise and pity its victims.

Unlike Sassoons' or indeed Owens' poems, however, there is no bitterness or anger in *Break of Day in the Trenches*. It is infinitely more matter-of-fact - as though Rosenberg feels that he is merely stating the obvious.

DEAD MAN'S DUMP

This poem begins with a description of artillery being drawn up a track towards the front. It is described as being rusty which denotes its age and the amount of use it has seen. The guns are given an air of authority with the use of the word 'sceptre', implying power; and also of sacrifice from the symbolism of the 'crowns of thorns', reminiscent of that worn by Christ at the Crucifixion. The guns serve a useful purpose, however: they halt the enemy who are described as brutish and, who would, otherwise be able to slay the poets' fellow soldiers.

The wheels of the limbers crush the bodies which lie on the road. This description of crunching bones is almost disturbingly realistic, leaving nothing to the imagination. The poet points out that in death, there is no difference between friend and enemy, and that in fact, they now lie together. He also implies that as the shells continue over their heads, there will be more deaths to come. The use of the word 'crying' as the noise made by the shells is worth noting, since this would normally be a sound associated with mourners, except of course, these men have no one to mourn them. Rosenberg could also be suggesting that the shells are sorry that these men are dead and are, either genuinely contrite, or are sad because they cannot kill them anymore.

Next he tells us that the earth has been waiting to reclaim these men ever since they were born. He suggests a sense of greed and urgency, almost a blood-lust on the part of the earth, which can only be satisfied and strengthened by a steady supply of the dead.

He seems to believe that the earth has taken the mens' souls and flung their bodies back, leaving them to decay. He questions who has removed the spirits of these men: was it some unseen being - like a God - or was it the war itself: were these men made soulless by the war, rather than by death. This section of the poem mourns the loss of so many young lives which are described as 'half-used'. It is as though he feels that life has been literally sucked out of these men, like a bee drinking honey. The manner of their deaths is described as 'swift', yet although this implies a lack of suffering, he also seems to be saying that this, almost indecent haste, leaves no time to appreciate their lives, worship their spirits, or mourn their deaths.

Now we return to the living, with an image of Hell. Those still alive are referred to as being thrown on a funeral pyre, denoting that they are living with the dead. They are able to walk through this scene of devastation as though they are fed and looked after by the Gods, untouched by what lies around them. He seems to suggest that what he is witnessing should be sufficient to make him die from fear, but he has not; so perhaps there is worse still to come. This denotes a sense of immunity to the sights that surround him, and possibly to death itself. He is surrounded by a cacophony of sound - all around him shells burst, as though the sky is raining death. He remembers that those who now lie dead were recently living and 'vigorous'.

However, for some, death does not come instantly. The injured, he says, are given time to dream of their home and loved ones and other such things as they have not allowed themselves to ponder, until now. The war and their experiences of it have prevented them from thinking such happy thoughts.

Next comes an image of a stretcher-bearer, whose face is 'splattered' with the brains of the man he is carrying. He puts down the stretcher and when he looks at the soldier again, finds that he is dead. This verse is heart-rending; the language used is simple and very descriptive, so that the reader can picture the stretcher-bearers' brain-splattered face and feel his sense of loss when he realises that the man no longer needs his care. This verse acknowledges that men were still capable of such feelings of caring and kindness, despite their surroundings.

This dead soldier is left with many others, who have been lying there much longer. The fact that this group of bodies is left at a cross roads is interesting. It could be a literal reference to a cross roads, where bodies are left, hopefully, to be collected and possibly buried; or it might also imply a metaphorical cross roads, where the dead may begin their next journey, presumably to Heaven, while the living return to walk through Hell. These bodies have obviously been lying here for some time as they have turned black with decay - as though they have been burnt. The grass, even the earth itself, appear to have more life in them than these bodies. The physical appearance of these bodies is another reference to Hell and fire.

Amongst the others, the poet spots the body of a man, who has obviously not been dead for very long. He imagines that the man would have heard the wheels of the limber as it approached and how, in desperation he would have reached out, longing for them to stop; or else for his life to end now, since knowing that help was so near and yet being unable to reach it was torture. The description of the dying man crying as life passed from his body, washing over him like a rising tide, even as he still hoped and prayed for help, is deeply moving. The reader can imagine the man's sense of desperation, knowing that help is to hand, while he lies dying and powerless to reach it. As the limber rounds the bend, the men hear the dying soldier's final cries - literally the last noise he will ever make. Then, as they pass, their wheels, which had given him a final thought of hope, graze his now dead face.

This is amongst the most poignant, brutal and realistic of all First World War poems. By portraying the war as a ceaseless, pointless Hell in which hope and youth are lost forever, it is simply and quite unemotionally, stating a fact. Even in the title, Rosenberg has managed to portray this needless waste, since the dead men are not mourned or buried, but dumped unceremoniously, to rot into the earth, their spirits having long-since been drained by the endless war.

The poignancy of this poem lies in the fact that, without sentimental language, Rosenberg manages to portray pity and sorrow at man's self-destruction. His uncompromising language makes this poem more realistic than many - but without bitterness or anger. Instead his tone is resigned - as though the carnage knows no end and he has already sacrificed himself, safe in the knowledge that the killing will go on. He sees no end in sight, but also cannot see a means of justifying what has gone before. He paints an image of a human tragedy unfolding, which there is neither the will nor the power to prevent. In this world, life and death have become confused as have Heaven and Hell, as he is no longer able to distinguish between the two.

This sense of tragic loss and waste is shared by many other poets - notably Siegfried Sassoon, Wilfred Owen and Charles Hamilton Sorley. One poem which bears some comparison with *Dead Man's Dump* is *The Death Bed* by Sassoon, in which he vividly describes the desperation of a dying man, clinging on to life, and the arbitrary nature of death which eventually claims him, despite the fact that he is surrounded by loved ones who are willing him to pull through. Finally, Sassoon reminds us how pointless the young man's battle for life has been, as in the distance, one can still hear the guns.

Sassoon's poem is an intense and beautiful portrayal of the dying man's final thoughts, tempered with the reality of the ongoing war, suggesting that where this young man goes, others will follow - again, as in *Dead Man's Dump*, there is no end in sight. Unlike many of Sassoon's other poems, however, there is no bitterness or blame here, but a powerful description of a young man passing, unwillingly and unfairly, from life to death.

Rosenberg, in *Dead Man's Dump*, gives us an image where life and death are blurred. As in many of his poems, he places himself more with the dead than the living - in this instance on a 'pyre' - a living hell. He portrays the living and the dead as spiritless. The life is drained from these men, not yet old enough to have lived and they are left to rot. His language and tone are harsh, not beautiful and even nature is given qualities enabling it to take life: the earth has been eagerly awaiting these dead men - as though through them it gains added strength; the shells are burning bees with a fatal sting; death is like an incoming wave which overpowers the young and consumes them. He is describing, with heart-rending realism, a world which, through its own self-destruction, has gone mad.

RETURNING, WE HEAR THE LARKS

This poem opens with the men marching back from the front to a rest-camp.
Rosenberg describes the night as sombre or gloomy and points out that the
soldiers fear the night because it heralds untold dangers. These men are
obviously exhausted as they drag their tired bodies back towards the camp, and
the comparative safety it holds. Here they will be able to sleep, even if only for a
short time, away from the danger and discomfort of the front line. The road
down which they march is described as blasted by poison, which denotes that it
has obviously been shelled, either literally by poison gas shells, or that Rosenberg
perceives all shells as deadly - like poison.

Then the tone changes as the poet hears birdsong. The repetition, three times, of
the word 'joy' symbolises the unusual nature of this emotion for these men,
which is reiterated by the fact that this is deemed by the poet as being strange.
The dark night no longer seems fearsome, but is now filled with beautiful
birdsong. An image is being created of these battle-weary men, who have
tramped, exhausted from the front line, and are completely overwhelmed by the
unseen beauty they have discovered. They turn their faces towards the blank sky
and the birdsong falls like a gentle shower of rain, soaking their senses with its
invisible harmony.

A jolt back to reality follows, as the poet states the bare fact that, just as
birdsong appears to be 'raining' from the sky, so could a shell - unforeseen until
it is too late. This takes the reader back to the realism of the poet's situation, in
that death, during the First World War, was as everyday and commonplace as
birdsong in peacetime.

Then comes partial reassurance as we learn that the only thing which has
dropped from the sky is the birdsong. However, he says, this is only the
equivalent to the shattering of a dream, because the danger which will destroy
them, and their dreams themselves, are both invisible, and will arrive
unannounced, one bringing beauty and peace, the other destruction. He
compares this sense of unseen, yet impending doom with that of a blind man,
who waits on the sand while the tide comes in, unable to move.

At the end of the poem, it is as though the poet is saying that behind every
thing of beauty lurks danger and death. He appears here to be criticising women
as he says that in their kisses they have a hidden danger. This could be an
allusion to the women who appeared to gladly send their men to war with a kiss,
or goaded them into joining up, little dreaming that such action would bring
death and destruction. He is not comparing a woman's beauty very favourably

with the lark's birdsong, but perhaps it is the uncomplicated nature of the song which endears it to the poet, rather than the physical attraction, and implied danger, of a beautiful woman.

Nature, in the form of birds, animals, flowers etc., is often used in First World War poetry as a means of forming a contrast between the beauty and peace of home, with the harsh realities of war. Examples of this can be seen in the works of many poets, for instance: Rupert Brooke, Edward Thomas and Laurence Binyon among countless others. The contrast here, however, is that many of these poets use these images of 'home' to symbolise a nationalist pride, and therefore justify, at least to some extent, the fighting (and, in some cases, to positively encourage it).

Rosenberg, on the other hand, as an experienced and war-weary private soldier, uses such images to portray the sense, demonstrated in this poem, that destruction lurks everywhere - even in nature at its most beautiful. This poem creates the impression that he feels surrounded, and overwhelmed, by death.

WILFRED OWEN

For many people, Wilfred Owen epitomises the image of the First World War soldier-poet and like Rupert Brooke, he has come to symbolise the waste and futility of the conflict. His death, coming just one week before the end of the war, coupled with the fact that his parents received the news of his demise on the day the war ended, has given him an almost iconic status. Owen's friendship with Siegfried Sassoon had a great impact on his life and poetry and has been well documented by many authors - most notably Pat Barker in *Regeneration*. Jon Stallworthy's choice of poems is fairly standard and shows all of them show Owen at the height of his ability, after his meeting with Sassoon at Craiglockhart.

BIOGRAPHICAL DETAILS

Wilfred Owen's early life was a mixture of happiness and disappointment. He enjoyed a close relationship with his mother, yet the family's lack of money prevent him from attending university, as he failed to gain the required scholarships. In order to escape these disappointments, in 1913 at the age of twenty, he left England and took up a teaching position in France. He was still there when the First World War began in August 1914. Initially, this event had little impact on Owen and he did not return to England until September 1915, whereupon he enlisted in the Artists' Rifles.

After his training, he was commissioned as a Second Lieutenant in the Manchester Regiment and sailed for France in December 1916. This was the coldest winter of the war and gave Owen a rude awakening as to the harsh conditions of trench warfare. In March 1917, he fell into a cellar and was concussed, resulting in a short hospital stay. The following month, he was blown off his feet by shell-fire and spent several days lying in a shell-hole, surrounded by the dismembered remains of a fellow officer. He seemed to recover from this experience, but it was noticed that he had become shaky and his speech was confused, which resulted in a diagnosis of shell-shock. He was sent to Craiglockhart Military Hospital in Edinburgh, where he remained until October 1917. During that summer, he met Siegfried Sassoon, who came to have a great influence over Owen, both personally and professionally. Owen became extremely attached to Sassoon and the older, well-respected poet did a great deal to advance Owen's poetic career.

Although Owen was declared fit in October 1917, he did not return to the front until August 1918. In October, he was awarded the Military Cross for gallantry. On November 4th, he was shot and killed while trying to lead his men across the Sambre-Oise Canal. One week later, the Armistice was signed, signalling the end of the war and it was on that day that his parents received the telegram informing them of their son's death.

ANTHEM FOR DOOMED YOUTH

This sonnet was completed on, or just before, 25th September 1917 and the final draft, of which there were many, bears several amendments by Siegfried Sassoon, whom Owen had met while both men were at Craiglockhart Military Hospital during that summer. Sassoon's influence over Owen's poetry can be seen in many of the pieces which he wrote during that period, although *Anthem for Doomed Youth*, in a different form, was first imagined by Owen as early as September 1916. During the summer of 1918, Owen began to assemble a Table of Contents, in preparation for the publication of his first volume of poetry. In this table, he listed *Anthem for Doomed Youth* under the title 'Grief', which shows his intended theme in this piece.

The first point of interest in this poem is the title, which immediately informs us that the poem is essentially a tribute to the young men who are 'doomed' by the war. Owen had, in many of his earlier drafts, referred to the men as 'dead' rather than 'doomed', and this alteration changes the entire emphasis of the poem.

The opening lines introduce the two threads which run throughout the poem: grief or mourning and the slaughter of war. Owen questions who will lament the dead, who have been shown no more respect than cattle, in the manner of their death. Even in asking this question, however, the reader is already able to sense that the answer is 'no-one', as there is an air of hopelessness here. Owen then almost contradicts this assumption, however, by reminding us that there will be mourners, but only in the form of guns and rifles. He personifies the weapons and turns the noises they make into the sounds of grief. So, the booming of the guns and rifle fire become the 'orisons' or prayers of a funeral service, although even these are described as 'hasty', which gives them less significance than they deserve. These men are not even afforded an attempt (or mockery) at a funeral: they are given nothing. 'No prayers or bells' will sound for them and again, Owen employs personification to tell us that the only 'choir' which will sing for these men will be in the form of the noises made by the shells. These metaphorical 'choirs' are, however, not really in mourning, because they are deranged and, therefore, their noises are those associated with the insanity of war, rather than with grief. The unmentioned element here is that many of the dead soldiers will have no funeral for the simple reason that they are 'missing' and there is, therefore, no body to bury.

The final line of the octet brings a change in the tone of the poem, leading us into the calmer, more reflective, sestet and contrasting with the noise and anger of the first seven lines of the piece. The 'bugles' are reminiscent of the playing of the Last Post, while the 'sad shires' serve to remind us that someone, somewhere will mourn the dead.

In the second verse, Owen continues with this quieter tone, in which he describes the more commonplace funeral rites, which we know these men will be denied. Now, however, he no longer seems angry, but remorseful. The candles which would normally be lit in a church and held by altar boys, are suggestive to him of the eyes of these young boys, which seem to 'shine', presumably with tears. He reminds us that these boys are saying a last farewell to the dead, while we are always aware, because of the title of the poem, that the dead soldiers are little more than boys themselves. Girls also mourn, and in their case, Owen remarks that the paleness of their faces is like the cover of a coffin (or a 'pall'). This reinforces the idea of extreme grief and sorrow, in that the girls are drained of colour - just like the young men for whom they mourn. Through the creation of an ethereal atmosphere, Owen has suggested that these devices of remembrance are not simply that, but they are also reminders of the level of loss experienced by the boys and girls and by the soldiers themselves: in all cases, they have lost their youth, their innocence and their hopes for the future. The flowers are particularly symbolic of this, in that they represent a beauty which will soon fade and die.

The final line of this poem depicts the closing of curtains, or 'blinds', over a window, which was a common habit at the time, in a house where someone had died. Here, however, Owen has also conveyed other suggestions. The slowness of the dusk, which will happen every single day, reminds us of both the time which it takes to grieve and the reality that, for many, like the dusk of every passing day, the sorrow will never end.

This is an undeniably moving poem, which evokes none of the deep bitterness which can sometimes be associated with Owen's verse at this time. There is anger here, undoubtedly, but it is interwoven and ultimately overpowered by his sadness. There is more than one recipient of his sorrow, in that while acknowledging the hardships of the soldiers, he has clearly not forgotten those at home who will have to learn to live with their grief. At the beginning of each stanza, Owen poses a question, which he then goes on to answer, although his answers give him no pleasure, since they are negative and distressing.

The regular rhyming pattern and rhythm of this poem help the reader to really focus on the words and their meanings, which, due to the number of drafts and changes through which this poem went, have been very carefully selected. All of this is further assisted by Owen's use of alliteration and assonance, which add to the soft, flowing tones of the piece as a whole. One of the few lines which remained unchanged through the last few drafts, was the final one, with which he obviously felt justifiably satisfied. The use of this sonnet form is also reminiscent of love poetry, showing Owen's depth of feeling on this subject and making the whole piece even more reflective and significant.

The subject, tone and atmosphere of this poem are reminiscent of much of the home-front or non-combatant verse which was written during the First World War. Such pieces include *The Fields of Flanders* by Edith Nesbit, *The English Graves* by G. K. Chesterton or *Lament* by Wilfrid Wilson Gibson. In these cases, however, because for various reasons the poets are all non-combatant, they are not only speaking of sorrow, loss and remembrance, but also of an incalculable gratitude. This is, quite understandably, not a sentiment which is found in *Anthem for Doomed Youth*.

A possible influence on Owen may have been Laurence Binyon's *For The Fallen*, which he is known to have read during 1915. In this piece, Binyon is urging his readers to remember the dead with pride and dignity. The most remarkable aspect of this poem is that it was written in September 1914, within weeks of the beginning of the conflict and yet it has gone on, at least in part, to become the most quoted and best known poem of the entire war, due to it's fourth verse:

'They shall grow not old, as we that are left grow old:
Age shall not weary them, nor the years condemn.
At the going down of the sun and in the morning
We will remember them.'

It is not inconceivable that Owen was remembering this verse, when he wrote the final line of his sonnet.

Anthem for Doomed Youth has, as stated earlier, been influenced by the direct involvement of Sassoon, but also it would seem by some of his poetry. Owen had read some of the older poets' works, in particular Sassoon's volume of poetry entitled The Old Huntsman and Other Poems which was published in 1917. This contains at least two poems which may have affected Owen, namely The Death Bed and The Last Meeting. Both of these poems are very different from Sassoon's customarily ironic or critical verses and are much more reflective and thoughtful in tone. In the first piece, The Death Bed, Sassoon describes the slow demise of a soldier in a hospital ward, explaining in great detail the various sensations of pain which this man has to tolerate and contrasting them with his thoughts as he experiences many different things, from rain to nightfall, for the very last time. His description of the moments immediately after the man's death are beautiful and moving:

'And there was silence in the summer night;
Silence and safety and the dreams of sleep.'

The alliteration and assonance used here and throughout this piece are reflected in Anthem.

The second poem, The Last Meeting, is more personal and was written by Sassoon following the death of David Thomas, a fellow officer whom Sassoon had come to admire. The final verse of this long poem describes how the poet will reflect upon this time in later years, when he remembers his lost friend:

'And, as it was in life, his name shall be
Wonder awaking in a summer dawn,
And youth, that dying, touched my lips to song.'

In common with Anthem for Doomed Youth, the focus of both of these poems is on loss and grief as well as facing an unknown future - for both the dying and those left behind. Without doubt, Owen respected Sassoon - both as a person and a poet - and there are those who believe that their meeting had perhaps the greatest influence on Owen's writing - other than perhaps the subject matter itself. In Anthem for Doomed Youth, Owen urges us to remember the dead and shows that by being touched to song himself, he had come of age as a poet.

DULCE ET DECORUM EST

This poem was begun at Craiglockhart in the autumn of 1917, although, like most of Owen's work, it later underwent many amendments. He addressed *Dulce Et Decorum Est* 'to a certain poetess', which was a direct reference to Jessie Pope, who had written patriotic, nationalistic and positively war-mongering verse at the beginning of the conflict. This poem was written as a direct response to this and shows the influence of Siegfried Sassoon in its tones of anger, resignation and criticism of civilians.

The first point of interest is the title, which is taken from the Roman poet Horace's *Odes* and literally means 'It is sweet and meet'. Owen completes the quotation at the end of the piece with 'Pro Patria mori', meaning 'to die for one's country'. This is an ironic title, intended to shock educated civilians by the poet's use of their comfortable latin phrases in a frightful context.

Dulce Et Decorum Est opens with a vivid description of men walking back from the front line, leaving the horrors of war behind them. This description paints these, presumably young men, as old and haggard. Owen describes them harshly as 'old beggars under sacks', which gives the impression of someone who is more like a tramp than a soldier, weighed down by uniform and kit. The 'sacks' in this line may refer to the blankets under which soldiers (and tramps) might sleep, or to the material from which many army supplies, such as uniforms, sandbags, and so on, were made. In this way, Owen may be implying that the men are weighed down by all of the trappings of the war. The downcast tone of the first two lines changes momentarily in lines three and four, as we realise that the men are marching away from danger and towards their 'distant rest'. The fact that their hoped-for rest is described as 'distant', may simply indicate that they have a long march ahead of them, or that they have been in the line of fire for so long that the very idea of being able to relax seems very far removed from their present and past circumstances.

Owen then returns to a less optimistic tone, as he begins to once again describe these men, who are, it would seem, in various states of dishevelment. He provides a telling contrast in his description of the mens' feet, when he tells us that some of them have 'lost their boots', but then describes them as 'blood-shod', implying that their boots have been replaced by blood. Whether he intends this literally or as a metaphorical representation of the idea that the men are steeped in blood, is open to interpretation. Whichever is the case, Owen presumably meant to dehumanise them, as one associates horses with being 'shod', rather than human beings and he continues this analogy when he describes them as 'lame'. According to Owen, in fact, these men seem to have lost all useful purpose: they are 'blind' and 'deaf', as well as being so tired that they appear 'drunk' with it. The gas shells (or 'Five-Nines') which continue to fall behind them, as they march away, have no effect, which is meant to demonstrate their complete exhaustion, but also reveals how they have become immune to the noises and dangers of the front line.

Unfortunately, the men's deafness to the shells, brings the inevitable panic when they find themselves in the midst of a gas attack. The second verse commences with the shouts of alarm and the order to fit their gas helmets.

Owen's description of this as an 'ecstasy of fumbling' initially seems peculiar. He may be alluding to that sense of rushing adrenaline which, in its sheer panic, almost gives the impression of excitement, or this may be a medical reference to 'ecstasy', as a suspension of one's normal emotional state, caused mainly by an intense pre-occupation with one idea or task. The notion that the gas masks are fitted 'just in time' supports this feeling of unsuppressed panic. However, not all of the men have actually succeeded in fitting their masks and one is crying out and staggering as though he is on fire, or affected by caustic 'lime'. Owen then changes the pronoun from 'we' to 'I', giving this section of the poem a more personal and haunting atmosphere. He describes seeing this man through the steamed up visor of his gas mask, as 'drowning' in the gas, which evokes a sense of helplessness on his part, and certain death on that of the victim.

Owen continues with this personalisation of his account, as he describes how the scene of this man 'drowning' has continued to haunt his nightmares. His reference to his 'dreams' shows that his war experiences were continuing to affect him, even while in Scotland. The fact that he has placed this statement in a single couplet and repeated the impression that the man is 'drowning', while he remains 'helpless', shows that this section of the poem, and its meaning, have a unique significance.

The pronoun changes back to the first person plural, as Owen now describes the physical effects of the gas on this man, and the impact on him of having to watch the victim's suffering. He tells us that the man, still alive, had been 'flung' into a wagon, which again dehumanises him, making him appear more like a beast than a person. His eyes 'writhe' in agony in a face which is described as 'hanging', which may be a literal account of his features, or may refer to the dead face of a hanged man. The ensuing narrative of the man's suffering leaves little to the imagination, as Owen builds the tension and anger in layer upon layer of revulsion, before abruptly stopping and changing the tone once again. He suddenly addresses himself directly to a 'friend', by whom we may infer than he means Jessie Pope, and implores this person to refrain from filling children's heads with the 'old Lie' that it is 'sweet and meet to die for one's country'. In describing Horace's words as a 'Lie', Owen is attempting to shock his readers by telling them that one of the beliefs which they have long held dear, is a falsehood. His addressing of Jessie Pope as a 'friend' is at once intentionally ironic and patronising.

Although this is a poem of irregular verses, it does have a fairly uniform rhyming pattern - with none of Owen's later prolific pararhyme - and some use of assonance (such as 'white eyes writhing' and 'devil's sick of sin') which helps to create the building tension towards the end of the poem. The aspect of being haunted by such sights and experiences also reminds us that when he first began writing this piece, Owen was a patient at Craiglockhart Military Hospital, where he was surrounded by men with visions of hell in their dreams.

Some of Owen's amendments between earlier drafts and this final version are interesting. This is especially true of lines 23-24, which had at one stage read:

And think how, once, his head was like a bud,
Fresh as a country rose, and keen, and young, –'

The change to these lines shows how angry and bitter Owen had become and how much he sought to shock and disempower those who wanted to glorify the conflict. Modern readers may appreciate Owen's emotions and, possibly choose to agree that he might have had some justification in directing his displeasure at Jessie Pope specifically, and others like her in general. However, one should bear in mind that in 1914, when Pope was writing some of the very pieces which have made him so angry, Owen himself had written a poem entitled *The Ballad of Purchase Money*, which contains the following verse...

'O meet it is and passing sweet
To live in peace with others,
But sweeter still and far more meet
To die in war for brothers.'

... and possibly draw a different conclusion.

EXPOSURE

The date for this poem is unknown, but it is thought that the events it describes took place in Winter 1917, and that he may have begun it at around this time, but in preparation for the publication of his work, Owen made numerous changes to it over the following year or more, probably finishing it in late summer 1918. This is born out by the fact that in his Table of Contents, which he prepared in that summer, this poem is still entitled Nothing Happens, so the title, at least, was undecided at that time.

In a letter to his mother dated 4th February 1917, Owen described the extreme cold he had experienced in the trenches, vividly describing the snow and icy wind. One of his men froze to death and many ended up in hospital. They were heavily shelled, although no-one was hurt as a result of this. In this letter he tells how the extreme cold affected him physically, literally making his feet feel dead. He also speaks of the unburied bodies and points out how the sight of them, sitting there, motionless day after day is enough to drain any soldiers' spirits.

The title of the poem is the first point of interest. It naturally refers to the exposure to the cold and the elements, but also to the fact that these men are exposed in other ways - to enemy fire, to constant potential danger, to boredom and ultimately death.

The first stanza opens with an ironic references to one of Owen's favourite poets: John Keats, whose *Ode to a Nightingale* begins 'My heart aches', although in Owen's case, he states that it is the brain which aches. In this first verse, Owen dramatically and immediately introduces the concept of suffering in extreme cold, with his reference to the fact that the icy wind cuts through the men, reminiscent of the bayonets used in battle. The wind is therefore seen as having the same killing potential as a knife or bayonet. The men are nervous because the night is so quiet and they worry that this denotes an imminent attack. They are in a salient, which is a place in the line which protrudes into enemy-held territory and is, by definition, prone to heavy fighting and difficult to defend. The ending of this verse, and all the following ones, perpetuates a sense of hopelessness, confusion and monotony.

The next two stanzas go on to further describe the awful conditions: the elements are given human or natural connotations, so the wind is mad - like many of those who are experiencing these hardships. The barbed wire is like a bramble, and the dark clouds at dawn are an army. He continues this metaphor later in the poem where the wind is nonchalant and the snow touches their faces, like fingers. The coming of dawn does nothing to lift their spirits, as might normally be expected, because nothing changes.

The description of the dawn as an 'army' is possibly an allusion, not to a real army of men, but to the clouds which gather like a regiment preparing for battle, although in this case, they are heralding the arrival of more snow. This adds to the belief that the weather and conditions are as dangerous to the men as the enemy. However, this reference could also be interpreted as a hallucination of a forthcoming battle when you bear in mind that the German army wore grey uniforms. This battle obviously does not materialise, because, once again, nothing changes.

The fourth verse introduces the more conventional danger of bullets, but Owen informs us that they are less dangerous than the cold. At least a bullet would mean a quick death while the cold only provides a long, unrelenting suffering. There is so much snow that it has become impossible to see, hence the air is 'black' - there is no hope and the blackness also represents the colour of death. The monotony continues with the snow being caught and drifted around by the wind, which reflects the fact that the men are also drifting and helpless.

Although by the fifth stanza, it is daylight and the sun is shining, the men are still suffering - there is no respite from the cold, or from the war and it is so hopeless that they begin to question whether death is actually already upon them and the whole experience is simply one of slowly becoming dead. In these dreamy moments, their thoughts turn in verse six, to the warmth - both literal and metaphoric - of home, as represented by the fires. But the doors are closed to these men and they are forced back to their unhappy reality. These last two lines could imply that they know there is no future and no way back from war and, therefore, to dream of home is futile. There could also be a reference here to the frequently held concept that, due to the complacency and lack of understanding shown by those safe at home, who are still able to 'rejoice', these soldiers now belong more with their dead and dying comrades than with family and loved-ones.

In the seventh verse, Owen raises the idea that men must die; that this is the only means of securing the things which men hold dear; that they bear no resentment for their plight and that they were in fact born for this very purpose. He tempers this, however, with the final line which tells us that even a love of God cannot survive these horrors. The poem ends on the same hopeless note - the future only holds more of the same; they will die here in the frozen mud and become unrecognisable, even to their friends. The closing lines perfectly demonstrate the finality of the piece and of the situation, since it is through your eyes that you experience everything and they reveal all your emotions. The fact that all of the men's 'eyes are ice does' not necessarily mean that they are all dead, but could be interpreted that they have nothing left on the inside - no emotion left to feel and nothing more to give.

The use of alliteration and assonance to describe the experience of cold and boredom is vital in this poem, so in the third stanza, the 'rain soaks' and the 'clouds sag stormy', which not only illustrates the weather, but also adds to the sense of monotony, since these words are dull and lifeless. In the fourth verse the ceaseless gathering snow is described as 'flowing flakes that flock' which not only perpetuates the relentlessness of the snow, but also compares it with a flock of sheep, drifting aimlessly, so again we have a reference to a harsh nature and the pointlessness of the war.

Owen has also used a regular verse pattern and pararhyme throughout, such as 'silent/salient', 'brambles/rumbles', which again adds to the feeling of repetitiveness. This is even further enhanced by the fact that the final line of each stanza is shortened, often duplicated and always thought-provoking.

This poem could be compared with Isaac Rosenberg's Dead Man's Dump. Both of these poems seem to confuse the living and the dead, making much of the pointless waste and futile nature of the war. Owen and Rosenberg demonstrate their sense of hopelessness in the future: they can see little reason in anything. The descriptions of the men, and their surroundings in both these poems are startlingly realistic, with nothing left to the reader's imagination, although Rosenberg's language is more harsh and gritty.

INSENSIBILITY

Probably written, or at least completed, in March 1918 while Wilfred Owen was at Ripon, this poem provides a description of various forms of 'insensibility' or indifference to the war and how these manifest themselves. It opens with the suggestion that the only soldiers who can die happy are those who have become immune to the war: who no longer feel warmth towards their fellow men. They have no pity or sympathy for those who suffer; they do not make jokes or feel sensitive to the fact that they are walking over the bones of their fallen comrades, although they can feel physical pain because they are aware that their feet have become 'sore'. This all implies that the men have been at the front far too long and that they have become insensitive to their surroundings. Owen says that 'the front line withers', which implies that it resembles plants which are shrivelling and dying, but he then reminds us that this is not the case, because it is the men who are dying and not the 'flowers', to which many poets often referred in their verses. He seems to acknowledge that although some of the men may be insensitive to their surroundings, the poet still finds plenty about which to be 'tearful'. However, his use of the word 'fooling' suggests a pointlessness to the poetry. The men have simply become spaces which, as they die, require replenishing; they are lists of 'losses' whom others believe should have been able to carry on fighting and yet, really, there is no one left who cares. These final three lines could be interpreted as an indictment of those at home, who read the casualty lists and wonder at the number of dead, but do nothing about it themselves.

The second verse describes men who have also ceased to care but these men have become unconcerned for themselves, rather than others. They simply feel nothing. This is because through such low spirits, a boredom with one's surroundings has become the best cure for the fear of being shelled. As such this could be described as a self-inflicted numbness or a sense of survival, caused by becoming inured to one's environment. Owen describes the shells as teasing and doubting the men which shows a certain amount of irony at the situation. In this way, he gives the shells a human quality - as though they deliberately choose their victims. This demonstrates the popularly held belief that one's well-being was as much a matter of luck or destiny as training or preparedness. In addition, he suggests that there is no logic in the decision as to who should live and who should die. Owen continues in this vein, in describing how 'Chance' decides such matters, almost as though preparing a balance sheet or a set of accounts, thus comparing such decisions with a mathematical equation. It would seem that the counting up of the men's wages is more difficult than the addition required by 'Chance'. Men who enlisted at this time were often referred to as 'taking the King's shilling', which was the amount that a new recruit was paid per day, so the addition of a man's salary would have been a simple equation. In the final line of this verse, Owen suggests that the reason that the 'arithmetic' of the dead is so easy is that no one bothers to keep count anyway: armies are simply destroyed, without anyone keeping a record of how many have been killed. This second verse, while continuing to comment on the collapse of morale at the front, also perseveres with the idea that there is no one who cares: it is not just that the men at the front have become insensitive - everyone has.

In the third verse Owen focuses on the men whose imaginations have been weakened to the point where they merely function, rather than living; they carry out their duties, but no more. They have nothing to burden them because they have lost the ability to think for themselves. However, this insensitivity goes further still, for these men feel nothing at all - not even physical pain, or the torment of death. They are surrounded by death and blood, but they remain unaware of its presence. The initial fear which accompanies a bombardment or an attack, has a momentary effect, which soon passes. Their 'small-drawn' hearts denote a sketched personality, made incomplete by their lack of feeling or emotion. The notion that battle can be cauterised or burned to prevent its continuation is interesting as it implies the healing of a wound and yet we know that this cannot work, because there can be no remedy. However, despite the Hell of battle, the men have become hardened to the point where they feel absolutely nothing and can even laugh at death. This verse paints an even more desperate picture than the previous two: these men have lost all sensitivity; they feel nothing; know nothing; care for nothing.

Next Owen describes the contentment of the men on leave, who are able to forget. They obliterate their memories of the war to the extent that they do not think about the men going over the top at dawn and dying in the process. Then he tells us about the men who are not trained to plan ahead. These men, one could assume, are the ranks, rather than the officers and NCOs, who would have undergone more rigorous training and have had greater experience, thus enabling them to think for themselves, rather than merely following orders. The more innocent men sing as they march, evidently oblivious to what lies ahead, while the trained man has enough imagination to keep quiet: he knows what will happen and that they have nothing to sing about, as dusk approaches. Dusk is traditionally associated with death, but in war poetry is generally less feared than dawn - a more popular time for attacks. However, dawn will always follow dusk in the 'relentless trend' by which night follows day. Owen describes the daytime as large, but the nights are huge, which shows how the darkness and the unknown still signify fear, even to those who have been trained. This verse may appear to be fairly damning of the ranking soldiers, until the reader remembers Owen's use of the word 'lad' in line four. This suggests someone of youth, as well as inexperience, and implies that Owen is referring to new recruits, who innocently march - and sing - on their way to the unknown front, while the worldly and experienced men remain silent.

The fifth verse suggests another category of men, with whom Owen associates himself. These are the 'wise' men, the educated or trained men, whose misfortune is that they cannot think without remembering the blood and death - it fills their every thought. He wonders, given this mental torment, how they should perform their 'task' of recording the war through poetry. Their only option is to attempt to see the war through the eyes of the men whom Owen had been describing earlier, namely those who have not be trained to think for themselves. These men have 'blunt' eyes, rather than sharp ones, which implies that they do not see everything. Their eyes are also 'lashless', or unprotected.

Owen goes on to say that whether living or dying, such men are not really alive: they are not significant individuals and the lives, or deaths, mean little. They are so lost to human feeling that they cannot even tell whether their own peace - or death - is any different from that of the old men who die safely at home. This verse describes, once more, Owen's central theme of the loss of feeling, which he compares with his own sensitivity and, again, with that of of the 'old men' - a common First World War euphemism for those responsible for the war. Up to this point one could argue that Owen seems to regard these men jealously. He almost envies their insensitivity, compared with his own troubled thoughts and feelings.

In the final verse, Owen describes the last category of insensible people - those who have chosen to keep themselves safe from the war. These people cannot be hurt by the war, not just because they have a physical remoteness, but also because they have made the conscious decision to remain detached. It is not that they are too stupid or simple to understand the horrors of the conflict, it is that they are too poor in spirit to care. Owen may seem to wish that these people were dead - the reference to them being 'as stones' in the second line of this verse could be interpreted either as a reference to their immobility and inaction or as a desire for them to be like tombstones. These people are so hardened to the suffering of the war, Owen states, that nothing can touch them: they feel no sorrow or compassion for their fellow man and they never will, no matter how much time passes, how many men die, or how many tears are shed. Owen's final line in this poem shows that, regardless of the attitude of these 'dullards', the mourning will go on for ever: the crying will never end.

This is a sad, moving poem, whose title immediately sets the scene, in that it tells us of Owen's theme here - the insensibility of various types of people. Owen lists them out, verse by verse, reserving - as in much of his other poetry - his greatest criticism for those on the home front, who have not been made insensible, but have chosen to become that way. Everyone is described as insensitive in some way, demonstrating a hopeless element which even affects the poets, who find it difficult to write of their experiences without becoming submerged in the horror and desperation of war. He excuses the actions of all of these men, however, because they all have a valid reason for becoming insensitive to the war: either to protect themselves, or because they are simply too young and inexperienced to know otherwise.

Many of the other poems written or completed at Ripon shared these themes of the incalculable losses (in terms of death and mental or physical suffering), mourning, horrors of war and the callous attitude of those at home. These poems include *Futility, Exposure* and *Strange Meeting*, which all paint vivid pictures of the trenches and death, while reminding the reader how pointless each death is. Here, Owen is more thoughtful and retrospective than in some of his earlier pieces, such as *Dulce et Decorum Est*, which were written while at Craiglockhart and more directly under the influence of Siegfried Sassoon.

The form of this poem is irregular: not only are the line and verse lengths uneven, but the rhyming pattern too. Owen has made some use of pararhyme here, such as 'shelling'/'shilling', 'red'/'rid' and 'stuns'/'stones'. This irregularity allows the reader to concentrate more on the words and their meaning, but it is also a less 'forced' form of poetry than a regular chiming pattern, which - in this instance - would be inappropriate for the message. Owen's use of pararhyme - for which he became renowned - also has the effect of making the reader unwittingly focus on sounds. Each verse in this poem features a different series of sound effects, some more obvious than others. For example the second verse features soft 's' sounds, making this feel like a gentle description of the numbness created by the war. In verse six, however, the soft 's' sounds are joined by a series of words featuring the letter 'm' (mean, simplicity, immune, mourns, man, many). Such repetition, even if only of a sound, creates a greater, although unwitting, concentration in the mind of the reader. The imagery in this piece reminds the reader of man's connection with nature, and by extension, of man's comparative insignificance. So, the 'alleys' are 'cobbled' with the bones of their comrades; it is not the 'flowers' which are dying, but the men; even the stars and the seas seem unfortunate as nothing can ever really be the same again - because no one will ever feel the same again.

FUTILITY

Probably completed in spring 1918, this poem tells us its theme immediately, in its title. Futility, or pointlessness sums up the poet's thought process that there is no purpose to man's existence. Owen had written letters to his mother during the exceptionally cold winter of 1917. In one of these letters, he had explained to her that a man in his Company had frozen to death while at the front - surely one of the most pointless ways to die. Although this poem was completed over a year later, it is not inconceivable that Owen was writing about his earlier experience. The memory of this event may also have served to remind him, as he read of more deaths, that in the intervening twelve months, nothing had changed - hence Futility.

The poem opens with a kindly request to move a dead man 'into the sun' so that its warmth might revive him. Owen immediately introduces the idea that the man had been a farmer, in that he had been woken by the sun before, reminding him that the fields needed to be sown. This all suggests that the setting for this poem is sunrise, as the farmer would normally have woken at dawn. Normally, in First World War literature, the coming of dawn is portrayed as a time of fear, as this was a popular time of day to launch an attack. Here, however, Owen gives the dawn a more traditional treatment, greeting it with hope for new beginnings, or in this case that the sun will be able to revitalise the dead.

The soldier's familiarity with the dawn not only stems from his farming days, however, as even while in the trenches, its warmth has previously roused him from sleep. Except that today, it has snowed and now even the sun cannot wake him. Still, Owen has faith in the power of the 'kind old sun' and hopes that somehow it will find a way to bring life back to this man. The 'snow' which Owen mentions in this first verse could be interpreted as a metaphor for death. He may, of course, be referring to literal snow - giving an impression of coldness and desolation. However, it may be that he is alluding to the snow as a blanket of death in that so much destruction has taken place, it has becoming impossible to find life, just as though death was covering the ground, like snow.

The second verse opens with a reminder that this friendly sun helps plants to grow and that it has provided sufficient warmth to bring the planet to life. From its very beginnings the earth has depended on the sun to the extend that, without it, there would be no life at all. This link between mankind, the earth and the kindly sun shows a bond of trust and necessity: man needs both the earth and the sun in order to survive and, therefore, regards them as his friends.

Next, Owen begins to question the power of the sun, wondering whether the man can really be so difficult to waken. He reminds us of the human qualities of the man's body, which he informs us is 'still warm', suggesting that the man has not been dead for very long. The man had been much beloved and for him to have survived childhood and become a man would have been 'dear-achieved', or difficult. Yet, Owen begins to wonder whether there is any hope at all.

Then he questions why the earth developed, whether there was any point, if all that would result was the destruction of men. There is a growing desperation in Owen's question, as though he really does not believe that man can have so little purpose. Finally, he wonders why the sun ever bothered to work so hard to create and nurture the earth in the first place. Everything is so pointless, so what was the purpose in creating any of it - earth or man - if all that would follow was death. There is an implication here, that in destroying man, the earth will also face destruction and the sun's work will have been in vain.

This is a sad and hopeless poem, made more so by the fact that its beginning is so full of promise. Initially, Owen seems full of expectation that the sun can perform a miracle and bring life back to the dead man, just as it does to the earth each spring when it 'wakes the seeds'. However, he then begins to doubt and question, not only the sun's ability, but also its purpose and value, if death is the only result. There is no more point in the earth itself than there is in the body of the dead man - which implies that the earth itself is dead. All of this shows the poet's despair that the world has changed so much: death should not go unheeded and yet there is nothing to be done, because there is no power with which to make things better again. In addition, this sadness derives from the knowledge that there are no answers to his questions. The relationship between man, the sun and the earth is frequently explored in literature - notably in Owen's Spring Offensive, where the sun is shown as having a calming and soothing influence over the men.

Owen's use of language is noteworthy. His tone is gentle and calm - reminiscent of thoughtfulness and also of death. He speaks of the sun as 'whispering', 'kind' and gentle, rather than harsh and burning. This gives a languid air to the first verse, forcing the reader to believe that the poet is deep in thought. The first verse is more hopeful than the second, a sensation aided by the use of assonance, which links the poets thoughts together, as in 'awoke'/'unsown'/'woke'/'snow'/'old'/'know'. This forms the first verse into one long train of thought, rather than a series of disjointed sentences. The second verse is more questioning, more stilted and doubtful.

Throughout, Owen also makes simultaneous use of both full rhyme and pararhyme, as in 'snow'/'know', 'tall'/'all' or 'now'/'know', 'star'/'stir' and 'tall'/'toil'. This provides both balance and disharmony, which corresponds with Owen's growing doubts and questions.

STRANGE MEETING

This poem has a dreamlike, or even nightmarish, quality which frequently causes confusion as to its real meaning. It is impossible now to say exactly what Wilfred Owen had in mind when he produced this piece and even the date of its composition remains somewhat of a mystery. None of this is helped by the suggestion that *Strange Meeting* is, in fact, unfinished. In the manuscript, the last line has been added later than the rest of the poem, in a somewhat rushed hand, suggesting that Owen possibly intended to write more, but either changed his mind, or simply did not get the opportunity.

The poem appears to open with a degree of optimism, as the narrator believes that he has got away from the battle, although there is an element of doubt even here, as it only seems that he has found sanctuary. The tunnel which he enters, however, gives this poem its first nightmarish element. He describes it as being gloomy, but the use of the word 'profound' here could have two meanings: either the tunnel itself is profound, or possibly, very deep and with some unusual significance; or else it is profoundly dull in appearance. He implies here that this tunnel has been in existence for some considerable length of time, dug into the rock to form an archway. However, this is unlikely and in all probability the tunnel has only been there for the duration of the war. This suggests that the war has been going on for a long time, or at least that it feels as though it has. There is also a sense of permanence about this tunnel, almost as though it has become a part of the earth itself.

He notices that there are men who appear to be sleeping here. It would seem that, although they are quite still, like corpses, some of them, at least, are alive as he describes them groaning. The men seem to be in a trance as he asserts that they are either too mesmerised by their own thoughts, or else they are actually dead and this is why they do not move. It seems as though external forces are preventing these men from being active.

The narrator then examines these 'bodies' and, as he does so, one of them appears to come to life. This man looks at him with pity, knowing that they both share the same fate. His eyes are frozen, as though he is dead and yet he raises his arms, wanting to help the newcomer. The notion that the person wants to 'bless' the narrator introduces a religious overtone which is then dashed by the nightmarish element that follows. The narrator suggests that the man's deathly smile reveals that they are in Hell. The use of the words 'sullen hall' reflects the 'dull tunnels' of the second line which makes the reader question whether this is all a dream or whether it is, in fact, reality.

He goes on to describe the 'dead' man's face as lined with years of suffering. However, this is all in the past as, down in the tunnel, there are no reminders of the war. The battle might rage above them but here there is no blood and no noise from the guns. Next, the narrator begins a conversation by stating that they do not need to mourn. This may be because he realises that they are all dead, or because he knows that to mourn is pointless as it achieves nothing. Alternatively, he may be implying that as he feels he is among friends, he s better off than many others and, therefore, he has nothing to feel sad about.

The man responds, agreeing that they have nothing to regret, except for the years they will not live to see: their future. This, again, may be because they are dead, or because they cannot consider themselves to be really able to live again in the future. The man speaks as though the narrator still has hope, in that he uses the present tense, but it would seem that all of his own hopes are behind him now. He speaks of his youth and, initially, seems to refer to chasing after beauty, possibly in the form of a woman, but then contradicts this by stating that such beauty is transient. Real beauty lies in life itself and yet this also has a darker side as life is really just the passage of time.

The man then recalls the laughter and sadness of life and that both of these emotions are now lost to him. This would seem to refer to the feelings of others, as well as himself. Others will not laugh now, or share his tears as all they are left with is the pity which the war has caused. Such pity may be the sense of mourning for the dead, or self pity for the various sacrifices which the war has necessitated. This passage reinforces the notion that the men are actually still alive, but that they will never be able to live as they did before the war: that their lives have been ruined by their experiences.

Some people, he asserts, will be able to live in deluded happiness, despite the destruction which the war has caused: they will have no feelings of guilt about the consequences of the war, or their part in it. Some, on the other hand, will become so bitter and angry that they will eventually cease to live themselves, becoming so wrapped up in their rage. It is interesting to note that he attaches a proportion of the guilt or responsibility to himself and the narrator for the destruction of their own lives and values. He speaks of the survivors as hunters, following orders, regardless of the consequences and assumes that nothing will have been gained by the war. There will have been no development or enhancement of life. Here he seems to imply that the men who have fought and survived will be unable to forget their role in the fighting and will continue to live afterwards as they have done in the army.

The man reflects that he used to be brave and mysterious when he was younger but as he gained knowledge and understanding he has become more powerful. This shows the importance of experience over strength. Owen seems to be implying here that being brave - which was something he was keen to prove about himself - is not what he thought it would be and that it is his intellect which gives him greater power. Before returning to France, Owen had felt it necessary to prove that he was courageous and yet the reality seems to have ben perhaps less rewarding or satisfying than he had expected.

Next, the man asserts that, through his newly gained wisdom, he has managed to avoid the ultimate downfall of his world and his old way of life. This older world has withdrawn into its own pride, where it is now unprotected. Here the implication is that, if nations had believed that by going to war, they would be made safe, they are mistaken. Nothing can protect these nations from their own vanity and conceit.

He states that, even when there has been so much fighting, death and bloodshed that no-one can progress further, he would be able to cleanse them again, by reminding them of the past and telling them of all the things which the war has made them forget. Here, for the first time, there is a hint of possible redemption as he suggests that there are some elements of humanity which not even the foul stench of war can have completely corrupted.

He goes on to say that he would, in fact, have sacrificed his very soul to save his world, without hesitation or restriction, but he feels that it is wrong to achieve such salvation through aggression: the cost of the war is too great. Owen's use of the word 'cess' is interesting in that he may be referring to the war as a cesspit or sewer. Alternatively, another meaning of the word 'cess' is a tax on land or commodities which may suggest an implication of the cost of the war itself - not financial in this case, but human. So, the man could be saying that he would happily sell his soul to save the world, but that war is not a means by which this can be achieved.

Then the man appears to suggest that those who have not fought or died are just as responsible for the war as those who have. Everyone has given something of themselves in tolerating such inhumanity and all must share the blame. This reference to a bleeding and yet unwounded forehead may also have religious overtones and may allude to the crucifixion of Christ when He is said to a worn a wreath of thorns around His head, which made it bleed, although no-one had actually physically injured Him. Owen's inference here could be that he perceives those who are giving their lives as saviours.

The man's assertion that he is the 'enemy' may not be literal. This may be a metaphorical suggestion that all men are the same in death. There could also be an inference here that, in the madness of war, friends and enemies are one and the same. In other words, there is now so little difference between the two sides that it is impossible to tell one from the other. Another implication here could be that the narrator may represent the people - both soldiers and non-combatants and the man is accusing everyone of having killed, regardless of the role or nationality, meaning that all of the people must take responsibility for the death and destruction. Despite this accusation, the narrator has failed to recognise the man who he has theoretically killed and this reinforces the notion that all of these men are alike. They share the same viewpoint and yet must try to kill each other, when they might just as easily have been friends. The speaker has recognised the narrator and recalls his expression as he killed him the previous day. He remembers that the narrator had seemed to look through him, rather than at him, which is another reference to the inhumanity of war in that the narrator appeared to not even be focused on the person he was killing. The man asserts that, although he had tried to defend himself against the attack, his hands had been reluctant. This implies that the man had had enough of fighting and, possibly that he welcomed death as a release from the war. Now all he wants for all of them is to be able to rest and here there is a definite suggestion of relief that finally he has found peace.

This is a complex poem which is open to several interpretations. Owen's state of mind might be better understood if one knew exactly when this piece was written, but as stated earlier, even here there is some confusion. Both Siegfried Sassoon (who helped compile the first volume of Owen's work in 1920) and Edmund Blunden (who edited a second edition in 1931) appear to have believed that *Strange Meeting* was Owen's last poem and was, therefore, probably written in the late summer or early autumn of 1918. Dominic Hibberd, on the other hand, points out that as this poem appears in Owen's Table of Contents which he compiled during the summer of 1918, it must been written before that time and probably before he completed *Spring Offensive*. He asserts that it may have been written as early as the spring of 1918, before Owen left for France. The manuscript, however, shows several alterations to the text which may have been added at a later date.

One of the many questions which arises upon reading this poem is: are the men involved actually dead and are they really in Hell or are they still alive, but living in such hellish conditions that they cannot tell the difference between life and death themselves? Either assertion could be correct and there are many sources of evidence within the text which reinforce both theories. For example, at the end of the poem, the speaker states that he has been killed by the narrator, which may imply that both men are dead and that the narrator has recently been killed himself, has 'escaped' the battle and is joining the other man in Hell. Alternatively, one could interpret this speaker as a vision, who haunts the narrator, reminding him of all the men he has killed - a vision from which he knows he will never escape. The second theory is reinforced by the suggestion in line 16 that the narrator still has some hope left in his life. Whichever interpretation one places on this poem, the inescapable truth of it, is the hopelessness of war: that even for the survivors, everything is lost. This sense of despair is the predominant feeling in this poem.

Another possible interpretation is that Owen was pointing out that his own life could never have the same meaning again. His reasons for returning to France were, firstly to prove his own courage and secondly to write about the war from first-hand experience, rather than the safety of England. In this poem, he may be implying that, as a poet, he will never be able to write again, as he has, by participating in so much destruction, destroyed his own humanity and ability to transfer that into a poetic form. In other words, the numbness created by the war means that he no longer feels the same about his own life and he has lost the power to put any feelings which he does have into words. For a man like Owen, to lose the will or capacity to write poetry could be construed as a fate worse than death.

In his Preface to his volume of poetry, which he never lived to see published, Owen spoke about pity as being one of his main subjects. In *Strange Meeting*, he also refers to this emotion, as the 'truth untold', implying that pity is the only real, or truthful emotion to survive the war and yet no-one speaks of it, possibly because they are ashamed of their own role in the conflict, or because they do not wish to show their feelings in case they are misconstrued as self-pity. Owen wrote this Preface during the spring or summer of 1918 and was clearly influenced by the idea that as a poet he had a sense of responsibility to tell the truth, stating that he had no concern for poetry and was only interested in war and pity. These sentiments seem to be echoed in this poem. He seems to be hoping that out of this suffering and sadness there must be some good, even if it is only the compassion which he hopes that one man has learned to feel for another, regardless of nationality.

The notion of the living and the dead somehow being able to communicate with one another and that they are all in a living Hell is a theme which other poets have touched upon. Ivor Gurney in *The Target*, for example, suggests that having killed a German soldier, he will, once inevitably dead himself, ask his victim which of them has felt the greater pain: the man who died, or the man who had to kill him. He describes the war as a 'bloody mess' and a 'tangle' which reflects Owen's suggestion that both sides are suffering equally and the living and the dead have both lost a great deal for seemingly no purpose. In *Dead Man's Dump*, Isaac Rosenberg portrays his pity and sorrow at man's self-destruction.

Throughout this poem he demonstrates that he believes himself to be living amongst the dead, in Hell itself and yet he is clearly still alive. Here both the living and the dead are spiritless, having both given up any idea of a life. Like Owen, Rosenberg shows us a world driven mad by its own wanton self-destruction.

Different people have different interpretations of *Strange Meeting*, many find it difficult or even impossible to completely understand Owen's meaning, and it remains one of his most impenetrable poems. In his volume of Owen's work, published in 1931, Edmund Blunden has stated that this piece is uniquely of and about the Western Front. He believed that Owen was writing about a scene which was both dreamlike and realistic at the same time. Blunden asserts that Owen's depiction of the dim, smoky tunnels, full of resting soldiers snatching a few moments of peace, captures the very essence of a soldier's existence on the Western Front. He goes on to say that Owen has created, from this scene, a living nightmare. So, Edmund Blunden would seem to have believed that Owen was writing about the realistic loss of a man's soul, snatched from him by the horrors and brutality of his existence, rather than a scene between two genuinely dead men in Hell. This interpretation, coming as it does, from another poet who shared many of the hardships of the war, provides a valuable insight into the complexities of *Strange Meeting*.

ROBERT GRAVES

Although he is one of the more well-known war-poets, Robert Graves is often neglected in anthologies. Here, Jon Stallworthy has chosen three fairly unusual poems.

BIOGRAPHICAL DETAILS

Robert Von Ranke Graves was born on 24th July 1895 in Wimbledon. He was educated at Charterhouse School, but postponed his entry into St John's College, Oxford to enlist in the Royal Welch Fusiliers at the outbreak of the First World War. Graves met another poet, Siegfried Sassoon, quite early in the conflict and the two maintained a long, although tempestuous friendship. His direct involvement in the war ended temporarily in July 1916 when he was so badly wounded that the Medical Officer thought him unlikely to survive. By the time it was discovered that Graves was, in fact, still alive, news of his death had already been sent to his parents. Great confusion followed, but eventually he made a sufficient recovery to return to France - albeit briefly - where he remained until he was struck down with pneumonia. During his recover in England, he was diagnosed with shell-shock and was sent to Osborne House on the Isle of Wight to recuperate.

When Siegfried Sassoon made his declaration against the war in July 1917, Graves travelled to the regimental headquarters in Litherland and pleaded, unsuccessfully, with Sassoon to retract the statement. Eventually, after Graves made an emotional appeal at Sassoon's medical board, the authorities sent him to Craiglockhart. This event, essentially, ended Graves's involvement in the war, as his lungs had been so badly damaged, it was impossible for him to continue to participate.

In January 1918, he married his first wife, Nancy Nicholson and they had four children in the next six years. Graves returned to study at Oxford, but finances were always a problem and the young family received a great deal of help from Siegfried Sassoon, as well as other friends and relations. In the meantime, Graves had become infatuated with the American poet, Laura Riding; they became loves and a peculiar ménage was set up.

Graves wrote his autobiography *Goodbye to All That* in 1929 and emigrated to Majorca immediately afterwards, taking Laura with him. This book caused much upset - especially to Sassoon, who objected to the way in which his family had been represented. The Spanish Civil War caused Graves and Laura to leave Majorca and eventually they split up. He then met and fell in love with Beryl Hodge - who was married at the time, although her husband very quickly agreed to a divorce. Nancy, on the other hand, would not accept the situation and refused Graves's appeals. He and Beryl moved in together and had three children before Nancy finally agreed to a divorce. During the second world war, Graves's oldest son, David, was killed while serving in Burma. After that conflict was over, Graves, Beryl and their children moved back to Majorca, where a fourth child was born. Unable to settle to a simple relationship, Graves continued to have affairs throughout his marriage, which remained, somehow, intact until his death in 1985.

SERGEANT-MAJOR MONEY

This poem was written in 1917, after June, since that is when the Arras offensive, mentioned in verse one, came to an end. At this time, Graves was in England. He had been severely wounded during the Battle of the Somme, on 20th July 1916; his wounds being so serious that he had actually been reported as killed in action. A letter of condolence was dispatched to Graves's parents and his name appeared on the casualty lists in The Times. However, Graves was not dead and sent a brief note to this effect to his parents from hospital in Rouen, whereupon they spent several harrowing days seeking official confirmation of their son's status and whereabouts from the War Office, before he was confirmed as alive on 30th July. The Times then published a retraction of Graves's untimely death report on 5th August. The wounds to Graves's lungs, coupled with the shock he had suffered, meant it took many months for him to recover and he did not return to France until January 1917. He was, however, soon back in England, suffering from pneumonia and was then found to also have shell-shock. Graves never returned to active duty again: the damage to his lungs was considered too serious for him to pass another medical board.

The poem was written quite clearly at some distance from the conflict, offering the poet the benefit not only of hindsight, but also of objectivity and humour, which might not have been possible had he been writing while in the thick of the fighting.

Sergeant-Major Money opens with a statement that reads like an excuse - almost like a child who has broken something and then says, "It wasn't me!" In this case, Graves is explaining that the story he is about to relate has nothing to do with his own battalion, but with one which was "alongside". There is an implication here that this gives Graves the right to be more critical of the actions of the others involved, and certainly to pass comment on them, because he and his own men had not been directly concerned in anything that had taken place. However, being as the action had happened in close proximity, he feels that he is able to give a truthful, as well as "frank" account of events. Graves informs us that, since fighting at Arras, this particular battalion have lost all of their officers, except for a "batty major" and an alcoholic colonel.

In the second verse, we learn that one of the replacement Company Commanders - in charge of "B Company", is totally inexperienced in everything except "gas drill". This leaves the sergeant-major (a man named "Money"), effectively in charge of B Company, since there is no-one else to take control. It would seem, however, that the sergeant-major is a bit of a tyrant, since Graves goes on to explain that he makes the soldiers "sweat blood".

The third verse reveals exactly how harsh the sergeant-major had been. His "humour", which Graves describes as "Old Army", but which is clearly out of step with the new volunteer and conscripted recruits, causes one soldier to shoot himself, while another goes insane. Whether the first man commits suicide, or has a self-inflicted wound, is not made clear, but Graves leaves the reader in no doubt that the new members of the Company cannot cope with the actions and methods of the sergeant-major. Nonetheless, he blithely points out, with extreme irony, that the sergeant-major manages to preserve "discipline" within the Company to the point that, when they return behind the lines to rest, the Colonel feels able to commend the men on the standard of their equipment.

In the fourth verse, Graves tells us that the diligence and oppression meted out by the sergeant-major has meant that the junior officers, who would have been young and inexperienced, have been able to be much less harsh with the men themselves: they can leave all the hard work to Money instead. However, eventually his bullying really takes its toll and two of the men kill him with their bayonets. This line, despite its content, is delivered with an element of humour, as though the location and method of the sergeant-major's death matter just as much as the fact that he has been murdered. The two men responsible for his death are portrayed heroically, creating the impression that they have done everyone else a favour, but we are also given the feeling that they are only acting naturally or instinctively.

Finally, Graves explains that, when it comes to analysing the death, there is no-one to be blamed. The officers had depended on the sergeant-major, because they lacked the experience and understanding to lead the men themselves. The killers had actually shown outstanding bravery, we're informed, although Graves doesn't make it clear whether this courage had been displayed on the battlefield, or in the act of killing the sergeant-major. Finally, Graves says that Sergeant-Major Money himself can't be blamed either, since he was only an old regular soldier, doing his best to adjust to life in a new army that had changed beyond his recognition.

This poem has a jaunty tone which belies its content, although the story is also told with a certain amount of tongue-in-cheek humour that may be intended to make the reader feel uncomfortable with the testimony that is being revealed. Everything else about the poem is regular and uniform and this also contrasts with the episodes contained therein. Graves's language is every-day and matter of fact, so the reader is left in no doubt as to the meaning of his words. The ranks he has chosen to portray also cover most areas of army life, showing us his perspective of their value. The Colonel is the most senior person mentioned and is portrayed as a drunk, who is only interested in the standard of the men's kit. Next comes the Major (not the sergeant-major), who is only mentioned once and, even then is revealed as "batty". Then come the subalterns, who would be Second Lieutenants and Lieutenants, such as the Commander of B Company. In this case, these men are newly trained and have just arrived as replacements for previously killed line officers. After these men would come non-commissioned officers (NCO's), such as Sergeant-Major Money, who is an "Old Army" soldier, meaning that his enlistment pre-dates the beginning of the war and the advent of Kitchener's New Army of volunteers. This means that, other than the colonel and the major, the Sergeant-Major would be the most experienced man present. Finally come the other ranking soldiers, consisting of junior NCO's, such as Sergeants, Corporals and Lance-Corporals and then, at the bottom of the pile, the privates. The fact that the more senior officers leave the Sergeant-Major to get on with his job would not actually have been that unusual, especially given that senior NCO's were generally more experienced than those who surrounded them.

Other poems which could be compared with Sergeant-Major Money would include any that give an unfavourable view of the army or senior officers. Such poems might include Base Details or The General by Siegfried Sassoon. In the latter poem, Sassoon employs a similar jaunty style to that used by Graves to convey the irony of the treatment of men by more senior officers. The main difference between the two poems would have to be that, while Graves tells his story simply and openly, Sassoon - as ever- lulls his readers into a false sense of security, making us believe that this is just an account of two men meeting "The General" on their way up to the front line. Only at the very end of the poem does he reveal that, thanks to the general's "plan of attack" both men are now dead. The poem lacks emotion and, like Sergeant-Major Money, is told in such a matter of fact tone, that the reader can easily believe this to have been an every-day event, which is rather the poet's intention.

Another poet who addressed this subject was Alan P. Herbert who, in his poem After Battle, is highly critical of the insensitivity of senior officers towards their men. Again, there is a sense of irony and bitterness here, but Herbert also manages to convey empathy and pathos, as he shows more understanding for the feelings of the men who have fought hard in battle and who like to be praised, but who also want to be left alone to consider their individual emotions and reactions, as only they can, since only they understand fully what has happened.

The tone of irony and satire that runs through all of these poems is possibly present throughout because the poets may have believed that straightforward anger or bitterness would not have been taken so seriously by their readers. However, to appear to mock such a situation actually has the - probably desired - effect of making the reader really think about each of the situations and their own responses.

RECALLING WAR

This poem was written in approximately 1938 and was one of only a handful of poems in which Robert Graves looked back retrospectively upon the First World War. At the time, of course, the Second World War was a cloud hanging darkly over Europe, but Graves remained somewhat aloof from this. He and his muse, Laura Riding, had been living in Majorca since 1929, but had been forced to flee in 1936 due to the dangers of the Spanish Civil War. They eventually settled in Northern France and it may have been this proximity to the battlefields of the First World War that made Graves look back to the conflict. Before the outbreak of the Second World War, however, he and Laura travelled to America, although they then split up and Graves returned to England in the middle of 1940. Graves's oldest son, David, from his first marriage to Nancy Nicholson, was shot and killed in Burma in 1943, while serving with the Royal Welch Fusiliers - the same regiment as his father.

The poem opens with a description of a scar on the skin, which has healed, but which has become "silvered" or whitened over time. This makes it now appear "clean", especially when compared with the remembrance of how it would have looked when the wound was fresh. The area of the wound, Graves says, only hurts in wet or damp weather and this is the only thing that makes him remember the injury at all. Graves goes on to justify this statement, pointing out that, even those who have lost limbs, or their sight, have become accustomed to these losses over the intervening twenty years and have compensated accordingly, managing as well, or better, than they did before. The war they fought, he comments, is really only a memory now - no different really to any other, such as the tracks left on the die of a hill by a walker, who might have stumbled and been frightened in the night, but in daylight, sees that there was nothing to fear. So might many, Graves ironically assumes, look back upon the war, who do not understand the true memories of those involved.

In the second verse, Graves ponders the nature of the war, which he had just, ironically supposed to be relatively insignificant, stating that it wasn't just an ordinary disagreement between countries. This had seemed more like a plague that had contaminated the world, making the whole earth appear downcast and dour, even when the spring had been at its height and normally nature would have made life seem more positive and uplifting. At such a time, when everything was so bleak, Graves asserts, men seemed to have no alternative, other than to join in and become antagonistic, matching the pessimism of the times with their own actions and attitudes. Graves also attributes to mankind a sense of chivalry and violence which, when coupled in this way, seems unattractive and incongruous, especially when also described as "boastful", giving the men the air of swaggering in their contemptuous behaviour. It is interesting to note that Graves claims that they had gained a "valiant yard", which unit of measure shows how futile had been their boasting and courage, to achieve so little. He goes on to claim that a natural death was unfashionable, since it meant that a man had been denied the opportunity of death while young and in battle. Death was the "patron" - or benefactor - of what Graves refers to as a "healthy" death (namely one in battle, rather than one as a civilian). The ending of this second verse seems very dismissive of anyone who wasn't a soldier, as though death outside of the conflict was an irrelevance and not to be taken seriously.

This criticism of civilians is common among the war poets, but for the emotion to have continued unabated for twenty years, seems unusual.

Continuing this train of thought into verse three, Graves comments that death and fear made excellent companions, keeping the men on edge at the temporary nature of their lives, to the extent that they could only focus on their bodies and ignored their thoughts. This made affection and attachments all the keener, seeming more significant than in the past and, although Graves has stated that the men "waived the mind", this seems only to apply to their present, during the war and did not prevent them from reminiscing about feelings from the past. Old thoughts flooded back to them, which may not seem that important, but at the time had been full of significance. Even these sweet thoughts however, had been mingled and intertwined with realities such as weaponry being at the ready and the knowledge that a doctor would have been on standby, waiting to treat the wounded. This makes Graves recall that the men had often abused God for the shortage of home comforts, which they had so freely recalled, or for the wounds which hurt them, but about which the doctors could do nothing.

In the fourth verse, Graves's anger begins to rise to the fore as he comments that the purpose of the war seemed to have been to return the earth to ugliness and sink all things of beauty: to extinguish all elements of happiness in faith and belief, through which the world had come to know and trust in itself. Despite any objections to the contrary, any declarations of love or faith, nothing could endure these horrors and, eventually, all would have been driven "mad" by their experiences.

The fifth verse sees a satirical note in which Graves describes the manner in which the "merry" guns would peck at the buildings, just like children "nibbling" at a "piecrust". The guns had also felled trees, which Graves equally likens to children hacking at dandelions with a twig. Next, he describes the machine-guns as being "toy-like" in their "rattle", as they cut through the "tin soldiers". These, he says, are exactly the same "visions" that will be used in the future when men seek to justify acts of war. Graves's use of the words "boastful" and "despair" make this ending both unattractive and mournful and possibly give us an insight into the poet's thoughts regarding the forthcoming Second World War.

This is a fairly straightforward poem to understand and Graves's message appears to be almost a warning that, although the First World War may appear to many to be nothing more than a series of distant memories, it is a great deal more serious than that for those who were involved. There is some subtle irony involved here, in that Graves initially comments that the wounded and maimed were not really affected by their injuries and then, later, he compares much of the damage inflicted by the weapons of war to the comparatively innocent harm done by children playing. These comments are intended to be critical of those who, in 1938, on the eve of another war, would belittle and undermine the efforts and sacrifices of a previous generation. Graves is recalling that he had only been young when the First World War had begun and that he had probably taken his youth for granted, only to realise how transient it was. He wishes, perhaps, to warn the next generation not to be so blasé about their own lives.

Recalling War could be compared with any First World War poem that was written after the conflict, which looks back on it, or deals with its consequences. Alternatives might include Edmund Blunden's *Report on Experience*, which was probably written in 1929, in which the poet decries the fact that men were led to war falsely, without being "formerly told" what they would have to sacrifice. He goes on to comment that, during the war, he had witnessed the destruction of the countryside and the fall from grace of beautiful women - although this may be a reference to fine women who became more interested in war and soldiers than might be considered ladylike. However, Blunden's poem ends on a fairly positive note, stating that God still "loves humanity" and will continue to do so.

Another poem which could warrant some comparison is Siegfried Sassoon's *To One Who Was With Me in the War* which was written in March 1926. This is a sad poem, full of memories, given in a conversational tone. Sassoon had written the poem as though he were trying to help his friend, Ralph Greaves (a pianist who had lost an arm during the war), come to terms with his losses and memories. However, in doing so, it would seem that Sassoon has reawakened his own recollections and found them to be more disturbing than he might have imagined.

Other poems that could be compared with *Recalling War* might include those written more recently by non-combatants, such as Vernon Scannell's *The Great War*, which has an angry, incriminating tone. Scannell fought in the Second World War, but states in his poem that on Remembrance Day, he does not recall that conflict at all, but the earlier war: "the one called Great", which is etched into this country's conscience. Another such poem would be Douglas Dunn's *War Blinded*, which details the human consequences of the conflict, but is also about society's blindness to war and its casualties. These later poems share one common emotion, other than perhaps anger and disappointment, and that is gratitude. This latter feeling is one that won't be found in many poems by combatant poets, who had little for which to be grateful.

THE PERSIAN VERSION

Background to the Battle of Marathon

Taking place in 490BC, this battle formed part of the Greco-Persian wars and was fought on the Marathon plain in north-eastern Attica (a historical region of Greece, containing Athens). In a single afternoon, the Athenians, supported by the Plataeans, drove back the first Persian invasion of Greece. The Greeks were greatly outnumbered by the Persian forces, but managed to defeat them, by reinforcing their troops to the flanks and thereby surrounding the Persian soldiers, who abruptly fled. According to Herodotus, the Greek and Plataeans lost only 203 men, compared to the 6,400 lost by the Persians. A legend grew out of this battle that an Athenian messenger was sent from Marathon to Athens to pronounce the victory, whereupon he promptly died of exhaustion. This distance, being around 25 miles, became the basis for the modern marathon race, which was re-created in 1896 with the competitors in the first modern Olympic Games competing over the same Marathon to Athens course. Herodotus, however, tells the story somewhat differently, as that of a trained runner, who was sent from Athens to Sparta before the battle had begun, in order to request assistance from the Spartans - evidently covering a distance of approximately 150 miles in two days.

The Persian Version

The Persian Version was written sometime between 1938 and 1945, making its inclusion in the First World War section of Jon Stallworthy's anthology a little confusing, as it was neither written during, nor about that conflict. Its content could really relate to any battle, since Graves's message here is that it is the victor who writes the history of a battle and may, therefore, say whatever he pleases. In this case, the battle was an enormous victory for the Greeks, but it really had little impact on the Persians, who had vast resources and were not going to be greatly affected by defeat in one "trivial skirmish", regardless of its significance to their opposition.

The poem opens with a reference to the fact that the Persians would not "dwell upon" their defeat at Marathon. Graves refers to the Persians as "Truth-loving", which immediately suggests that the Greeks, on the opposing side may have been contrasting in their manner: namely liars, or at least may have exaggerated the importance of their victory. Graves reiterates this theory, going on to describe the Greeks as having "theatrical tradition", which suggests again that they might be inclined to embellish, or enhance their roles. He describes "that summer's expedition" from the Persian perspective as "a mere reconnaissance", thereby severely belittling its significance, while to the Greeks it had been a "grandiose, ill-starred attempt/ To conquer Greece", showing the difference in the two viewpoints.

Graves describes some minor details of the battle, such as the outflanking of the Persian forces, but makes light of this as only an insignificant element of the battle. He goes on to explain that the Persians treated the battle with "contempt", before telling us that they would "refute" the "claims" made by the Greeks. The Persians, he says, would claim that they had won, and they declare this by stating that in spite of the Greeks having defended their land well, and the "adverse weather" conditions, the Persians all fought "magnificently together", thereby diminishing the battle's outcome, compared to the manner of its fighting, and relegating it to nothing more than the "trivial skirmish" mentioned at the beginning of the poem.

As demonstrated in this poem, by extinguishing the Greek's delight and glory in their victory, the Persians effectively manage to rewrite their own "version" of the battle, extending their efforts to the point of becoming a triumph.

In applying this message to other wars (while remembering that Graves was writing after the First World War and during the Second) one could interpret his meaning here as a criticism of all propaganda, showing that, depending upon one's perspective, anything can be turned into lies and exaggeration, created to suit the person writing it. Graves's portrays his message with great irony, especially at the end of the poem, meaning that he certainly expected his audience to take him seriously.

This poem could be studied in conjunction with *Triumphal March* by T.S. Eliot, in which the poet seems to examine the cost of war, by looking back over the literal number of items and armaments employed during the fighting. Both poems were written retrospectively with an ironic tone and contain elements of the attitude of the victorious side being unrealistic in their claims.

EDMUND BLUNDEN

One of the most regularly anthologised poets of the war, Edmund Blunden spent more time serving on the Western Front than any other poet included in this collection. His experiences had a profound effect on his personality and he remained deeply troubled by his war-time memories for the remainder of his life.

BIOGRAPHICAL DETAILS

Edmund Blunden was born in London on 1st November 1896. The eldest child of schoolteachers, Charles and Margaret Blunden, he spent a very happy childhood, especially after his family moved to Yalding in Kent , where he was able to enjoy the countryside. Edmund was initially educated at the local village school and then at Cleaves Grammar School. Here, one of his teachers suggested that the academically gifted Edmund should sit the entrance exam for Christ's Hospital - a school of 'public' standards, without the high fees. He passed this examination and began his education there in the autumn of 1909. He then won a scholarship to Queen's College, Oxford, but by this time the First World War had begun, so Edmund postponed his university education and joined the Royal Sussex Regiment as a Second Lieutenant.

Blunden arrived in France, following his training, in the spring of 1916 and before long he found himself on the battlefields of the Somme. In November 1916, he was awarded the Military Cross and was then made Intelligence Officer. He also took part in the Third Battle of Ypres, also known as Passchendaele and it would be fair to say that, of all the soldier-poets, it was Blunden who spent the most time in the trenches. Early in 1918, he was sent back to England, to a training camp near Stowmarket in Suffolk.

Although he missed his comrades from the trenches, while there, he met and fell in love with Mary Daines and the two were married in June. By the time Blunden was recalled to his battalion, the war was already over, although he was obliged to remain with his unit until he was demobilised in February 1919. Blunden decided to resume his education at Oxford and also introduced himself to Siegfried Sassoon. In July, Mary gave birth to their daughter, Joy, although she died tragically at the age of just five weeks. While at Oxford, Blunden became friends with fellow war poets, Robert Graves and Robert Nichols, as well as continuing to build his friendship with Siegfried Sassoon. Although Blunden and Mary had two more children, their marriage was becoming strained, so in 1924, when he was offered the position of Professor of English at Tokyo University, he sailed for Japan alone, leaving his young family behind.

While in Tokyo, Blunden had an affair with a young teacher named Aki Hayashi and when he returned to England in 1927, she accompanied him, although their relationship was by now platonic. He and Mary were divorced in 1931 - the same year that he became a tutor of English at Merton College, Oxford. Two years later, he married again - this time to a writer named Sylva Norman. Neither of them had very much money, so Siegfried Sassoon paid the first year's rent on their new marital home. Before long, the relationship with Sylva, while still affectionate, was no longer sexual and during the Second World War, while she was away, Blunden began a relationship with an undergraduate named Claire Poynting. Sylva reluctantly agreed to a divorce and in 1945, Blunden and Claire were married. At about this time, he also fell out with Siegfried Sassoon over the latter's divorce, and they did not speak to one another for three years.

Claire and Edmund had four daughters and they travelled a great deal, especially in the Far East, as Blunden took up various job offers. They finally returned to England in 1964 and two years later, Blunden took over from Robert Graves as Professor of Poetry at Oxford University. Ill health finally caught up with him and in 1974, Blunden died following a heart attack. At his funeral a runner from his First World War battalion laid a wreath of poppies. Blunden was deeply affected by his experiences during the First World War and this is reflected in both his poetry and prose.

TWO VOICES

Originally entitled *The Survivors*, this poem was written about the Battle of the Somme, some time after it actually took place, making this a poem of memories. Blunden served with the 11th Battalion of the Royal Sussex Regiment and saw action over many months on the Somme battlefields. He was deeply affected by his war experiences, having spent longer in the trenches than any of the other mainstream soldier-poets.

The poem opens with a direct speech in which one of the "two voices" simply states that there is "something in the air". The scene for this speech is a "large parlour cool and bare", suggesting that the somewhat serene setting is somewhere behind the lines, far enough away from the guns that they cannot be heard. Nonetheless, these words create an atmosphere of dread and "tumult" amongst those present. Despite their feelings, however, the men present remain in "silence", awaiting their orders, which the speaker, whom we now realise to be an officer, finally gives. His manner in pronouncing these orders is "wryly gay", which suggests a certain irony or mocking to his outward air of good humour. This officer may be assumed to be a staff officer, since he doesn't accompany the men, but issues them with orders to march on their way.

In the second verse, we are told of another voice, which announces the fact that the men are to go "South". At the same time as this announcement is made, there comes the noise from a howitzer being fired. We may assume that this is a British gun, since Blunden speaks of it as though it were being fired from nearby, rather than of the sound of a German shell falling. He places this conversation in a "light hut", which suggest somewhere a little closer to the front lines than the "large parlour" of the first verse. This also creates the impression that this place is not, perhaps, so secure as the "parlour" of the first scene, as a "light hut" would afford little protection from shell-fire. In a contrary moment, just as the voice tells him this bad news, of their imminent move south, and the howitzer is heard to fire, Blunden also hears "skylarks" singing, which feels quite out of place amid the doom, gloom and noise. Again, we may assume that the speaker is an officer, because Blunden has him pick up his "riding-crop" before going out into an orchard, full of "bloom and scent", which feels rather incongruous, given the situation.

In the third verse, the "story" has moved forward from the "bloom" of the spring to the "misty light" of the autumn. In the intervening months, Blunden's regiment (part of the 39th Division) had been involved in fighting around Thiepval Wood on the Somme and he describes this fierce scene as a "roaring night" of memory. Looking back, he can recall both the angry guns and the quiet voices, both of which had been responsible for destroying the "flower" alongside which Blunden had fought. This "flower" not only represents the literal "bloom" of the "apple-trees" and the dense thickets of Thiepval Wood itself, but also all the young men who perished, fighting on the Somme battlefields. Blunden's recollections of that battle centre around the wood "and all its worst", and the voices of the two men to whom he had listened not long before the silence was shattered.

This poem shows Blunden at his most fascinating and complete. We can see the haunting of his mind by his memories of the "worst" of the war, even though he actually tells us very little about what actually happened. The Somme was Blunden's first experience of battle and proved a baptism of fire, for him and many others. At the same time, we can also witness his appreciation of nature and its ability to survive and flourish, in spite of the war. This is a strong feature of his memoir Undertones of War and can be seen here when he describes the skylarks singing and the apple trees blossoming, regardless of the guns blazing around them. Then, there is also Blunden's feelings towards his fellow soldiers. We can see his poor opinion of his superior officers, who are shown to be offhand and uncaring in verse one, treating their orders as ironic, rather than serious. However, his feelings for his fellow soldiers and junior ranks are very different: their brief mention here is as the "flower" - a simple description which implies that they hold all hopes for the future.

We know from the testimony of others, including Siegfried Sassoon, that Blunden was among the most haunted of the "soldier-poets" and that he rarely gave voice to his experiences. Occasionally, however, in his poetry, we get a glimpse into his memories. In this poem, Blunden's language is melancholy and evocative, especially in the first verse, which is replete with internal rhymes ("waited", "gay", "phrase", "bade", "ways"), helping the reader to feel a part of the scene which is being created.

When comparing this poem, one could look at any other piece which looks back on the war, or specific scenes such as Recalling War by Robert Graves, The Silent One by Ivor Gurney or Blunden's own Report on Experience. Each of these gives the viewpoint of a soldier-poet who experienced trench-life at first hand, survived the war and wrote about it afterwards. There are differences here, however. Graves is issuing an angry warning at the outset of the Second World War, seeing that the sacrifices and mistakes of his generation are about to be repeated. In The Silent One, Gurney, writing from the confines of a mental institution, shows a sense of regret for the passing of the days of shared comradeship, when all that mattered was survival. In *Report on Experience*, Blunden offers a list of man's shortcomings, but gives us hope for the future in the form of God's love. None of these poems offers the blank, dull acceptance of lost youth and innocence which is portrayed in *Two Voices*, where we can see and feel the poet's pain in recalling a time when he had faith in nothing more than the certainty of death, and a fear of survival, with all of its terrible memories.

THE ZONNEBEKE ROAD

The road mentioned in the title of this poem, according to Undertones of War, ran across the front-line trenches. At the beginning of the poem, the men are waking up to their first morning in these trenches, in the bitterly cold winter of 1917. The poem opens with a reference to the morning light, which seems faded or shrunken, almost as though the morning itself is dying, because it has been starved of goodness. This picture of early morning bears no resemblance to the customary bright cheerfulness of daybreak, with all its hopes for the day ahead. But then, as Blunden points out, the days are no longer young, which implies that neither is the war, or the men. This shows a sense of cold, depressing hopelessness right from the very beginning of the poem.

The faces of the men reflect this feeling of despair, which appears in their features like a physical pain, despite the fact that the most fearsome time of day - dawn itself - has now passed. Dawn, with its half-light and semi-wakened men was always a popular time for an attack, hence the men would have to "stand to" immediately before dawn, just in case. Once this time of day was over, they would "stand down", relax a little more, have breakfast and begin the day's chores. However, the fact that this dreaded time has passed without incident, does nothing to cheer the men or remove their pain.

Due to the fact that the men have been on duty in such extreme cold, their hands have frozen to their rifles, although one man, Stevens, who is obviously an older and much-respected man, just seems to carry on regardless, taking all these discomforts in his stride. Blunden suggests that the other men, who seem more despondent, should take heart from Stevens. He then points out that he has always found this particular part of the trench frightening, ever since he first saw it. This, he asserts, might be because of a collapsed dug-out, which reminds him of a grave: maybe he assumes that men have been buried there when it fell in. He also seems to believe that whenever the men are in a trench long enough for others to have died there, the place develops a melancholy atmosphere. This sadness serves no purpose, however, as the men will still have to go on living and dying there.

Next, he describes an intersection of the trench, which is particularly unsafe. Like many trenches, this communication trench has been given a nickname - "Haymarket". In this instance, two communication trenches led back to the support line - the other was named "Piccadilly" and Blunden notes, both here and in Undertones of War, how the Germans had managed to pinpoint their position with disturbing and costly accuracy.

He observes the dusty snow being blown along the road. It is not welcomed, as it might have been when the men were younger, but reminds them of how cold it is. Even the rocks and stones must feel this extreme of cold, and yet the skies obviously hold yet more snow which has still to fall and make them even colder. Blunden gives these clouds a threatening air, as though they are doom-laden. The whole earth seems overwhelmed by the cold: the broken trees look like teeth sticking up from the frozen ground; the man-made cracks and holes in the earth are like the grotesque open mouths of gargoyles, which if they could speak,would cry out in their pain. It would seem that nature is conspiring against the men now: not only is it so bitterly cold, but they are trapped and overpowered even by the barbed wire in front of them. Blunden describes the wire as being like a bramble or the dead stems of bindweed - both plants have a reputation for taking over flower-beds and eventually destroying the other plants that grow there.

Already, however, it is dusk and everything becomes grey again. The trees along the roadside have no branches, so they seem like dark columns, almost like they are standing to attention, guarding the road. Blunden believes that, despite its devastation, the men would prefer to be back in Ypres itself, but this is only the first night of their tour of duty: they must endure another seven such nights before they will be relieved.

The final section of this poem is open to interpretation. Firstly, it is unclear who the poet is addressing here. It may be nature itself, which seems to conspire against the men, or it may be the non-combatants, sitting quietly and safely at home. The idea of hearing the screams of the dumb would fit in with either scenario, as would death clashing - neither feat being really possible. The following line lists four dead or destroyed items - grass, willow trees, homes and men - once again, however, this does not help clarify Blunden's intended target. Then the final two lines are equally ambiguous. He seems to imply that the men are made of sterner stuff; they will grit their teeth and look upon their tormentors with contempt. It is for the reader to decide to whom these lines are addressed. There is every possibility that Blunden was almost challenging nature to do her worst, because the men, in whom he had so much faith, would rise above every challenge. Alternatively one could argue that Blunden had recently been home on leave and had become angry at the complacency he had found there. This poem may, therefore, be suggesting that the men at the front are entitled to look upon those at home with scorn, especially as they have to tolerate so many hardships.

Throughout this poem, Blunden makes references to nature, and in particular its harsher qualities. This scene would have taken place during Blunden's period of service in the Ypres sector in the winter months at the beginning of 1917 - the coldest period of the First World War. He gives some of the natural elements an almost human quality - so stones flinch; trees resemble teeth; daylight oozes away like blood from a wound; the black tree stumps look like sentries. Equally, he gives natural qualities to his war-like surroundings: the barbed wire, for example, is like a bramble or a dead weed. This technique resembles that employed by Wilfred Owen in his poem *Exposure* which describes the same period of the war. Owen, for example, portrays the wind as a knife, the wire as a bramble and the clouds are seen to be gathering like an army waiting to attack. This goes to show that both men, having experienced this particularly harsh winter, felt that nature itself had turned against them, adopting war-like qualities. The main difference between the two poems is that in Owen's all hope has gone - nothing makes any difference anymore, hence his repetition that there is nothing happening. Blunden's men have just one hope left - although that is not a very positive one - but he asserts that they can and will rise above their surroundings and conditions, because they are more worthy. Like Owen, Blunden's language in this poem depicts perfectly the extreme cold and desolation of that winter. His portrayal of the icy, frozen, broken earth makes the reader wonder how men could survive, yet Blunden assures us that they will - even if only through sheer determination.

VLAMERTINGHE: PASSING THE CHATEAU, JULY 1917

The poem opens with a quote from Keats's *Ode on a Grecian Urn*, which compares the image carved onto an Urn and thus preserved forever, with the actual content of that image and an imagined but realistic scene. The fourth verse of Keats's poem provides inspiration for Blunden's piece, as does the event, described in his memoirs *Undertones of War*, in which he describes walking past Vlamertinghe Chateau and seeing it standing almost intact and surrounded by flowers in full bloom. Thus, like Keats, Blunden is describing an image of beauty, effectively frozen in time and contrasting this with the guns, blood and death of reality.

The second line is also a reference to Keats's *Ode*, in that the image he is describing is one of sacrifice, where a heifer (a young cow) is being lead to an altar. In Keats's poem, he asks who is coming to attend this sacrifice, and Blunden answers him: it is the soldiers. They go up to the front line to be killed and Blunden seems to consider that there is a sacrificial element to these deaths, which suggests that their lives are being taken for some sacrilegious purpose. Death is, therefore, seen as an intentional, rather than accidental waste.

Next, Blunden questions whether the flowers are to commemorate the dead, and seems to imply that the presence of so many blooms reminds the passing soldiers, who are still alive, that they may soon be dead. In the next line, by using the word "may" instead of "must" at the beginning of his questions, he changes the emphasis. He now questions why the living should be reminded of their own immortality, rather than simply being able to enjoy the beauty of the flowers, especially given the horrors and discomforts of their daily lives. He then reminds us how unusual this scene is, as generally speaking, the earth has been transformed into just mud.

Then he turns his attention to the outside of the building itself, which seems stately and regal. It is possible that the pride and "borrowed" elegance of this building are described in this artificial way because this chateau may have housed the senior officers who sat and planned the sacrifice of the soldiers. The house has remained intact despite the guns, but then in Undertones of War, Blunden describes the chateau's orchards as the perfect place for artillery to be concealed. His description of the guns as "lowing" takes us back, once again, to Keats as he describes the heifer making this noise as she is taken to the sacrificial altar. It would seem, therefore, that Blunden is associating the noise of the guns with the act of sacrifice.

At the beginning of the second verse, Blunden gives a description of the flowers, using vivid imagery and colour, which contrasts well with the imagined scene which awaits the men at the front. Again this device was similarly employed by Keats, who not only describes the scene depicted on the urn itself, but also imagines the town from which the people present may have travelled. There is obviously a profusion of flowers at the chateau as they have formed a carpet covering the ground. This reminds us of the first line again, where Blunden describes the flowers as covering the sides or "flanks" of some creature, which is the case of Keats's piece is the heifer. In Blunden's poem this may be a reminder of the graves of the dead which would normally be covered with flowers although the chateau hides no bodies so the carpet is more cheerfully described. This is followed by the suggestion that there are millions of poppies and this may be a reference to the number of dead. By this stage of the war poppies were becoming synonymous with the conflict in the eyes of many poets (such as John McCrae and Isaac Rosenberg.)

The next line continues this flowery theme, as these colours describe the pinks and bright reds of roses and poppies. There is a type of rose named Damask which is pink and has an ancient history, having been mentioned by previous authors including Shakespeare. The colour of poppies could easily be described as vermillion, which is a bright reddish-orange. These are vivid cheerful colours which continue to enhance the sense of a happy scene.

Finally, in the last two lines, Blunden's tone changes as the pastoral language gives way to a more colloquial form. He suggests that the colour of these flowers is too bright and strong. It should, he proposes, be more dull - possibly more like the colour of blood. This dulling of the colours would also reflect the grey and depressing nature of his world. This ending, although spoken quite cheerfully, contrasts with the brightness of the beginning of this verse, and brings the reader down to earth sharply. Blunden does this by simply reminding the reader that his world is not colourful, but dull.

The title of this poem is the first point of interest as Blunden tells us, in a straightforward fashion, exactly where he is, what he is doing and even when he is there. Thus, he very quickly and simply sets the scene, giving the reader an image of what might be to follow before one even starts to read the poem. The influence of Keats is immediate as the first line is a direct quotation, and the remainder of Blunden's poem contains references or inferences which link back to *Ode on a Grecian Urn*.

The form of this poem is also interesting in that a sonnet has a conventional rhyming scheme and this provides a paradox similar to those within the poem. For example, the scene which Blunden describes is one of beauty, which contrasts with the horror of reality. Similarly, this orthodox form of poem contrasts with the unorthodox scene which it describes, thus attracting the reader's attention and making one give greater consideration to the poem's contents.

This poem could be compared with *Anthem for Doomed Youth* by Wilfred Owen. Both are sonnets, and both describe an unorthodox or unlikely scene. Owen quite directly describes the men as dying like cattle, while Blunden is more subtle: his description of the guns as brutal and his association of this with the noise of cattle makes the reader think more deeply about his implication. Blunden is describing a realistic scene, which somehow seems out of place. Owen, on the other hand, is describing a scene which cannot happen: a proper Christian burial, with choirs and bells, during the war. Owen implies throughout that the men deserve to be shown the respect of a decent funeral, but because of the war, this is denied to them, and other things must become symbolic of their death. Both poems also contain religious overtones: Blunden's contains the reference to sacrifice and flowers being used in remembrance, while Owen's sonnet has the central theme of lost funeral rites, which have been replaced by the trappings of war.

Like much of Blunden's writing, one is struck in this poem by his pastoral theme and close affiliation with nature, especially given his surroundings. *Undertones of War* is littered with examples of Blunden observing something horrendous or sickening, followed by him noticing a flower, a tree or a blade of grass, which has somehow managed to survive the destruction of everything around it. The end of this poem has something of Siegfried Sassoon about it, in that Blunden has spent the whole poem creating an image of serene and vivacious beauty which he ultimately shatters in the final two lines, by completely changing his tone and language.

REPORT ON EXPERIENCE

This poem was included in Blunden's volume entitled Near and Far, which was published in September 1929, the theme of the piece being an older man recalling experiences from earlier in his life. At the time of writing, Blunden was probably in his early thirties, meaning that he was hardly an old man himself and yet the poem is written as though he were much more advanced in years. Although this would go on to become Blunden's most anthologised poem, the poet himself was not entirely satisfied with the composition, referring to it as "unpremeditated", suggesting that he had no particular plan in mind when he wrote it.

The opening of the poem comes from a combination of two other texts: Shakespeare's Henry VI Part One, Act Three, Scene Four, in which the title character proclaims "When I was young, as yet I am not old"; and a contrary twist of Psalm 37, Verse 25, which reads "I have been young, and now I am old; yet I have not seen the righteous forsaken...". The meaning of this opening verse is, essentially, the betrayal of Blunden's generation, which he perceives as "the righteous" and regards them as having been "forsaken". This generation, which is given the quality of a single youth, is described as having lost its "health", its "honour" and its "quality", all of which would have been enormously prized. In the final line, Blunden makes it clear that he includes himself with this generation of the betrayed, but also that their current situation is different to that which they had been promised.

In the second verse, Blunden goes on to describe the physical scenes he had witnessed, giving an account of a "green country", which served a purpose to those who lived there. Despite this, the country had been destroyed by "guns and mines" to the point were the villages had disappeared, as had all the animals. He closes this verse with the ironic statement that this situation was a "peculiar grace", implying the pointlessness of the circumstances whereby those who would have benefitted by and prized the country, had been responsible for destroying it.

In the third verse, Blunden changes the subject once again, turning now to women, who he generalises with the name of "Seraphina", giving them an angelic quality. This, however, refers to their former selves, which had a certain superiority: a way of looking, a compassion and a tone of voice which made them seem like a creation of God's. However, the war has made woman's smile distorted, and her voice become lifeless. She has become promiscuous in her ways, which behaviour seems "new" to Blunden. While this "harlotry" and general falling from grace of the female sex may be a direct reference to prostitution, it could also be an allusion to the way in which women became more interested in the war and in the men who were fighting, which might have seemed rather unladylike to him. Either way, he asserts that the behaviour of women seemed "new" to him at the time, implying a certain amount of innocence on his part.

The final verse appears to have a more positive note, as Blunden attributes some of the "disillusions" he has previously listed, to the fact that God is proving his love for "humanity". However, given the fact that everything which Blunden has mentioned is negative and tells of the ruin of mankind, his affirmation of God's love seems rather ironic. Nonetheless, he does close the poem positively, asserting that above everything else, the survivors of the war may still enjoy a belief or "faith"; the joy of "life" itself, and the goodness of the "sun": simple pleasures in which the dead may no longer participate.

One can understand why this poem became so popular and so anthologised as, despite its occasionally harsh messages, it does appear to end in a more optimistic tone. Ten years after the end of the war, this would probably have been a most welcome emotion for the poet to portray and one which audiences would have appreciated However, one should also bear in mind the poet's own dissatisfaction with the piece and the fact that he felt it was "unpremeditated" or unplanned, suggesting perhaps that he wasn't entirely happy with the messages he ended up portraying.

One could compare this poem with others that were written looking back on the conflict, such as Recalling War by Robert Graves, or those written much later, like The Great War by Vernon Scannell or MCMXIV by Philip Larkin, although none of these others carry the same mixture of sadness and irony which Blunden manages to achieve. Graves's overriding emotion is really anger, as he warns a future generation against making similar mistakes to his own. Scannell also features anger, mingled with gratitude in his poem. Larkin, like Blunden, focuses on the changes which the First World War brought to society in general, claiming that the "innocence" that was lost on the battlefields will never be rediscovered: men will never go so willingly or unquestioningly to their deaths again.

It would be pleasant to believe that Larkin was right and also that Blunden really did find "virtue in the sun", but in reality neither was the case. Men still did their duty in future wars (and do so today - although perhaps not so blindly). Blunden remained haunted by his experiences, which would affect every aspect of his life and those of many of the 'forsaken" with whom he had served.

Richard Aldington

Although his work was popular at the time, Aldington is often not included in anthologies of First World War poetry and the choice of poem given by Jon Stallworthy is an unusual one.

BIOGRAPHICAL DETAILS

Richard Aldington was born Edward Godfree Aldington at 50 High Street, Portsmouth on 8th July 1892. His father, Albert was a solicitor's clerk and bookseller and when Edward was only an infant, he and his wife Jessie moved to Dover in Kent, where the young boy grew up in the company of his younger brother and two sisters. At a very young age, Edward took a dislike to his given names and decided that he would be known as Richard. He initially attended local preparatory schools at Walmer and St Margaret's Bay, before joining Dover College in 1904, where he remained for the next two years. In 1910, Aldington won a place at University College London, although he failed to complete his degree, being forced to abandon his university career after just one year due to a decline in his family's finances. By this stage, Aldington had already begun writing poetry, his early inspirations coming from Oscar Wilde and John Keats.

After a brief spell as a sports journalist, Aldington soon began to earn a living from poetry and literary criticisms. In 1912, he began to meet other literary "names", including W B Yeats, Ezra Pound, and Hilda Doolittle (known as H.D.). Later that year, Aldington, H.D. and Pound founded the imagist movement and in 1914, Aldington's work appeared in Des imagistes. Following several months spent on the continent, H.D. and Aldington were married on October 18th 1913 in Kensington Register Office.

When the First World War began, Aldington tried to enlist in the Honourable Artillery Company, but was refused on medical grounds. Frustrated, he spent his time working as secretary to Ford Maddox Ford, helping with the latter's novel, The Good Soldier. H.D. was equally infuriated by her husband's situation and her distress was complete when she gave birth to a stillborn daughter on 21st May 1915. By the middle of 1916, medical regulations had been relaxed somewhat and Aldington was able to enlist as a private in the 11th Battalion of the Devonshire Regiment, embarking for France on 21st December. After six months at the front, Aldington was sent home for officer training and was then commissioned into the Royal Sussex Regiment in November 1917. While he was in London, however, Aldington began an affair with Arabelle Yorke, an American art student. Shortly after Aldington returned to the trenches, H.D. also took a lover, composer Cecil Gray, with whom she bore a child.

By the end of the war, Aldington had been promoted to the rank of Acting Captain, but was also suffering from shell shock and the after-effects of exposure to gas. Aldington's relationship with H.D. was now irretrievably broken down, and he settled with Arabella in Berkshire, although he and H.D. would not divorce until 1938, remaining friends until her death.

In the late 1920s Aldington, now separated from Arabella, moved to France, where he became friends with Nancy Cunard, who was living there, having established The Hours Press in Reanville just outside Paris. By 1928, Aldington had found a new love, in the form of Brigit Patmore and had also begun writing novels instead of poetry.

His debut novel, *Death of a Hero*, was published in 1929, to critical acclaim. This, like many of his ensuing novels, contained recognisable caustic portrayals of some of his friends, many of whom would not remains friends for very long.

The early 1930s found Aldington and Patmore travelling around Europe while the former continued to write at a feverish pace, although by the middle of the decade, he had tired of Europe and decided to settle in America, returning regularly to London and Europe for visits. During one of these, he met Brigit Patmore's daughter-in-law, Netta, and they began an affair (although she was still married to Brigit's son, Michael, at the time). When both of their divorces were finally settled - Aldington's from H.D. came through in the summer of 1938 - he married Netta in a quiet ceremony in London within three days. Their daughter, Catherine, was born less than two weeks later.

The family settled firstly in New York and then in 1940, they moved to Washington DC and he found work as a freelance screenwriter. After the war, the family returned to France and Aldington turned his hand to writing biographies on famous historical and literary figures, including the Duke of Wellington and D.H. Lawrence.

In the autumn of 1950, Netta left Aldington, which led to him having a breakdown, following which he did little writing for four years. At this time, he wrote another biography, on T.E. Lawrence, called *Lawrence of Arabia: a Biographical Enquiry* and this book would cost Aldington his reputation. In this biography, Aldington accused Lawrence of assisting in the creation of his own heroic status and brandished him a liar and a charlatan, as well as a homosexual. A group of influential Lawrence supporters, including Robert Graves and Basil Liddell Hart attempted to prevent publication of Aldington's book and, when this failed, they ensured as many bad reviews as possible, guaranteeing poor sales and lasting damage to Aldington's reputation.

From then on, Aldington lived in poverty, with his daughter in a small cottage purchased for him by a friend, at Sury-en-Vaux, where he died on 27th July 1962.

BATTLEFIELD

Although there is no given date for this poem, we may assume from its content and phrasing that it was written during the First World War rather than after the conflict had finished. The poem was certainly published in Aldington's volume entitled *Images of War* in 1919. Although his poetry - especially that written later in the war - generally exudes an element of anger or bitterness about the conflict, there are those who claim that Aldington had less cause to feel such an emotion than others, stating that he spent little time in the trenches. Certainly by the end of the war, he was serving with the Signallers (a much less dangerous task than being in the infantry) and at the end of the war, he wrote to his semi-estranged wife, H.D. (fellow poet, Hilda Doolittle), that he was relieved that no-one had died at his hands.

The poem opens with a description of the cold, creating a stark atmosphere, devoid of hope. Aldington describes the "wind" as "piercing", which immediately calls to mind the way in which bullets and shrapnel would pierce the flesh of the men. The word "chill" adds a suitable note of menace to this description, as well as relating back to the notion that those killed by the "piercing" weapons would naturally lie cold in the ground. The poet goes on to relate how the wind causes the snow to be blown about, but he alludes to the flakes as "grains", which makes them seem additionally harsh and uncompromising, allowing nothing for the softer, melting qualities normally associated with snow in the reader's mind. Then Aldington completes this initial description, informing us that the ground over which the wind blows and the snow falls is "shell-rent", implying that it has been torn apart and made unrecognisable by the frequent bombardments that have taken place.

Into this scene of cold misery, Aldington injects a brief interlude of hope that there are "houses" within his "sight", thus allowing the reader to believe that people are still able to live close to the lines and that, therefore, things may not be so bad as they might have seemed in the opening lines of the poem. However, these hopes are immediately dashed, as Aldington goes on to describe these houses as "smashed and desolate" revealing not only their ruined condition, but also the fact that they have been deserted by their owners. This heightens the sense of isolation which Aldington is creating within this piece.

The second verse opens with a further allusion to the barren nature of the countryside, where there are no longer any trees to bear fruit, nor crops growing in the fields. The thorns that would have covered the brambles now take the form of barbed wire, as there are no longer any shrubs to be found. Additionally, Aldington tells us of the sights and smells surrounding him in the form of "rotting clothes and sacks" which may be a reference to the uniforms once worn by now dead soldiers and the sand-bags that are all around. However, there is also no escaping the notion that these "sacks" could also be a description of the men themselves, and that the "rotting clothes" would have been their uniforms, which now decay along with their bodies. The only things that thrive here in this desolate environment, are the "crosses" whose number increases rapidly and without thought or concern for the damaged surroundings.

At the close of the poem, Aldington switches from English to French, telling us "Here lies... here lies one German soldier, Pray for him". The first three times he repeats "Ci-gît" (here lies), denoting presumably the frequency of the crosses and the fact that on a headstone, the wording would normally begin "Here lies...". This is in French, we may assume, because the graves are those of French soldiers, except for the final one, from which he quotes in full. This German soldier has presumably been buried by the French (hence the wording on his cross) and we may assume was unable to be identified. The notion that the French wanted those who saw this grave to pray for the dead German soldier, shows that, despite everything that Aldington has earlier described, there remained an element of humanity among the men concerned, even if they were slowly obliterating their surroundings.

This is a short, fairly hopeless poem in which Aldington creates an atmosphere devoid of life and promise for the future. However, at the very close, he offers a small chance of something more optimistic, showing us that, despite their desolate surroundings and that they had been enemies in life, the soldiers felt that they shared enough experiences to warrant a common prayer in death.

EDGELL RICKWORD

Another poet whose influence at the time of the First World War did not last. Despite this, *Winter Warfare* is shown in several anthologies.

BIOGRAPHICAL DETAILS

John Edgell Rickword was born on 22nd October 1898 at 28 Head Street, Colchester in Essex, the youngest of the five children of borough librarian, George Rickword and his wife Mabel Thomas (née Prosser). Rickword attended Colchester Royal Grammar School from the age of ten and, as a teenager enjoyed reading books by H G Wells, George Bernard Shaw, William Morris and others, whose views converted him to socialism.

When the First World War began in August 1914, Rickword was still only fifteen years old and was obliged to wait until September 1916, just before his eighteen birthday, in order to enlist in the Artists' Rifles. Following his training at Hare Hall, Gidea Park in Essex, Rickword was commissioned as a Second Lieutenant in the 5th Battalion of the Royal Berkshire Regiment, embarking for France in January 1918. Initially he moved in and out of the front line, serving in quiet sectors, but on 19th March, was wounded in the shoulder. His wounds were not severe and Rickword rejoined his regiment five days later. On May 12th, Rickword was wounded for a second time and was invalided back to England, only returning to France in September 1918. On 14th October, he participated in action on the Haute Deule Canal, which resulted in him being awarded the Military Cross, his citation reading as follows:

"For conspicuous gallantry and initiative near Dourges on 15th October 1918. He volunteered to cross the Haute Deule Canal and make a reconnaissance. After crossing

the canal at Pont-a-Sault, his presence was discovered by the enemy, who kept him covered with their machines guns. In spite of this he worked his way along the eastern bank of the canal and brought back most valuable information, which enabled his company to form a bridgehead."

In January 1919, Rickword developed septicaemia in his left eye, which resulted in the removal of that eye to prevent the infection from spreading. His removed eye was replaced with a glass one and Rickword was invalided out of the army. In September 1919, he went to Pembroke College, Oxford, where he found himself in the company of several other war poets, including Edmund Blunden and Robert Graves. He was also introduced to Siegfried Sassoon, who assisted with the publication of Rickword's poems. He didn't complete his degree, however, leaving Oxford after just one year, upon his marriage to Margaret (Peggy) McGrath in October 1920. The couple had become lovers the previous year and Peggy gave birth to Rickword's daughter one month before their wedding. A second daughter was born in March 1922 and these early years of Rickword's marriage were contented and productive in terms of his writing, as he contributed regularly to both the Daily Herald and the New Statesman. In 1921, he also published his first volume of poetry, entitled Behind the Eyes, which title comes from a love poem called Intimacy, written to Peggy. However, domestic bliss was short-lived, as in 1924 Peggy suffered from a nervous breakdown which resulted in her confinement to a mental institution, while their two daughters were placed into foster homes.

Following this, Rickword moved into a flat in London and, together with Bertram Higgins and Douglas Garman, founded the Calendar of Modern Letters, a literary periodical which featured work by D H Lawrence, Robert Graves and John Crowe Ransom among many others. Rickword also published two further volumes of his own poetry, Invocations to Angels in 1928 and Twittingpan three years later, at which point he ceased writing verse, in favour of politics.

Rickword joined the Communist Party in 1934 and became founder and editor of The Left Review in the same year, representing the British section of the Writers' International at the 1937 Madrid Conference, during the Spanish Civil War. Rickword remained a well respected editor and literary critic among his contemporaries, but was relatively anonymous as far as a wider public audience was concerned.

In the 1940s, Rickword became a bookseller, firstly in Kent and then in London. He was remarried in 1944, following Peggy's death, to Doris Russell Back and became manager of Collet's bookshop in Hampstead ten years later. Rickword left the Communist Party following the Soviet invasion of Hungary in 1956. In 1960, Doris's health began to decline and she died four years later of a brain haemorrhage. Rickword lived the remainder of his life with Beatrix Hammarling in North London, although his sight failed completely in 1976. He died from cancer on 15th March 1982.

WINTER WARFARE

Although there is no given date for this poem, we may assume that it was written about Rickword's first (and only) winter in the trenches, which began in January 1918.

The poem opens with a reference to "Colonel Cold", by which Rickword personifies the weather, giving it the rank of a senior officer, and thereby immediately telling us his opinion of those in command. The cold is described as striding "up the Line" in the same way as a snarling officer might, with nothing but contempt for those he encounters. The "colonel" is given frosty "tabs" on the shoulders of his uniform and the "spurs" on his heels are made of "ice". Again, this personifies the weather, while dehumanising the senior staff officers, who seem to be made of nothing but frozen matter. At the same time, these descriptions also refer to the icy nature, or aloofness that some felt typified the senior officers. Rickword goes on to explain how the "Colonel's" "glare" effects everything with which he comes into contact, from the "horses" to the "men" and even the "lice" that live on them. In this way, Rickword is trying to convey not only the extreme cold of his surroundings, but also the hostility which men encountered from their "superiors".

In the second verse, we learn that "Colonel Cold" had gone right up to a "forward post", where the men had been left so cold, that their skin had actually felt like it was "burning". So severe had been the sensation of being frozen, that the mens' fingers had become "stuck" to metal and their "toes" had become "frozen" inside their boots. This description encourages us to think of the colonel as truly harsh and unrelenting - just like the weather that he represents as the men are made to stand on duty, frozen to the spot. Rickword makes further use of personification and metaphor here, describing the steel as "biting" which nonetheless allows us to understand the pain of attempting to peel away one's fingers from the cold metal.

After this, in verse three, the cold continues out into no man's land, where it deposits snow and frost onto the barbed wire, making it appear like "fleecy wool". The iron stakes in the ground are given the appears of "sugar sticks", which give the impression that they would probably break if touched, even gently. Here, the personification becomes slightly more friendly (although no less deadly). Rickword's description of "fleecy wool" is much less harsh than his earlier accounts of the cold's frozen attributes and the "sugar sticks" even call to mind the stripy candy canes that hang on Christmas trees. However, readers should not be fooled by Rickword's change of language here: he is still being cynical with regard to the harshness of the senior officers.

In verse four, the tone of the poem changes slightly, as does the perspective. Now, the cold "colonel" has stopped and stands alongside "Hauptman Kälte" - his German counterpart - whose role is exactly the same. These two "characters" are observed by their men, whose eyes are covered with frost as they watch the glistening ice and frozen landscape. The officers are described as "gaunt" suggesting a haggard appearance, devoid of humanity. Now we can see that the inhumanity of both the cold conditions and the service officers affects the men universally, on both sides of no man's land, regardless of nationality.

Verse five continues along the same lines, as the officers now move about, their "spurs" on their heels "tinkling" in the cold. This reminds us of the first verse, where the "spurs of ice" were first mentioned, showing that nothing has changed. The brutality of the officers is touched upon once more, as they are referred to as "glassy-eyed", showing that they don't notice the suffering of those around them. Those who remain in no man's land, who have been "torn" by shrapnel wounds, are further stabbed by the cold, but they are also left feeling abandoned: the reader knows that the senior officers are not really in no man's land - only the dying and dead live there.

This is a very angry and bitter poem in which we learn as much about the poet's feelings towards his senior officers as we do about the conditions in the trenches during a harsh winter. Rickword's language is savage and uncompromising, leaving the reader in no doubt that his sympathies lie with the private soldiers. He brings home some of his feelings by using literary devices such as alliteration, assonance and sibilance, drawing the reader into the situation. So, for example, in verse three the repeated use of "s" sounds creates a softer atmosphere than in the previous two verses, which only really serves to lull the reader into a false sense of security, as the two officers representing the cold are still present and threatening. Additionally, Rickword makes use of harsher sounds, such as the repeated hard "c" of "Colonel Cold" and hard "g" of "gaunt", "grey", "glassy", "glinting" etc., all of which give the impression of being rather sinister. The ongoing metaphor, of the officers representing the cold, not only introduces

Rickword's opinion of the former, but also allows for great use of personification throughout, as natural elements are given human qualities, while the officers and men are effectively dehumanised by their experiences of both the elements and the war.

Winter Warfare appears at first glance to be quite a simple, jaunty poem, full of irony and black humour, yet it is really rather clever, in that almost everything that Rickword says here can be given two meanings. Throughout the poem, where each verse takes the form of a simple sentence, the poet may either be referring to the senior officers or to the weather, both of which are depicted harshly and neither of which respect the men, regardless of nationality.

This poem could be compared to several others within this genre looking at either nature or the treatment of soldiers by their officers. Such poems might include *Exposure* by Wilfred Owen, *The General* by Siegfried Sassoon or *The Zonnebeke Road* by Edmund Blunden. Looking at Owen's poem, *Exposure*, this features a vivid description of the trenches during the extremely cold winter of 1917. Like Rickword, Owen personifies some of the natural elements, so the wind is "tugging on the wires", for example and is later described as having an air of "nonchalance". Unlike Rickword, Owen uses no humour or irony, focusing instead on the monotony involved in being so cold while "nothing happens". In *The General*, Sassoon tells the story of two soldiers named Harry and Jack, who happen to meet their senior officer, but who are now dead, thanks to his "plan of attack". Sassoon was renowned for his bitter, ironic poetry, enhanced here by the jolly metre of the piece, which, like *Winter Warfare*, belies the content. *The Zonnebeke Road* is set, like *Exposure*, in the winter of 1917 and here Blunden paints a picture of hopelessness. Again, personification is used, so stones "flinch" and the trees resemble teeth. Blunden speaks of the cold as having "pierced" the men, which language is reminiscent of that employed by Rickword.

In *Winter Warfare*, it could be argued that Rickword has combined certain elements from all of these poems, including humour, satire, personification, metaphor, anger, bitterness and a jaunty, jolly rhythm, through which he has created a piece that is wondrous in its complex simplicity.

E. E. CUMMINGS

One of many American poets in this anthology, Cummings has become famous for his use of lower-case letters throughout most of his writing.

BIOGRAPHICAL DETAILS

Edward Estlin Cummings was born in Cambridge, Massachusetts on 14th October 1894, the oldest child and only son of Edward Cummings and his wife, Rebecca Haswell Clarke. Edward Cummings Snr., was a professor of Sociology at Harvard University, although later in life, he became a Unitarian Minister. A second child, a daughter named Elizabeth, was born in 1902 and Edward, or Estlin, as he was known to his family, seems to have passed a happy and secure childhood, becoming especially fond of his father, although it was his mother who introduced him to poetry. Following his initial education at Cambridge Latin High School, Cummings went to Harvard, where he studied English and Classical Studies, graduating in 1916. While there, he wrote several poems, which were published in the Harvard Monthly.

Following his graduation, Cummings volunteered to serve in the ambulance corps. However, in September 1917, while serving on the Western Front, he was arrested on suspicion of spying. He had spoken out openly against the war and in favour of Germany and was therefore interned in a detention camp, where he was held, without charge until late December. Cummings returned to the United States, but was almost immediately drafted into the Army. He was stationed at Camp Devens in Massachusetts until the end of the war, serving with the National Guard.

During 1918, Cummings began an affair with Elaine Orr, the wife of one of his friends from Harvard. On December 20, 1919, Elaine gave birth to Cummings's daughter, Nancy, who would be his only child. Following Elaine's divorce, the couple married in March 1924, although the marriage only lasted nine months. After their divorce, Elaine moved to Ireland, taking Nancy with her and prevented Cummings from seeing his daughter until 1946.

Cummings spent much of the early 1920s travelling in Europe, especially in Paris, where he had stayed at the beginning of his time with the ambulance corps. In 1926, Edward Cummings Snr., was killed in a car accident which also left Rebecca Cummings seriously injured. This sudden loss had a severe impact on Cummings who missed his father's influence over both his life and his work.

By now, Cummings had published several volumes of poetry and was working on his first play, entitled HIM. In 1929, Cummings married Anne Barton, although this was another short relationship and the couple separated three years later, by which time Cummings had met Marion Morehouse, who would remain his partner until his death, from a stroke on September 3rd 1962.

Cummings is perhaps best known for his supposed abandonment of capital letters and punctuation, although in fact, he frequently used both.

"my sweet old etcetera"

Although there is no known date for the composition of this poem, it was not published until 1926 and Cummings's reference to 'the recent war' would suggest that it was written after the end of the First World War. Like many of his poems, this one is written with almost no punctuation and this, coupled with the frequent insertion of the word 'etcetera' makes the poem difficult to read, understand and analyse. Therefore, the first thing to do, is to rewrite the poem, with punctuation, omitting all of the 'etceteras' (with the possible exception of the final one, the meaning of which is clearly sexual and is entirely up to the individual reader to interpret!) For myself, I would write the piece as prose, as I also find Cummings's verse form very distracting, but this is also a matter of personal choice. Therefore, my own re-written poem would read as follows:

[My sweet, old Aunt Lucy, during the recent war, could – and what is more did – tell you just what everybody was fighting for. My sister, Isabel, created hundreds (and hundreds) of socks, not to mention shirts, fleaproof earwarmers [and] wristers. My mother hoped that I would die bravely, of course. My father used to become hoarse, talking about how it was a privilege, and if only he could. Meanwhile, myself, lay quietly in the deep mud (dreaming of your smile, eyes, knees and your...)]

In this way, it can be seen that this poem is really just a series of recollections of how the First World War affected a family. 'Aunt Lucy', it would seem, was good at explaining the causes and reasons behind the war, to everyone and anyone who would listen. Whether she was correct in her assumptions is not made clear, but the ironic, almost sarcastic tone of the poem, suggests that, perhaps, she was not. Meanwhile, sister Isabel knitted or sewed away, as though it were an Olympic sport. Once again, however, the 'etceteras' suggest that the usefulness of some of her garments was, perhaps, questionable. Shirts and socks are no doubt valuable, but 'fleaproof earwarmers' and 'wristers' have dubious merits.

The mother sounds potentially heartless until one remembers the 'etcetera' in this context. Her attitude then becomes typical of her time, so that if her son must die, she wants him to do so with courage and not dishonour the family, which in those days would have been perceived as something of great importance. The 'etcetera' here could also be replaced with something like 'or be wounded' or words to that effect, demonstrating the ironic insignificance of these supposed 'details'. In other words, Cummings could be implying that to die or be wounded 'bravely' would be better, in the eyes of the mother than to be seen as a coward and, perhaps, suffer from shell-shock, or have to retire from battle due to some other less 'worthy' reason. This attitude is quite shocking for today's reader to interpret, but is not that unusual for the time.

Then comes the father, who talks himself 'hoarse', about how honoured men should feel to fight and that he would gladly join them if only he were younger and more able - 'if only he could'. Although Cummings may not use conventional rhymes or verse forms, there is an internal rhyme here as the word 'hoarse' rhymes with 'course' in the previous line, joining the two parents and their attitudes together. The theme of older 'armchair warriors' is quite common amongst the soldier-poets, who would often deride these men who could talk a fine war, without having ever experienced one themselves.

Finally, Cummings reaches the description of himself, lying in 'the deep mud'. He does not give an account of himself fighting, or really suffering in any way, but chooses instead to create an image of himself dreaming about his sweetheart. This is the one place in the poem where Cummings has used capital letters, which signifies the importance of his sweetheart and also of her Etcetera! To the sex-starved soldier (or in Cummings's case ambulance driver) on the Western Front, dreaming about a wife or girlfriend was often the nearest they could get to gratification and, possibly the first etcetera within the parenthesis implies that he wasn't only dreaming!

"next to of course god"

Unlike many of Cummings's poems, this has a relatively traditional verse form, being a sonnet, in which the poet has used some rhyme, although the metre is somewhat unconventional. In common with most of his poetry, he has used little punctuation, and where he does, this signifies the greater importance of those sections of the poem. Cummings also uses some internal rhyme within the speech, such as 'acclaim' and 'name', which gives this part of the poem more a flowing feeling, contrasting well with the jarring rhyme of the piece.

In order to better understand this piece, one could re-write it, incorporating punctuation where applicable, in which case my version of the poem would read as follows (although yours might be different):

['Next to, of course, God, America, I
Love you: the land of the pilgrims', and so forth (Oh
Say can you see by the dawn's early...) (My
Country 'tis of...) Centuries come and go,
And are no more. What of it? We should worry!
In every language – even deafanddumb –
Thy sons acclaim your glorious name. By gorry,
By jingo, by gee, by gosh, by gum.
Why talk of beauty? What could be more beaut-
Iful, than these heroic, happy dead,
Who rushed like lions to the roaring slaughter?
They did not stop to think, they died instead.
Then shall the voice of liberty be mute?'

He spoke. And drank rapidly a glass of water.]

I have read several analyses of this poem, which proclaim it as a patriotic verse, which description ignores completely the irony and cynicism contained within these lines. Cummings's background was one of pacifism. During the First World War, he had served as an ambulance driver and had been imprisoned for several weeks under suspicion of spying, mainly because he had spoken out against the war and in favour of Germany. It seems to me highly unlikely that a man who would take such a position, would write a supposedly patriotic poem.

The poem takes the form of a speech (with the notable exception of the final line), presumably made by a politician. It opens with the speaker pronouncing that, other than God, he loves America more than anything. Cummings interweaves excerpts from two American anthems here, namely The Star

Spangled Banner and My Country 'Tis of Thee, touching also upon the country's history, by referring to the pilgrim fathers, although he derides them, by describing their input to their country's history simply as 'and so forth'.

Cummings's speaker goes on to wistfully say that time passes, but that really this is insignificant. Then, the speaker points out that everyone, even those who cannot speak or hear, proclaim the glories of the American nation. The ensuing proclamations are supposed to demonstrate the excitement in which the country is beheld: it is too much for words! He then wonders about those who question the nature and courage of the men who have died in the war. He praises their bravery, describing them as 'lions', who did not hesitate when their country called, but rushed to their deaths. The point of this statement is entirely ironic, in that Cummings believes they should have questioned the war – as he did, they should have paused to think, rather than rushing blindly to their deaths. However, the final line of the speech is also enlightening in that, while the speaker asks whether these deaths would have caused the 'voice of liberty' to die too, Cummings really means that there is no voice of freedom here at all, since these men were not really 'free' to fight; they were drafted, and the alternative was to be pilloried as a coward.

The final line, outside of the speech suggests that the speaker has spoken quickly or hurriedly and now needs a drink in order to slake his thirst. In this way, Cummings is able to imply that the speaker himself doubts the content of his own speech and has rushed through it, perhaps fearing an adverse reaction from his audience.

The poem is laden with irony and cynicism, showing that Cummings was not unpatriotic, but was questioning the blind type of patriotism or jingoism that had driven men to fight and die in the name of their country, without really understanding the reason.

"i sing of Olaf glad and big..."

[It is worth noting that in my version of his anthology Oxford Book of War Poetry, Jon Stallworthy has published a version of this poem with the swear words deleted. This, I feel, detracts from the meaning of the poem and the anger of the poet. Regardless of any offense such publication may cause, the poet intended it to be read with those words intact and they should be left in place.]

This poem was first published in 1931 and Richard S Kennedy, in his biography of the poet, entitled *Dreams in the Mirror*, states that the background to this poem was based upon Cummings's own experiences of the military, after he was drafted into the army in January 1918 (although others have wrongly cited this date as July). In common with many of Cummings's other poems, the poet has dispensed with most of the punctuation and capital letters in this piece. The exceptions are quite significant – as ever – and in this case demonstrate a link, in the poet's eyes, between his central character, Olaf, and Christ, since these are the only names which are capitalised.

The poem opens with a reference to 'Olaf' as a large, warm-hearted, cheerful person, which immediately conjures up an image in the reader's mind and encourages us to like this character. It is also worth noting that the poet does not merely speak of Olaf, but 'sings' of him, suggesting that he wishes to cry out his praise loudly for the world to hear; to rejoice in the man that was Olaf. He describes Olaf very carefully as a 'conscientious object-or', specifically and unnecessarily hyphenating the word 'objector', thereby giving this phrase another meaning. In this way, we could be led to think of Olaf simply as an 'object' of his conscience, thereby de-humanising him very early in the poem.

What follows is a series of foul and degrading tortures at the hands of various men, beginning with the colonel, then the non-commissioned officers (the 'noncoms') and finally the other ranks. The acts performed upon Olaf are disgusting, beginning with a beating, then a dunking in ice-cold water. This is followed by prodding with dirty toilet brushes, then more beatings from his fellow soldiers. By this time, Olaf is naked, but he maintains his dignity and his perspective, still refusing to obey the rules of the army, by kissing the American flag. The colonel (represented here by the 'silver bird', which is the military insignia for that rank) now finds this tortuous beating too severe and excuses himself on the basis that he needs to shave, although this is clearly not the real reason for his departure.

Other officers now take over the beating of Olaf, crying out as they kick him, until both their voices and their boots are worn out. The officers then encourage the first-class privates to the ultimate desecration – namely they rape Olaf with red-hot bayonets. Nonetheless, the now kneeling Olaf maintains that he will not succumb.

At this point, the president (presumably of the United States) hears of this man's treasonable statements and has him thrown into jail, declaring him to be a coward. While in this jail, not surprisingly, Olaf dies.

Cummings goes on to say that, in prayer, he claims to 'hope to see' Jesus Christ, but he has the same feelings now for Olaf. This is mainly because Olaf, he states, was much braver than Cummings himself, suggesting that the poet feels some element of cowardice in his own position over the war. Possibly this would be because he volunteered for the ambulance corps, rather than the army and once drafted in 1918, he remained in the USA, never really being obliged to test his pacifism in the field of war. Perhaps he is wondering whether he could have stood up to questioning and maintained his principles as bravely as Olaf.

Finally, Cummings asserts that Olaf is 'more blond than you', by which he directly points a finger at the reader, or the population at the time of writing, at least. By 'blond', I would suggest he means white, or in this instance, true, so really he means 'true to his beliefs', which again implies that Olaf – or the true conscientious objector, who refused to fight, regardless of the cost to his own person – was, in Cummings's eyes at least, the bravest and truest of all men.

John Peale Bishop

Another American poet, who served in Europe during the First World War. John Peale Bishop is often featured in older anthologies, making this an unexceptional choice on the part of Jon Stallworthy.

BIOGRAPHICAL DETAILS

John Peale Bishop was born in Charles Town, West Virginia on May 21st, 1892, the oldest child and only son of John Bishop, a physician from New York and his wife, Margaret Miller Cochran. A second child, a daughter, also named Margaret, was born in 1896 and the family lived happily in this Southern town, where John's father taught his son to paint and appreciate poetry. This idyllic childhood was shattered by the death of John's father, when the boy was only nine years of age. Six years later, John's mother re-married Dr Alfred M Smith, another physician, from Missouri, and the family moved to Washington County, Maryland.

John Peale Bishop attended Princeton University later than most students, entering in his 21st year, in the autumn of 1913. While there, Bishop became great friends with F. Scott Fitzgerald, who greatly admired the former's literary abilities, using him as the model for the character Tom D'Invilliers in his debut 1920 novel, *This Side of Paradise*. While at Princeton, Bishop edited the Nassau Literary Magazine, to which he contributed several of his poems, including *They Should Have Gone Forth With Banners* first published in February 1917 and which is in many ways a finer war poem than the more usually quoted *In The Dordogne*.

Upon graduating in 1917, Bishop enlisted in the US Army, and travelled as a First Lieutenant to the war in Europe, where he was commanding officer of a Prisoner of War Escort Company. Other duties after the war, included the disinterment and re-burial of American soldiers. By the time he returned to America in 1920, Bishop's stepfather, Dr Alfred Smith, was dead, leaving his mother widowed for second time. Bishop resumed a career in writing, becoming a member of the editorial staff of Vanity Fair and beginning a short, destructive affair with Edna St Vincent Millay, which she ended, much to his disappointment. In 1922, he married Margaret G Hutchins, from Ohio, whose father, Robert, was a wealthy manufacturer of iron implements based in New York. Margaret, an actress, was no stranger to travel herself, having spent most of the previous year touring England, France and Italy. She had also done voluntary work in Europe during the First World War. Shortly after their marriage, the couple moved to France, where their three sons were born: Jonathan on October 27 1927, and twins Robert and Christopher on March 22 1930.

The family returned to America on 27th September 1933, moving to an apartment in Park Avenue, New York, before relocating to Connecticut, then New Orleans and finally settling in Cape Cod in 1935. Bishop was appointed Chief Poetry Reviewer for The Nation, although he continued to write poetry and prose throughout his life, despite being plagued by frequent illnesses which meant his output was perhaps not as prolific as it might have been. During the Second World War, Bishop was appointed Publications Director of the Office of the Co-ordinator of Inter-American Affairs. He died of a heart attack in 1944, a few weeks before his 52nd birthday.

IN THE DORDOGNE

This poem is somewhat mysterious, essentially because, although it appears to be describing clear scenes of devastation caused by the First World War (note the mention of men being gassed), there are also references to the Bible, and to previous periods of history. In addition, the area in which the poem is set: namely, the Dordogne, saw no fighting during the conflict, and is not the scene of any American cemeteries on which Bishop may have been employed during the months after the war, therefore making this piece something of an enigma.

The poem is set after the First World War, possibly when Bishop was working with the burial teams, whose gruesome task was to disinter the bodies of American soldiers and re-bury them in cemeteries. All references to the war are in the past tense, rather than the present, so we may assume that this poem was written some considerable time after the war – perhaps even after the poet had married and returned to live in France with his young bride.

It is a poem of memories, beginning with the simple, mundane remembrance of rising before dawn and shaving by dim candlelight. The men, it would seem, are billeted in some ancient castle or chateau, which appears to be haunted – although whether these 'ghosts of a dead dawn' are their former comrades or hail from a previous era, is unclear. Bishop goes on to reveal that, although he and the other men have risen, their colonel continues to sleep, which may imply an element of bitterness or anger towards the more senior staff, who remain indolent while others work – or die - during times of conflict. Here, the ancient scenes are interwoven with the more modern, as Bishop and his comrades observe stone statues and imagine wise men ('mages') bringing 'gifts of gold' – a clear biblical reference, which in this case refers to the golden leaves of autumn. However, a gust of wind shatters these illusions, leaving the scene as a simple autumnal one, no less beautiful than its predecessor, despite its realism.

Bishop then turns his attentions directly to the First World War, referring to the 'hundreds' who returned from battle each day, either 'wounded or gassed'. The dead, he claims, were buried by the castle wall. However, we now come to an anomaly, as he states that the wall was 'within a stone's throw of Perigord', which is in the Dordogne region in the West of France. At the same time, he has also mentioned that the colonel is sleeping 'in the bed of Sully', which may be a reference to Maximilien de Bethune, duc de Sully, whose home was the Chateau de Rosny-sur-Seine in Yveline, near Rouen, which would be an extremely long stone's throw to Perigord, but would have been a possible location for Bishop immediately after the war and is very close to Neuilly-sur-Seine, where the Bishops settled following their marriage. I think that we must, therefore, allow for some poetic license here, in that Bishop had perhaps wanted to refer to historical events and scenes in the Dordogne region and had, therefore, incorporated these into his poem.

In the penultimate and most beautiful verse of the whole piece, Bishop describes his sadness at the misconceptions of youth. He says that, because they had been brave, the soldiers had essentially believed they were worthy of anything; that their deaths would signify something of great importance to mankind, perhaps like that of Jesus Christ (note the reference here to the 'Virgin' Mary). However, even before one gets to the final verse, once senses that disappointment lies in store, for the simple reason that these young men hoped for too much.

The final verse brings the anticipated let-down, coupled with a reminder of the aforementioned anger and recrimination towards the indolent Colonel. We now know that the young men were not granted immortality, but that they 'rotted' under the tower, where they had been buried. Bishop then changes the tone of his poem, creating a closing scene of serene mourning, pride and dignity. It is worth remembering here Bishop's role immediately after the First World War, of re-interring the dead in the beautiful American cemeteries. The notion that with each evening, the falling sun leaves behind 'veils' of 'azure' and 'blue' and that the 'clear silent streams' and 'delicate border of poplars' guard and surround these fallen heroes provide us with as worthy an image of a nations' grief, as Owen's 'drawing down of blinds'.

DAVID JONES

Like Sassoon and Graves, David Jones served in the Royal Welch Fusiliers, but unlike them, he was not an officer, which makes his view of the war and interesting study. He is often omitted from poetry anthologies for the reason that many debate whether his lengthy work *In Parenthesis* is poetry or prose.

BIOGRAPHICAL DETAILS

Walter David Michael Jones was born in Brockley, Kent on November 1st 1895, the youngest of the three children of printer's overseer, James Jones and his wife Alice (née Bradshaw). James Jones was of Welsh descent, having been born at Holywell in Flintshire, although he had lived in or near London for several years and his wife came from Rotherhithe.

David, as he became known, took an early and keen interest in art and entered several competitions and exhibitions as a child. At the age of fourteen, he joined the Camberwell Art School, where he realised that his future lay in the world of fine art. Despite this keen interest, however, Jones was uncertain as to exactly what direction he should follow, although this problem was temporarily set aside with the outbreak of the First World War, when he enlisted as a private in the Royal Welsh Fusiliers, embarking for France on 2nd December 1915.

Jones saw action on the Somme, taking part in the attack on Mametz Wood on 10th and 11th of July, during which he was wounded in the leg and invalided back to England. He returned to France in October 1916, but was sent back to England permanently in February 1918, suffering from severe trench fever and was demobilised on January 15th 1919.

After this, Jones accepted a grant to work at Westminster School of Art. In 1921, he converted to the Roman Catholic faith and began working with Eric Gill, who shared many of Jones's religious and artistic opinions.

In 1927, Jones began writing In Parenthesis, although it was not published until ten years later, with an introduction by T. S. Eliot. Critics find it difficult to categorise In Parenthesis as it seems to be neither poetry nor prose; it is almost two hundred pages long and is written in seven parts in the form of a journey.

Jones also painted and exhibited in both Europe and America, as well as around Britain. In 1952, a second book, The Anathemata was published. Jones also wrote several essays on the subjects of art, history and literature.

Although Jones lived alone, he was not a lonely man and was highly thought of by his many friends, who respected his sense of humour, his generous spirit and his vast knowledge. Despite this, he lived in poverty and suffered at least two serious breakdowns, as well as chronic insomnia. Jones died on 28th October 1974 at Harrow in Middlesex.

from IN PARENTHESIS

Jones began writing In Parenthesis in 1927, although it was not published for a further ten years. In the introduction to this work, he referred to it, not as a poem, but as a 'writing', being as it is a mixture of poetry and prose and is almost 200 pages long. Where it appears in a First World War poetry anthology, it is always as an extract, although even that content varies from one editor to another. It is written in seven parts and takes the form of a story about the training and battle experiences of a group of soldiers, notably the central character, John Ball.

In the excerpt chosen by Jon Stallworthy, Jones describes a battle scene, using a combination of pastoral and religious imagery, coupled with the colloquialisms of the everyday infantry soldier, such as Jones himself. His description of going over the top is vivid and evocative, especially when it comes to the death of 'Mr Jenkins'. The account of this episode is lyrical and shocking in equal measure, such as his allusion to the officer's tin helmet as an 'iron saucer', which tells the reader what is being described, but also calls to mind, in a somewhat graphic and sickening manner, some sort of implement from which one might drink tea. The reader is drawn into the scene and longs for Jenkins to success as he 'grope[s] for air', while knowing instinctively that he will not. Finally, of course, he dies and Jones marks this, clearly devastating event, quite simply by telling us that 'Sergeant T. Quilter takes over', which at once diminishes this death to the realms of just another war-time fatality.

LAURENCE BINYON

Although he was too old to fight, Binyon served during the war as an orderly and Red Cross volunteer. Before any of this, however, he wrote one of the most moving and evocative poems of the entire conflict.

BIOGRAPHICAL DETAILS

Robert Laurence Binyon was born in Lancaster on 10th August 1869, the second of the nine children of Quaker and local vicar, Frederick Binyon and his wife Mary (née Dockray). The family moved to London, where Frederick became assistant curate at St. Paul's in Hammersmith, while Binyon and his brothers won scholarships to St Paul's school. Following this, Binyon and all of his brothers attended university, with Binyon himself going to Trinity College, Oxford. He was a published poet by the age of sixteen and won the Newdigate prize for poetry in 1890, while he was still at university.

Following his graduation, Binyon began work at the British Museum in the Department of Printed Books, before transferring to the Department of Prints and Drawings in 1895. Binyon's main areas of expertise were Chinese, Japanese and Indian art and he was responsible for enlarging the museum's collections within these genres. Despite his interests in this field, Binyon's first love would always be poetry and he published several collections in the 1890s, becoming friends with W B Yeats and Thomas Sturge Moore, among many others.

On 12th April 1904, Binyon married Cicely Margaret Pryor Powell, the daughter of Henry Pryor Powell, a merchant banker, and his wife Helena. Early the following year, Cicely gave birth to twin daughters named Agatha Margaret Eden and Helen Francesca Mary. The couple had a third daughter, Nicolette Mary in 1911, following which, they moved from 8 Tite Street, Chelsea to 118 Belgrave Road, Pimlico where they lived for the next eight years. Family life for Binyon provided a source of great happiness, marred only by financial problems, which forced him to take on additional reviewing work.

Having instigated a sub-department of Oriental Prints and Drawings at the British Museum, Binyon went on to become its first head in 1913. The following year saw the outbreak of the First World War and on 21st September, The Times published a poem by Binyon entitled For The Fallen, which contains one of the most quoted verses of poetry ever written in the English language. Given the extremely early date of composition and publication within the war, this poem is remarkably prophetic and, when read as a whole, provides a haunting tribute not only to "The Fallen", but also to the poet himself.

Binyon was too old to enlist, at the age of 45, but he served, nonetheless, as an orderly in military hospitals in France during 1915 and 1916 and then worked for the Red Cross, reporting on work being carried out by British volunteers.

After the war, Binyon returned to his work full-time at the British Museum and the family moved into a house within the museum grounds in 1919. Binyon continued to write poetry, publishing several more collections during the 1920s and also wrote several plays, including Arthur, which was staged at the Old Vic in 1923, with music composed and conducted by Sir Edward Elgar.

In 1929, Binyon travelled to the Far East on behalf of the museum to take charge of an exhibition of British Watercolours in Japan. By the early 1930s he was considered to be one of England's foremost literary figures, serving on the committee of the Royal Society of Literature. In 1932, he was promoted to become the Keeper of the Department of Prints and Drawings, where he remained until his retirement from the museum the following year, when he was also made an Honorary Fellow of Trinity College. In the 1933-1934 academic year Binyon served as Norton Professor of Poetry at Harvard University.

When Binyon returned to England in the summer of 1934, he and Cicely settled in a farmhouse in Berkshire, where he continued to enjoy writing poetry. Other occupations included the organising of art exhibitions and travelling. Binyon died of bronchopneumonia on 10th March 1943 and was mourned by those who knew him as a "warm" and "happy" man, who loved both "truth and beauty". He also, very probably, appreciated the fact that, while age may have wearied him, he had at least been allowed to grow old.

FOR THE FALLEN

For The Fallen has become one of the most famous poems of the First World War, as its fourth verse is quoted at countless Remembrance and memorial services around the world. The remainder of the piece, however, remains largely unknown, overshadowed, perhaps, by the resonant poignancy of these four lines.

The poem was written within a few weeks of the beginning of the war and was published in The Times on September 21st 1914 at a time when the British public were focused on news of the battles taking place around the Marne and the Aisne. The reports of casualties among the men of the British Expeditionary Force in these early weeks of war brought home to the general public the sense that the anticipated victory over Germany - which at the time almost no-one doubted - would not come without considerable human cost.

The poem opens with the immediate introduction of two strong and prevalent emotions at the time: namely pride and gratitude. Binyon likens these sensations to the way in which a mother might feel "for her children", thus personifying the country and humanising events, making the ensuing line even more emotional, as he describes the nation's mourning "for her dead", who lie "across the sea". In this way, Binyon also brings home the remoteness of these deaths, reminding the reader that the soldiers concerned have lost their lives in the service of "England", but while far from their beloved homes and mothers. This emotive languages continues, as Binyon goes on to describe the dead as though they were, quite literally, the children of England, as though they had once been joined, both literally and spiritually, implying that their deaths cause both parties a physical and emotional pain. The final line of this first verse makes it clear that, in Binyon's opinion, England's "cause" was that of "the free", or the right and just, which was a not uncommon viewpoint at the time, being as may people thought that England had truth and justice on her side.

The second verse opens with a celebration of death, in which the language seems quite contradictory, as Binyon describes the drums that sound as both "solemn", and at the same time causing a "thrill", which may be interpreted as a feeling of nervous pulsation, rather than excitement, almost representing, perhaps, the reverberation of the drum itself, as it is beaten. Death is then described as impressive or respectable, even to the point of being given regal status, which raises the stature of the dead to a level well above that of the living. Binyon creates the impression that these deaths will create such great "sorrow" that this will be heard in the highest heavens. Nonetheless, he states, despite man's desolation over the deaths, there is also cause for a certain amount of pride in the manner in which the soldiers have died. Although there will be "tears", he admits, these will be mingled with a sense of "glory".

In the third verse, Binyon goes on to describe the soldiers themselves as happy, "young" and upright. He paints a picture here of healthy, honest men who marched to war undeceived as to their task or their purpose. Binyon accounts for these men as dedicated to their cause, regardless of the fact that they were greatly outnumbered and states that they died bravely, facing their enemy. Readers should remember that Binyon is describing here the original British Expeditionary Force, which numbered just over 100,000 men and was vastly outnumbered by the conscripted armies of Germany against whom they found themselves opposed.

The fourth and most famous verse really requires no explanation. It stands alone as a quoted piece, recited at memorials and remembrance services around the world to reflect the feelings of those who are left behind. The fact that Binyon sees the future for the living in terms of weariness and condemnation, demonstrates a sense, which was more common at the beginning of the conflict, that those who gave their lives, were in some way, gaining something by their sacrifice. Nonetheless, he tempers this with the acknowledgement that the dead have surrendered their old age and, by extension, the life they would have had in advancing to maturity. He also admits that the dead will always be remembered, whether in the morning or the evening, they will be in the thoughts of the living.

In the fifth verse, Binyon recounts all the things that the dead can no longer do. For example, he says, they cannot laugh with their friends, or "sit" with their families at home. Equally, there is no place for them at work, because they have died overseas. The notion stated here, that the dead are merely sleeping, rather romanticises the state of death, ignoring any pain and sorrow that might have been caused along the way. This verse feels rather out of place, almost as though verses four and five have been switched around, as verses one to three are all about the dead men and the effects of their deaths, while verse four is about how they will be remembered. Then in verse five, Binyon reverts back to a discussion of the men again.

Verse six focuses, like verse four, on the feelings of those left behind, whose emotions run high when they contemplate their lost loved-ones. Binyon asserts that these feelings of grief run through the very core of the nation, like a "well-spring" or a gushing outpouring of emotion, that is, somehow kept "hidden from sight". Despite this reticence to express their sorrow openly, the feelings are there in the "innermost heart" of the nation's people and are as familiar to them as the stars are to the night sky.

In the final verse, Binyon continues with the idea of the familiarity of the stars, reminding us of their endurance,which he compares to that of the memory of the dead men. These soldiers, he says, will continue to "march" through time as ghostly figures in heaven and when everything else has faded into oblivion, they will still be there. In this way, Binyon gives the dead soldiers a degree of immortality not afforded to the living, showing us that this is what they gained through their sacrifice. This final verse, probably the most haunting of the poem, shows how the dead were observed in the early days of the war: the optimism remained and the praise for their sacrifices outweighed anything achieved by the living.

Despite the many profound and lasting messages contained in this poem, it is actually quite sketchy in terms of its quality, with only the fourth and final verses really standing out. That being said, those two verses alone warrant the positioning of this piece among some of the finest in this genre. It is possible to compare this poem with other First World War poems, such as *Into Battle* by Julian Grenfell or *The Dead* by Rupert Brooke. Grenfell's poem could be seen as a celebration of life, in which sense it bears some similarities to For The Fallen. Grenfell, like Binyon, speaks of war in glorious terms and makes definite reference to those who die becoming increased by their actions. However, there are few allowances for sentiment or grief in Grenfell's poem, presumably because it is written from the perspective of a professional soldier, rather than a civilian onlooker. Brooke, meanwhile never actually saw action prior to his death en-route to Gallipoli and his poems contained in the 1914 Sonnets were written very early in the war. In *The Dead*, Brooke tells of the richness of the dead and how the act of dying brings with it enhancement greater than money can buy. He also speaks with pride of the "Nobleness" with which he feels his generations is endowed and how the fighting of the war, and if necessary the deaths that this will entail, actually brings these men back to their "heritage". Brooke's perspective is even more romanticised than that of either Grenfell or Binyon, as he had not yet seen either of their realities: the loss of many young men, or the reality of having to fight.

For the Fallen has, through its fourth verse, become probably the single most famous poem of the Great War, although few people realise on hearing it how early it was written, or that this verse is only part of a much longer piece. At the time, most other poets, especially of Binyon's generation, were writing nationalistic calls to arms, such as Harold Begbie's *Fall In*, published just three weeks earlier, which became so popular that it was set to music and a "marketing campaign" was organised involving the sale of badges and posters. This makes Binyon's piece all the more remarkable, despite its occasional flaws, because he somehow captures an emotion that would eventually epitomise the nation's feelings about their men. While some of the language contained in the rest of the poem may seem rose-tinted and unrealistic, given the time of its composition, this is actually a genuine reflection of the thoughts of many, resulting in a remarkable and haunting poem. Although the world remembers and recites the fourth verse, it is really the final stanza that provides the most moving tribute to "the fallen", acknowledging their endurance and strength through the darkest of times; their extraordinary heroism and the legacy of grief that would continue to touch the world.

EZRA POUND

Born in America, Pound lived most of his life in Europe and was in England throughout the First World War.

BIOGRAPHICAL DETAILS

Ezra Weston Loomis Pound was born in Hailey, Idaho on 30th October 1885. His father, Homer Loomis Pound, ran the government office in Hailey, although his wife Isabel (Weston, from New York) disliked living there. As a result of this, when Ezra was still an infant, the family moved to Philadelphia, Pennsylvania where Homer took up a position as an Assistant Assayer for the US Mint, performing chemical tests on metals. When he was thirteen, one of Ezra's aunts, Frances Weston, took him on a tour of Europe, which introduced the boy to many sights and experiences that would later influence both his work and his life.

Pound studied firstly at Hamilton College, where he received his Bachelor of Philosophy and then went on the University of Pennsylvania, which led to a Master's degree in Romance Philology. While there, he met Hilda Doolittle and they were very briefly engaged to be married in 1907. Doolittle, better known as H.D. broke off the engagement the following year, after her father expressed his disapproval of Pound. Doolittle then became romantically involved with another woman, Frances Gregg, although she would later briefly marry another war poet, Richard Aldington. She and Pound, however, remained friends and he promoted her poetry.

In late 1907, Pound took up a position as a teacher at Wabash College in Indiana, but after only four months, in February 1908, he was dismissed following a scandal involving an actress. Not long after this, in April 1908, he left America for Europe, settling in London, after first travelling on the Continent. Almost immediately, Pound settled into life among the young modernist poets and writers, eventually becoming the 'secretary' to W B Yeats, with whom he lived during most of 1914 and 1915.

On April 20th 1914, Pound married Dorothy Shakespear, whom he had met at one of his lectures at the London Polytechnic a few years earlier. Dorothy, an artist, was the daughter of the novelist Olivia Shakespear, who was, herself, a close friend of W B Yeats. At around this time, Pound also met T S Eliot for the first time, in what would become a long collaboration.

After the First World War, Pound became increasingly dissatisfied with London and, in 1920 he in Dorothy left for Paris where they remained for the next four years, before moving on to Rapallo in Italy. In 1923, however, Pound met Olga Rudge and they began an affair, which resulted in the birth of their daughter, Mary two years later. Dorothy herself had a son, named Omar in 1926, although whether Pound was his father remains unknown and the boy was raised by his maternal grandmother. When Pound and Dorothy moved to Rapallo, Olga Rudge followed shortly afterwards and settled nearby.

By this time, fascism was on the rise in Italy and Pound turned his literary attentions to this new social and economic philosophy. In 1933, he met with Mussolini and from that moment, he idealised the fascist dictator and his politics. Six years later, Pound briefly returned to America, but did not remain long. His parents, now quite elderly, had retired and moved to Rapallo to be with their son (his father would die there in 1942), and his daughter Mary had been born and raised as an Italian. America, therefore, had little to draw him back.

During the Second World War, Pound made radio broadcasts on behalf of the Axis powers, which were disapproving of America's involvement as well as being anti-Semitic. In 1943, Pound was indicted in his absence, by the U.S. Government, for broadcasting Axis propaganda. As the war progressed, Pound fled to the north of Italy, where the Fascist regime still had a stronghold. However, in May 1945, as Mussolini lost control, Pound was arrested by Partisans and handed over to the Americans in Pisa where he was kept in a wire cage, prior to being shipped back to the U.S. to face trial for treason.

Once he was returned to America, Pound was found to be incompetent to stand trial, on the grounds of insanity. He was, therefore, confined to St. Elizabeth's Hospital in Washington D.C. There remains some controversy over whether

Pound faked his insanity to avoid being tried for treason, which could have resulted in him facing the death penalty, if found guilty. The plea of insanity meant that he could be held at St. Elizabeth's indefinitely, but his incarceration was not exactly onerous as he had a private room and was afforded as many visitors as he wished, including conjugal visits from his wife, who had loyally moved to Washington to be nearer to her husband. In addition he was free to continue writing and in 1949, he was awarded the Bollingen prize for poetry.

Pound was released from St. Elizabeth's in 1958, following the intervention of many prominent American writers and poets. He immediately returned to Italy to live with Olga and their daughter Mary. In the final years of his life, Pound suffered from depression, lapsing into long, protracted periods of silence and self-doubt. He died in Venice on 1st November 1972.

from HUGH SELWYN MAUBERLEY

This extract, selected by Jon Stallworthy for inclusion in the Oxford Book of War Poetry, comes from a long poem written in numbered sections - these two being numbers four and five. *Hugh Selwyn Mauberley* was written in 1920 and has come to represent Ezra Pound's farewell to England, which had been his home for the previous twelve years. However, this is no disguising his distaste for the country in these lines, as he refers to her as 'an old bitch gone in the teeth'.

The poem opens with a relatively blank statement that 'these' men fought regardless, believing that they were protecting their homes. Pound then goes on to offer more detailed explanations as to why men had chosen to fight in the Great War. These include a lust for adventure, a fear of appearing weak or cowardly, a fear of fear itself, which later became a love of killing. For some, he asserts, a dream of killing, which might first have seemed appealing, soon changed, once the reality of war became known. These explanations seem to make it clear that men fought for many different reasons: some honourable; others really quite selfish, and that a man's reason for fighting could easily be affected by his experiences, thereby changing his outlook. (Pound's naivete and inadequate experience of his subject is shown by the fact that his misses out another of the most frequent reasons why men enlisted which was for the money: a regular income was important to many in 1914 and the Army offered them just that.

Pound goes on to say that some men died for their country - 'pro patria' - but not sweetly or well. These latin references may be taken from Horace's Odes, or it is possible that Pound had read Wilfred Owen's *Dulce et Decorum Est*, which was published posthumously in his first volume of poetry, in 1920, edited by Edith Sitwell and Siegfried Sassoon. Either way, he disagrees with the statement 'Dulce et Decorum Est pro Patria Mori', which translates as 'it is sweet and meet to die for one's country', to which Owen had referred as 'the old lie'.

Pound suggests, aptly, that the soldiers spent their time during the war 'eye-deep in hell', which could be taken both literally and metaphorically. In the trenches, the men would have stood, literally up to their eyes, or if they were lucky, slightly higher, in the mud. Metaphorically speaking, the war was undoubtedly hellish and one could say that the men became submerged in their environment, losing all sense of normality, drowning almost, in the cesspit that was the Great War. (Incidentally, this phrase became the title of a highly acclaimed book about First World War trench life by John Ellis).

In Pound's opinion, the men had been deceived into believing 'old men's lies', and when they returned home, the lying continued. His use of the words 'old lies' does lead one to wonder whether he had in fact read Owen's poem, although this is pure conjecture. At the end of this section of the poem, Pound's anger is definitely aimed towards the statesmen and figures of authority. A general election had been held on 14th December 1918, only one month after the Armistice, which may have seemed an almost tasteless haste, and could be the cause of the words 'liars in public places'.

He then returns to the efforts of the younger generation, recalling their 'daring' and the 'wastage' of so many 'young' lives, with so much still to live for. Pound would have been around thirty-five when he wrote this poem, and one can easily imagine that the loss of so many young men, in their late teens or early twenties, would have had a profound effect upon him - as indeed it did on others of a similar age, such as Siegfried Sassoon. The line 'fortitude as never before' which stands isolated from the rest of the poem, has an air of sadness and retrospection about it, as though the poet is casting one final glance at the lost youth, before turning his gaze, once again, towards his anger and those whom he holds responsible.

The final verse of this section speaks of changes to society, although from the fact that Pound was leaving England, one would have to assume that he did not approve of these amendments. He speaks of 'disillusions' and 'confessions', but also of 'hysterias' and the sinister and macabre-sounding 'laughter out of dead bellies', which suggests that the dead mock the survivors and, perhaps, that in Pound's view at least, the dead were the lucky ones, because at least they did not have to return to a country that was prepared to lie to its heroes.

In the second section - part five of the poem - Pound continues along the same theme, commenting that, among the multitude of men who died, it always seemed to be the 'best' ones who were taken. Then comes his comment upon the country for which they died, which he now, clearly holds in contempt. However, his anger is not limited to the nation, but also to the 'civilization' which he claims to be 'botched'.

The penultimate couplet reminds us, once again, of the dead, who represent all that had been good about the nation - when she had a 'good mouth', and before she was 'gone in the teeth', or corrupted. Their young, alert, 'quick' eyes, or lives are now buried beneath the earth. But, he adds in the final couplet, it has all really been for nothing - or at least for very little. Pound states here that they gave their lives for some 'broken statues', by which we may infer either statesmen or politicians, or possibly memorials, and for 'a few thousand battered books' which is probably a reference to history or tradition.

There is no escaping Pound's anger in this poem: he does nothing to disguise it. What is equally difficult to escape, however, is the knowledge that, however fine and grand his words may or may not have been, Pound would, within just a few years of writing this piece, embrace both fascism and anti-semitism, which makes this poem just so much fashionable rhetoric.

T. S. ELIOT

Born in America, Eliot took no part in the First World War, although he became a British citizen in the 1920s.

BIOGRAPHICAL DETAILS

Thomas Stearns Eliot was born in St Louis, Missouri on September 26th 1888. He was the youngest of the six surviving children of Henry Ware Eliot, who owned a successful brick manufacturing company, and his wife, Charlotte. There was an age gap of eight years between Thomas and his next oldest sibling, Henry and, as Thomas suffered with a congenital double hernia, his mother and older sisters were very watchful of him. While in Missouri, Thomas attended the Smith Academy in St Louis, before leaving in 1905 to attend the Milton Academy, near Boston, prior to joining Harvard where he studied English Literature, graduating in 1910. Following this, he spent a year in Paris, returning to post-graduate studies at Harvard the following year.

In 1914, Eliot was invited to study at Merton College, Oxford and while in England, he met, among others, Ezra Pound, who would greatly influence Eliot's work in years to come. He also met Vivien Haigh-Wood and, following a very short engagement, the couple were married in June 1915. The Eliot family were not pleased with their son's choice, especially when Vivien's history of illness became known to them. Matters were made worse by Vivien's refusal to travel to the US during the war, resulting in an enforced detachment between Eliot and his family.

The newlyweds initially lodged with Bertrand Russell, with whom it has been alleged Vivien had a brief relationship. Then, in 1917, with their finances needing a boost, Eliot took a job at Lloyds Bank, writing poetry in his spare time. He published his first book Prufrock and Other Observations, later that year.

The following few years were difficult. In 1919, Eliot's father died, without the two men ever really healing the differences between them that had existed since Eliot's marriage. This was followed by a breakdown in Vivien's health, which in turn led to a similar turn of events for Eliot himself who, under doctor's orders, went to a sanitarium in Switzerland to recover. Despite all of these difficulties - or maybe because of them - it was during this time that Eliot wrote The Waste Land, which was published in 1922.

In 1925, with Vivien again in poor health, Eliot became literary editor of the newly formed publishers, Faber and Gwyer, which would go on to become Faber and Faber. This was followed in 1927, by two decisions which shocked friends and family alike: the first was that he was baptized into the Church of England; the second was that he became a British citizen. Literary success followed, although this was not mirrored in his private life, as his marriage was steadily deteriorating. In 1932, Eliot was offered the opportunity to deliver the Norton Lectures at Harvard and he took the chance to spent a year away from Vivien. Once he returned, he considered them as separated, although they did not divorce due to his religious beliefs. In 1938, Vivien was committed to a mental hospital in North London, where she remained until she died in 1947. Although he was still her husband, Eliot never visited her there. During the Second World War, he served as an air-raid warden, although he wrote no more major works of poetry after 1943.

In 1957, Eliot married Valerie Fletcher, who had for many years been his secretary at Faber and Faber, where he was now a director. Eliot died of emphysema on January 4th 1965 and, according to his wishes, his ashes were scattered at East Coker in Somerset, the place from which his ancestors had originally left to go to America.

TRIUMPHAL MARCH

This poem was first published in 1931 and appears to describe a scene at the end of the First World War, which bears some similarity to the one described in Wilfrid Wilson Gibson's poem Baccanal. Both pieces hint at Greco-Roman gatherings and lavish celebrations which appear somewhat out of place in the circumstances of so much loss. Much of Eliot's poem, however, seems to be metaphorical, as it is hard to believe that there really would have been a 'temple', 'virgins' or a 'sacrifice', for example.

The poem opens with a metaphorical list of items in this supposed parade. Eliot repeats the word 'stone' three times in this first line, which may be a references to tombstones, memorials or death - or all three. The other items are equally representative of war: the metals may be used to make weapons or medals; the oakleaves may represent the US military system for denoting that a soldier has receiving the same medal more than once; 'horses' heels over the paving' would have been a fairly common sound during the war, as the cavalry and artillery both used horses.

He then goes on to recount some of the other adornments of the march, which seem so numerous that they threaten to overwhelm the city. They seem to be waiting for one particular person, and their wait is a long one. Prior to the passing of this long-awaited person, an enormous quantity of army paraphernalia seems to pass by, which the poet lists numerically. This must be a metaphorical parade as, if one really had to wait for this quantity of equipment to pass by, the wait would be interminable, so we must assume that this is really Eliot's point: that the war consumed vast quantities of apparatus. Even then, however, the much anticipated arrival does not appear, as first, there seem to be other dignitaries, none of whom actually appear to be that important, but they must all pass through before 'he' finally arrivals. We might assume that 'he' - a lone rider on horseback - represents the war dead. His eyes seem at once 'watchful' and 'indifferent', as though he doesn't trust this crowd, but he also doesn't care about why they are all there to greet him.

In the final verse, we are introduced to a character named 'Cyril', who may be a survivor of the war whose nerves have become so shattered that he cries out 'crumpets' for no apparent reason, when he is taken to church. The 'light' which is requested at the end of the poem may be a metaphor for reason, or sense, in that the poet may be asking for someone to make sense of everything that happened during the war. The line of French at the end translates as: 'And were the soldiers forming a guard of honour? THEY WERE FORMING ONE' which suggests an element of pride in the actions of Cyril, or of the 'he' who was mentioned earlier in the poem.

I have seen this poem referred to as 'experimental', which does it more credit than I feel it deserves. Even as a poem laden with irony and metaphor, this still seems nonsensical and I can see little purpose or meaning in it, other than the waste of life, which subject has been better covered elsewhere.

G. K. CHESTERTON

One of England's greatest 20th Century writers and a renowned wit, G K Chesterton is best known today for his Father Brown detective stories. However, his poetry of the First World War shows a different side to this larger-than-life character, whose compassion and patriotism are self-evident. As a non-combatant, he is often omitted from anthologies of First World War poetry, which does him, and his work, an injustice. Jon Stallworthy's choice of poem is perhaps Chesterton's best-known, and it shows both his patriotism and humour, although it is not, perhaps, his best.

BIOGRAPHICAL DETAILS

Gilbert Keith Chesterton was born on 29th May 1874 in Kensington, London. His father, Edward, was an auctioneer and surveyor and Gilbert was the oldest of two sons, his brother Cecil being five years younger. He passed an extremely contented childhood and while very fond of his mother, Marie, was devoted to his father, referring to him, quite simply as 'perfect'. Initially, he attended Colet Court, before entering St Paul's School at the age of twelve. He loved art and literature, although he was slow to develop - his voice, for example, had not broken by the time he left school. At the time, doctors decided this was due to the fact that both physically and intellectually, Gilbert was larger than normal and, therefore, would take longer to mature.

After leaving St Paul's, Chesterton studied illustration at the Slade School of Art and then attended University College London, although he did not obtain a degree. In 1896, he began working for a London publisher, as well as undertaking some freelance journalism, neither of which paid tremendously well. Following a very long engagement, he married Frances Blogg. They enjoyed an extremely happy marriage and were devoted to each other. Initially they lived in Battersea, before moving to Beaconsfield in 1909. During this time, Chesterton continued to write prolifically and became good friends with many other literary figures, including Hilaire Belloc, and George Bernard Shaw.

Chesterton was a large, well-built man, who was renowned for his eccentricities of dress. He was also deeply religious and would convert to Catholicism in 1922. The writing for which Chesterton is best known today - namely the Father Brown stories - first appeared in magazines before *The Innocence of Father Brown* was published in book form in 1911. By 1914, the stress of overwork began to take its toll and Chesterton became seriously ill, suffering a complete breakdown, which lasted until the middle of 1915. The war years were difficult for Chesterton, a naturally sensitive man, who worried greatly, not just for his brother Cecil, who was fighting in France, but for all the young men who had answered their country's call. After the armistice, when all seemed well again, he received word that his brother had died of wounds on 6th December 1918.

Chesterton became increasingly angry that so many men, like Cecil, had died and yet the same men who had sent them to die were still ruling the country. In the early 1920s, Chesterton and his wife travelled widely, before celebrating their silver wedding anniversary in 1926. Chesterton died in 1936, leaving behind a grieving widow, who survived him by only two years and a wealth of poetry and prose, which rivals that of any 20th Century author.

ELEGY IN A COUNTRY CHURCHYARD

Published in 1922, *Elegy in a Country Churchyard* is probably a parody of Thomas Gray's poem *Elegy written in a Country Church-yard*, a mid-eighteenth century masterpiece that has become one of the most frequently-quoted poems in the English language. At the end of the First World War, just after the Armistice, Chesterton's brother Cecil died of nephritis. This illness, which is an inflammation of the kidneys, had begun while Cecil was in the trenches, but he had refused to seek medical help or leave his post, thereby resulting in his death. Gilbert Chesterton was deeply affected by the death of his younger brother, as well as by the deaths of so many other young men and although he believed that the war was just and right, he found it difficult to justify death on such a massive scale. His patriotism, which remained steadfast, was limited to those who really served their country, not to the politicians, who talked about service, while expecting others to make the commitments and sacrifices. As time progressed, especially after the hastily convened December 1918 General

Election, Chesterton became increasingly embittered that the men who had taken the country to war, were still in charge. Many of these politicians, including David Lloyd George, the Prime Minister, had also been involved in the Marconi Scandal in 1912, which had resulted in the prosecution of Cecil Chesterton for criminal libel.

Although the tone of this poem is ironic, there is no escaping Chesterton's anger, directed towards the stately men of England, whom he holds responsible for the fate of all the others. The poem opens with a reference to the men who did not fight, but remained in England, working for their country. Chesterton points out that those of this group who have died "have their graves at home", suggesting an element of privilege in this position. He goes on to portray an idyllic image of their rural churchyards, where nature is allowed to remain abundant, reminding both the living and the dead of their positions and of their very Englishness.

In the second verse, Chesterton describes the men who have "fought for England", by which he means the soldiers, and most specifically those who have given their lives for their country. He refers to these men as pursuing "a falling star", which suggests that by the time he wrote this poem, Chesterton may not have been feeling so certain as to the reasons why these men had gone to fight. Although Chesterton had been certain throughout the war that the conflict was a necessary battle of good versus evil, it would seem that once the fighting was over, he became more disillusioned. That is not to say that Chesterton was any less patriotic or supportive of the men who had fought, but he would seem to have started questioning the political motives behind the war itself. He goes on, in this second verse, to point out that the graves of these Englishmen are on foreign soil, which in similar tones to those implied in the first verse, would seem to be deemed a detrimental position, as to be buried in England, would have been their greatest reward. There is also an implication here that their deaths are England's loss, that England is all the poorer for their parting.

In the final verse, Chesterton turns his most satirical eye upon the politicians who "rule in England". These are the men who continue to take charge, despite their culpability for the war. They did not fight or work for their country, but merely sat in private meetings, full of supposed solemnity and pomp, although there is an implication that they have achieved nothing of any purpose. It seems rather strange for a man with such strong religious convictions as Chesterton to be wishing these rulers dead. However, this really only goes to demonstrate the depth of his anger against the men whom he believed to be responsible for the fate of so many others, but who had been allowed to continue living their lives with impunity.

Another poet who adopted a similar tone was Rudyard Kipling in his poem *A Dead Statesman* (part of *Epitaphs of the War*), in which he is openly critical of the politicians who he accuses of having "lied" in the first place to "please the mob" of young men who had originally wanted to go to war. They had done nothing useful towards the conflict, but now that it is over, and they are dead, they must face the men who they betrayed. Kipling allows that the "dead statesman" of his poem has developed a conscience, which Chesterton does not permit to his politicians, although this is possibly because his rulers are still alive and still believe themselves to have been right. Both poets use very simple rhymes and rhythms, almost making their poems seem like nursery rhymes in their simplicity. It is also interesting to note in Chesterton's poem, the repetition of the word "England" at the end of every other line, showing the importance to him of this aspect and how patriotic Chesterton was.

RUDYARD KIPLING

Best known for his children's stories, such as *The Jungle Books* and *Just So Stories*, as well as the popular poem *If*, Kipling's life and later work was greatly affected by the impact of his son's death in the First World War.

BIOGRAPHICAL DETAILS

Rudyard Kipling was born on 30th December 1865 in Bombay. His father, John Lockwood Kipling was an artist as well as a professor of architectural sculpture, while his mother, Alice had, before her marriage been one of the famous MacDonald sisters, whose renown stems from the fact that four of the sisters married extremely well. The first six years of Kipling's life were spent idyllically in India until, in 1871, he and his three year old sister Alice - known to the family as 'Trix' - were sent back to England to the home of Captain and Mrs Holloway in Portsmouth. Although Trix fared reasonably well, Kipling did not, as he was often neglected and bullied by Mrs Holloway.

His torture ended in 1877, when his mother returned from India and the following year he began attending the United Services College at Westward Ho! in Devon, which was meant to prepare him for service in the armed forces. Neither this, nor university were suitable, or affordable for Kipling or his family, so he returned to India in 1882 and became assistant editor of a a local newspaper. He also began writing short stories, which were either reproduced in newspapers, or in small collections. In 1889, wishing to advance his literary career, Kipling returned to London, where he began writing in earnest. He was also introduced to a young American, Caroline (Carrie) Balestier, to whom he was married in January 1892.

Their first daughter, Josephine, was born in December of that year, while they were living in Vermont, USA, near to Carrie's family estate. During this time, Kipling wrote *The Jungle Books*. Another daughter, Elsie, was born in 1896 and later that year, the family returned to England and settled in Devon for a short time, before buying a house in Rottingdean, near Brighton. The couple's third child, a son named John, was born in August 1897 and by this time, Kipling had become a famous author.

In 1899, the family visited New York and, while there, both Kipling and Josephine developed pneumonia and both were extremely ill. On March 6th Josephine died, aged just six years. Kipling, however, was still so ill that his doctors decided not to inform him until he was sufficiently recovered to take the shock of this news. By the time he was told, Josephine's funeral had already taken place, but the loss of his beloved and remarkably beautiful daughter overshadowed the rest of his life. The family returned to England that summer, but found it impossible to settle at their old house, without Josephine. So, in 1902, Kipling purchased Batemans - a house in Burwash, East Sussex, where he lived for the remainder of his life. In 1907, Kipling was awarded the Nobel Prize for Literature and his career had reached its zenith.

As the First World War began, Kipling, always an Imperialist, became involved with the War Propaganda Bureau and visited training camps and the trenches. Meanwhile, John Kipling, although only just seventeen, had tried unsuccessfully to enlist. His father approached a family friend, Lord Roberts, who was Colonel-in-Chief of the Irish Guards and asked for his assistance in the matter. This was duly granted, John was commissioned as a Second Lieutenant and sailed for France in August 1915. He was killed at the Battle of Loos on September 27th, within weeks of arriving at the front. His body was not found and Kipling would spend the rest of his life trying to discover the truth about John's death, and to make amends for his part in John's enlistment. He became involved with the work of the Imperial (now Commonwealth) War Graves Commission and wrote two single lines of text which that organisation used on many memorials and gravestones: 'Their Name Liveth for Evermore' and 'Known Unto God', which is inscribed onto the headstones of unidentified soldiers. Life, both personally and professionally, would never be quite the same for Kipling and, although he continued to write, his reputation had suffered a great deal immediately after the First World War. He died suddenly on 18 January 1936.

EPITAPHS OF THE WAR

Epitaphs of the War was first published in 1919, but was started in April 1918, and takes the form of a series of short poems, written in memory of and paying tribute to those who died during the First World War. Generally speaking, the tone of these poems is less patriotic or jingoistic than much of Kipling's earlier verse, such as his 1914 piece For all we have and are, in which he had encouraged the young men to enlist and fight for their country. Kipling's perspectives of the war were greatly affected by his own experiences both before and during the conflict, so we can see the influences of his Indian upbringing as well as the impact of the death of his only son, John.

EQUALITY OF SACRIFICE

A simple couplet in which the poet poses a question regarding the even-handedness of war. Unlike the days prior to the conflict, it matters not whether one is a "have" or a "have-not"; both are expected to give to their country in equal measure. In this way, Kipling is effectively pointing out that, at least in his opinion, the class barriers were being broken down by the war. This didn't just apply to the men in the trenches, but also to those at home who suffered losses in equal measure, regardless of how rich or poor they might be. It must be said, however, that what Kipling fails to take into account here is that when a poor family loses their breadwinner, the results can be long-lasting and catastrophic.

A SERVANT

A couplet in which Kipling explains the relationship between an officer and his servant. In this case, the two men have been together since the beginning of the war, so they would have an intimate knowledge of each other and although they would be of different ranks and backgrounds, a friendship would almost certainly have developed between them. Kipling describes the relationship from the perspective of the officer and does not hesitate to inform us that the servant was "the better man". This not only betrays Kipling's opinion of the lower ranks, but also that of many officers, who greatly respected the men who served under them.

A SON

In this couplet, Kipling offers a sanitised, idealised vision of the death of "a son".
We might reasonably assume that he would have been referring to the death of
his own son, John, who was killed on 27th September 1915. At the time,
however, John was listed as "missing, presumed killed", leaving his parents
wondering as to the fate of their son. When Kipling wrote this couplet, however,
he had almost certainly given up any hope of John being found alive and,
presumably found solace in the belief that his son had died happy. The notion
that the soldiers at the front were "laughing" might well also have suited Kipling's
pro-war stance. Indeed, he goes on to imply that the men who serve and are
being killed are having a more enjoyable time than those at home. He wishes
that he could understand how they could laugh on such occasions, so that he
might be able to participate as well, during such difficult times. Whilst one can
sympathise with the feelings of a grieving parent which are displayed in this
couplet, it is difficult to understand the complacency with which Kipling
dismisses the feelings of the men at the front.

AN ONLY SON

Another couplet which focuses on the loss of a son in war. This time the loss is
of an "only son", which is exactly what John Kipling was to his parents. Now,
Kipling writes from the perspective of the son, but relating only to the loss as felt
by the mother. He describes the death of the "only son" so effectively, bringing
about the death of the mother, who dies "of grief" for her boy. Despite her grief
and the fact that she will die, she still blesses "her slayer" - namely her son -
because her love for him is so great that even their combined deaths cannot
destroy it. This is another rather sanitised vision of war in which Kipling places
as much emphasis on the plight of those at home, as of those at war. Indeed, he
almost suggests that those who die in war are guilty of causing this dreadful,
final and ultimately murderous grief to their mothers.

EX-CLERK

A short poem, in which Kipling tells the story of a former Clerk, or office worker
- although the piece could apply to any worker. The poem opens with an
entreaty that the reader should not "pity" the clerk, and even though at this stage
we do not know his fate, Kipling's request seems somewhat callous. He goes on
to say that by joining the army, the Clerk has found freedom from his previously

slavish life. Through this freedom, he then gained a power of "body, will and mind" and through this, he was able to demonstrate good humour, friendship and love. Out of this love, the man went to his own death and through his death has finally found contentment. This is a terribly presumptuous poem on the part of Kipling, who assumes that the clerk would have felt like a "timid slave" in his previous role and that, therefore, everything which he found through his service with the army would have been an improvement. While army life suited many, it was certainly not for everyone and some were utterly miserable even before they had embarked for France. Again, Kipling is providing a sanitised, "home-front" version of army life, which suits his ideals, rather than the reality. It may have served him well to believe that men, including his son, had found contentment and peace in death, but he says nothing of the manner of their dying.

THE WONDER

Like "Ex-Clerk" this is another short poem on how a man may be improved and increased by his service in the army. Here Kipling comments that a man who enlists effectively donates his "body and spirit" to the whims of "harsh Instructors" and that when their training is complete, these men will have gained "a soul". This implies that those who did not serve their country had no soul; that they were much less worthy in the eyes of God. Kipling goes on to comment that if earthly beings, such as the "harsh Instructors" could achieve such changes, how much could be done by God himself? There would appear here to be a questioning of the moral and religious commitment of any man who did not enlist and serve his country.

HINDU SEPOY IN FRANCE

In this simple couplet, Kipling pays tribute to the Indian soldiers who served in France during the First World War. Kipling's birth and early upbringing in India gave him strong connections with that country and its people, who answered the call of the Empire at the beginning of the First World War. In this couplet, Kipling makes the point that while "we", meaning the British, may not always have understood the ways of the Indian people, our debt to them for their bravery, outweighs any misconceptions.

THE COWARD

One of Kipling's most famous Epitaphs, this couplet tells of a man sentenced to death for cowardice. Told from the perspective of "the coward", we learn that he was afraid to face death feeling that it was a certainty and also because he had seen so much of it that he knew how dreadful it would be. Nonetheless, he must face it now, because he is being led out to his own execution, by other men. Ultimately, however, he will not die surrounded by his comrades, as he might have done in battle, but "blindfold and alone". This couplet is a strange blend of sympathy and criticism. Kipling seems to sympathise with the attitude of the man, allowing that to "know" death makes it harder to face. Yet at the same time, the tone of the poem also implies that the man deserves to die "alone" because he failed in his duty. When reading and studying this particular Epitaph, students should bear in mind that attitudes towards those "shot at dawn" were very different then to what they are now.

SHOCK

This short quatrain would appear to be about shell-shock, or the after-effects of the war in the form of "shock". The subject of the poem finds that he can recall nothing about his life - his identity and powers of speech have gone and a visit from his wife and children does not help him to recall anything. The man dies, followed by his mother and, in her arms, he manages to find peace and remember everything. This is another rather rose-tinted image of a traumatising situation. Kipling portrays the man's eventual salvation through his and his mother's deaths as being somehow cleansing, without mentioning the intervening torture. Like A Son and An Only Son, Kipling focuses on the relationship between parents and children (specifically mothers and sons), implying that this outweighs any other commitments such as marriage and children. This reflects the loss of his own young son, who had not yet developed any other serious bonds or ties outside of those which he had with his parents and sister.

A GRAVE NEAR CAIRO

The first part of this couplet takes the form or a plea or prayer to the "Gods of the Nile" that the man in the "grave" of the title should be permitted to "get out", or leave his final resting place and, presumably, return to life once more. There is almost an element of panic here, leaving one to wonder how the "stout fellow" met his death. We are, however, informed that he was courageous in life, as Kipling goes on to say that the man was neither shameful nor afraid. This is a rather peculiar poem, whose message would seem to be that the brave and upright men do not deserve to die.

PELICANS IN THE WILDERNESS
A Grave Near Halfa

This quatrain is written from the perspective of the man in the "grave near Halfa". He tells of how the sand in the desert covers his grave, leaving no signs for anyone to grieve over, including his own children. As such, the implication here would seem to be that both the man and the battle in which he fought and died will be forgotten. The final couplet carries with it a further sense of regret, suggesting that only the living and the young are really significant. The narrator implies here that each day he is able to return, like an angel, to see his children continue with their lives. As in other Epitaphs, Kipling once again creates the impression that death is by no means final and that those who die in battle or in war are in some way increased by their sacrifices.

TWO CANADIAN MEMORIALS

I

In this short poem, Kipling returns to a familiar theme: namely that those who die in war are made larger by their sacrifice and he goes on to say that the living should neither grieve for the dead, nor offer them any particular reverence for having died. We may assume that in saying this, Kipling feels that the dead receive sufficient reward simply through having made "the ultimate sacrifice" and, therefore, need no additional admiration from anyone else. the poem ends with Kipling's assertion that it is not actually "death" that brings about the end of a man, but "fear". In this way, he is presumably asserting that the men who die bravely are not really dead, but will live on forever, while those who are more cowardly will not be afforded such immortality. As in so many of Kipling's Epitaphs, we are offered a very rose-tinted version of death in battle in which the poet shows no real understanding of the truths of warfare.

II

The second of the Canadian Memorials focuses on the fact that the men of Canada had travelled a great distance to fight in a war which might not seem to have concerned their nation, because that was the honourable thing to do. Having died to protect "a world aflame", these men now lie buried in foreign soil, far away from their home country. However, from their graves, these men now hope that the living will continue to "keep" or maintain the world which the dead fought so hard to win. In this poem, Kipling really pays great respect to the Canadian forces, who were known throughout the war for their courage and devotion. They managed, for example, to capture ground, such as Vimy Ridge, which had been fought over by the French and British without success.

THE FAVOUR

In this poem, Kipling again refers to his theory that death comes as a relief for many soldiers. Here, he puts the soldier in the position of narrator, stating that he (the soldier) could not bear to wait for death, so felt relieved when it claimed him early in the conflict. Kipling implies that the aspect of waiting for death is actually worse than dying itself. The soldier suggests that death has left others to live, who the man considers to be more worthy than himself. Once dead, death speaks to the soldier, informing him that although he will not have any descendants, and his name will die out, he has at least protected his honour by dying bravely and in battle, serving his country. The Favour of the title presumably refers to the service done by death to the soldier and again this poem shows that Kipling felt that the most important aspect of war was to die with dignity and honour intact.

THE BEGINNER

This short poem is another one written from the perspective of a deceased soldier. In this instance, the soldier concerned reveals that he died in his very first moments of action, and that he had been in the front line trenches at the time. This implies an element of bravery, that the man concerned had faced death with such evident willingness, despite his inexperience. The poem continues with an afterthought, that children who are watching avidly, as though the war were a theatrical play, should pay attention to what is happening in front of them. This could be seen as Kipling encouraging the youth of society to focus on the war, almost to the point of enjoying it. The theatrical element of the poem is enhanced by the title, which not only refers to the inexperience of the dead soldier and the children but also to those actors who open a play, who are traditionally called "the beginners".

RAF (AGED EIGHTEEN)

As in the previous poem, Kipling focuses here on youth and inexperience, as well as an element of those who participate in the war having fun, while fighting. Here, he creates an image of a very young pilot who appears to gain so much enjoyment from his profession that he is able to laugh while he flies. Kipling also explains the pilot's youth, telling us that he still has some of his "milk-teeth" which enables the reader to understand his extreme youthfulness. The way in which the pilot kills is not the same as an infantryman, as he deals in a more remote form of death. Having completed his work, however, the young pilot is free to return home to behave like the youth he still is. This is effectively a poem in which Kipling tries to explain and justify the way in which youths, like his own son John, who were little more than children, were expected to do the work of men. This poem must have been written after April 1918, when the Royal Flying Corps (RFC) became the Royal Air Force (RAF).

THE REFINED MAN

In this poem, Kipling may be referring to the "common office" of the mens' latrines which would have been fairly well hidden from the enemy. In the case of his narrator, however, the man here is described as being too "delicate" to use the "common office" and Kipling suggests that the man has therefore chosen to fulfil his needs elsewhere. Unfortunately, the man has been spotted by the enemy and killed. Now dead, he wonders why others might find this situation humorous. He clearly continues to believe that he was perfectly entitled to make the choice that he did, even though it cost him his life, because he stood by his principles. There is no doubting that many other soldiers would have found such a situation amusing, as the black humour of the trenches would have found endless resources here for jocularity. Whether Kipling is agreeing with the "refined man's" perspective or with that of the men who might mock him, is not altogether clear.

NATIVE WATER-CARRIERS (MEF)

[The letters MEF stand for Mediterranean Expeditionary Force]

In this quatrain, Kipling recalls a Greek myth in which Prometheus stole fire from Zeus to give to man. Zeus, angry with Prometheus, decided to destroy mankind by drowning, leaving only two survivors on Mount Parnassus. This myth formed the basis of one of the Greek's versions of Creation. Here, Kipling equates the anger through which Zeus had destroyed mankind with the evident anger now being displayed towards man, who seems to be destroying himself by fire, in the form of war.

BOMBED IN LONDON

A simple couplet in which one must not forget the significance of the title. Kipling is reminding us of his sense of togetherness: that by being "bombed in London", civilians are no different to the serving soldiers. In the poem itself, he tells of a man who, try as he might to escape from "conscription", cannot hope for success, because thanks to the bombs, it is everywhere. In this way, he implies that civilians cannot hope to evade their responsibilities, but he also suggests that they wouldn't want to, once they realise the fact that the war is all around them anyway.

THE SLEEPY SENTINEL

A quatrain in which Kipling describes the fate of a man who has been caught sleeping while on duty. He describes the man's original duty as "faithless", or disloyal, implying that he received nothing in return for sitting and watching out into No Man's Land. However, he now seems to regret that he has nothing to watch over and no duty to perform, because he is dead. The reason he is dead is because he fell asleep while on duty, and death gives him the ironic opportunity to sleep as much as he wants. In death's sleep, there is no-one to tell him off for not doing his duty and he seems to regret this. Finally, we discover that the man literally died because he was asleep. Although this may mean that he slept and missed an oncoming assault, only waking too late to achieve anything, it is more likely that Kipling is suggesting that the man was executed for dereliction of duty. His turning of this episode into a ditty, giving it the rhyme and rhythm of a nursery rhyme, implies that Kipling somehow condoned this episode and justified the action taken against the man by belittling the outcome of his actions.

BATTERIES OUT OF AMMUNITION

In this couplet, Kipling is being critical of the workers at home who insisted on keeping to their designated hours, despite the need for additional manpower to produce the required ammunition. Here the poet suggests that if any of the workers should find themselves mourning for a loved one who has died in battle, they will only have themselves to blame, because they would not work the extra hours. This may seem like a harsh indictment, but it was not unusual for Kipling and those of his generation and class, who felt that all efforts should go into winning the war, even if the workers were not being paid for their time.

COMMON FORM

Perhaps the most famous Epitaph of them all, Common Form is a simple couplet written, as were many, from the perspective of the dead soldiers. Here, there could be more than one interpretation to Kipling's words, as he may be suggesting that if anyone might wonder about the soldiers' deaths, the answer stands in the lies of their elders. By this he might be implying politicians, senior statesmen or officers. Another interpretation, however, has infinitely more personal connotations and revolves around the death of Kipling's only son John, in September 1915. At the time of his death, John had only just turned eighteen and had experienced a great deal of trouble gaining his commission, due to his appalling eyesight. Kipling helped John overcome these obstacles, by using his influence and underestimating the significance of his son's problems with his vision. Therefore, it is possible to read this poem as a very personal self-criticism of Kipling's own role in the death of his son, although whether he intended that interpretation, is a matter of conjecture.

A DEAD STATESMAN

Rather than being the Epitaph for a dead soldier, Kipling deals here with a man who might be deemed responsible for the many deaths he has elsewhere been describing. He explains this dead man as being either incapable or unwilling to contribute to the war in any way other than by lying to the general population. The dead man's problem, however, is that now the war is over, all of his statements are being revealed as lies and now that he is also dead, he has to face up to the men whose blood is on his hands. He wonders what further excuses he can use now to serve his purpose among these more worthy young men. Here, Kipling makes the assumption that a dead statesman would be prepared to

admit to his fraudulent ways, which seems unlikely. However, he pays the man
no compliments, by also assuming that the dead man would continue to lie
simply to save his own reputation.

THE REBEL

This poem is about a man who has just died and gone to Heaven. Upon his
arrival there, he had contemplated begging for another chance of life, but had
refrained and had chosen instead to laugh at the way in which God looked down
so thoughtfully upon mankind. Now, however, as he settles into Heaven, he
realises that what he is really seeing is not worth mocking, as he is witnessing
God's "shame" at the plight of man. This forms an indictment over the role of
religion in the war, as well as giving us an insight into Kipling's perspective on
faith, which would appear to have been unfavourable.

THE OBEDIENT

Written, almost certainly in conjunction with The Rebel, this poem portrays a
different perspective of a man who manages to retain his faith, despite receiving
no signs from the Gods that they are listening to his prayers - or even that they
are aware of his existence. To a certain extent these two poems could be seen as
the poet attempting to show that God is as much to blame for the war as
mankind. By doing this, Kipling might hope to justify his own earlier
perspectives on the war - that men should fight and serve their country.

A DRIFTER OFF TARENTUM

The next three poems or Epitaphs have nautical themes, beginning with A
Drifter Off Tarentum in which we learn the sorry fate of a man lost at sea. He,
the vessel that carried him and all of his comrades sink to the bottom of the
ocean. Once there, all they find are the relics of other men and ships, leaving the
man with no hope for his own salvation. So, he gives in, sacrificing himself to
death, floating back to the surface to be fed upon by the seagulls. Rather a
depressing piece, devoid of hope, with classical overtones in style and subject
matter, Kipling forces the reader to recall here the men lost at sea, who have not
yet been mentioned among his other Epitaphs.

DESTROYERS IN COLLISION

In this brief poem, Kipling speaks of the "fate" of a heavy fog that draws two ships together to collide, simply because they cannot see one another. In this instance, however, these are not enemy vessels, but are both on the same side. He describes one of the sailors as "hurrying to my bride", by which he may mean the sea, although this may be a metaphor for the fact that the young men on board had their futures ahead of them. Here, the reader is supposed to understand the irony behind the fact that, despite the war, these men were not killed by their enemies but by their "friends".

CONVOY ESCORT

Another nautically-themed poem in which the person concerned, whom we may assume to be dead, since this is an Epitaph, describes himself as a "shepherd" or a leader of men more foolhardy than himself. Their bravery, he claims, had been aimless and those who were not courageous were fearful. As their leader, he laid down regulations, but none of the others obeyed him and yet they survived. He, however, perished because he was stubborn and intransigent. This is probably an Epitaph to an officer in the Navy, who would have done his duty in an old-fashioned way, not necessarily suited to the new recruits now under his command. Kipling may, at the end, be describing a sinking ship on which the captain remained, while the men around him escaped to safety. There is a definite air of respect, rather than mocking within this poem, as in the other naval epitaphs, showing Kipling's evident regard for the Senior Service.

UNKNOWN FEMALE CORPSE

This, and the next poem, deal with the cost of war to women and, in Unknown Female Corpse, Kipling spares his reader no details. He gives a short but vivid description of the woman's corpse which is not only without a head, but is also minus a foot and a hand. This makes the corpse unidentifiable and, therefore, remote since she has no name. Nonetheless, in death she offers a warning to the men who make war, that they are in fact, killing their own mothers. This statement could be taken literally, as women were killed during the war, or it could be metaphorical, implying that in witnessing so much death and losing so many of their sons, each mother dies a little and loses a little piece of herself.

RAPED AND REVENGED

In this second poem about the hardships faced by women in war, Kipling tells a sorry tale of a woman who is brutalised by one soldier, but when another witnesses this he arranges her revenge, in the form of the deaths of "an hundred" of her attacker's comrades, described here as "heathen hosts". The implication here is that the men concerned have learned a hard lesson in how to treat women. It is however, interesting to note Kipling's use of the word "freeborn" to describe the woman, suggesting that a servant would not be afforded the same degree of consideration. This may also imply that British and Allied women are somehow more worthy than the females of the enemy countries.

SALONIKAN GRAVE

A simple poem in which Kipling evokes how illness can be just as deadly in war, as a bullet, or a shell. At the beginning of the poem, Kipling is essentially describing the boredom that might be associated with much of the First World War, which was not all about fighting and during which a great deal of time was spent waiting for something to happen. Having watched many days turn into night with monotonous regularity, this man now turns to night himself, as he faces death, not by violence, but from "fever" which over "time" has brought an end to his life.

THE BRIDEGROOM

One of the saddest of the Epitaphs, The Bridegroom reveals the story of a young and newly married man, who has exchanged the arms of his bride for the embrace of death. In the beginning, he begs his bride to forgive his falsehood, that he should be effectively "deceiving" her with another, although at this stage, Kipling does not reveal who this other person might be. In the second verse, we get clue that the other person involved is death, since the man has been haunted by its presence for so long, even before he met his new bride. The "marriage" which Kipling speaks about in the third verse, is the one between the young man and death, which is described as a certainty that has been long "delayed" by a series of miracles. Nonetheless, he and death have finally come together in a union that cannot be divided, since death is absolute. The young man urges his bride to carry on with her life in the hope that time will help her to forget the pain of his death. At the same time, however, he admits that the "immortality" which he has gained will not be pleasant but will be something to be endured.

We may presume that this is, at least in part, because the life of an immortal is so lonely. We are reminded in the poem of the transience of youth in wartime; that even the very young and carefree were forced to become old before their time and that death snatched happiness from the most deserving.

VAD (MEDITERRANEAN)

A lyrical poem in which the subject is the nurses who served overseas during the First World War. Here, Kipling paints them as "virgin" women, "drowned" in a metaphorical sea of wounded men. They have no immediate families to "mourn" their departure, since they are too young to have really lived and formed such ties. Nonetheless, they repair the men in their charge and return them to war, or else they help those who are dying and whose salvation will be sought "in vain" by their loved ones. Kipling creates a contrast between the men who will be mourned and the women, whose absence no-one will evidently notice. This is a rather rose-tinted perspective of the role of the VAD, seen here as only saviour and helper of the young men in her charge, but taking no account of the hardships faced by either the women in this role, or the men whom she served.

ACTORS

[The subtitle places this quatrain to an inscription on a memorial tablet in a church in Stratford-upon-Avon, the birthplace of William Shakespeare.]

There is an unsurprising Shakespearean tone to this quatrain, the meaning of which is that, effectively, actors are admitting that, compared to those who have fought and died for their country, they really serve no useful purpose. Kipling speaks of the actors as being the "servants" to those who have fallen in honour of their country, but leaves the reader feeling that there is a sense of inadequacy even in that.

JOURNALISTS

[As with "Actors", the subtitle places this Epitaph in the Institute of Journalists]

This single line Epitaph simply states that newspaper writers no longer serve a purpose, showing the poet's opinion of that profession and presumably its influence on the war.

ELIZABETH DARYUSH

The first of only two female poets in this collection, Elizabeth Daryush's pedigree as the daughter of Poet Laureate, Robert Bridges, is possibly the reason for her inclusion, at the expense of other, more well-known, and some might argue, better poets.

BIOGRAPHICAL DETAILS

Elizabeth Daryush (née Bridges) was born on 5th December 1887, in London. Her father, Robert Bridges had been a physician, but was also a poet and was made Poet Laureate from 1913 to 1930. Elizabeth's mother was Monica Waterhouse, whose father Alfred had been a famous architect - his best known design probably being the Natural History Museum and London. Elizabeth was the oldest of three children, her sister Margaret was born in 1889 and brother, Edward, three years later. When Elizabeth was still an infant, the family moved out of London to Yattendon in Berkshire, where she was privately educated.

By her early twenties, Elizabeth was already a published poet, producing three volumes of work between 1911 and 1921 although later, she would disown these poems, which were published under her maiden name. In 1926 Elizabeth married a Persian government official called Ali Akbar Daryush and for the first three years of their marriage, they lived in Persia. Upon their return to England, they settled at Boars Hill in Oxford and the 1930s would become her most productive period of writing with her poems often taking the form of criticisms of the upper classes. Her popularity faded in the 1940s and she died in 1977.

SUBALTERNS

A subaltern is an officer in the British Army, below the rank of Captain. This is usually the title given to the most junior of officers, such as Second Lieutenants, reflecting their lower status among the officer ranks. Nonetheless, the subaltern would be responsible for a Platoon of men and would also have to assist the more senior officers in running the Company. Due to their junior rank, many subalterns were quite often younger than the men they were leading, and some of them would have entered the war straight from school in their late teens.

This poem was written after the war as a conversation between a woman who seeks to glorify the role of men in battle and former soldiers who reveal their realities. In the opening verse, the woman makes a somewhat gushing statement, that the thought of men fighting in battle makes her heart thrill. This seems like a rather careless and immature statement, leading one to believe that it was probably made by a young women, innocent in the ways of the world. The subaltern in question then response that his thoughts of war are not warm and glowing and she supposes, but are cold recollections of an initially optimistic time, made barren by experience. It is interesting to note that he regards his happier moments as having been "bought" with, presumably other mens' lives, or his experiences of horror.

The second verse continues with the woman now suggesting to a subaltern that he must feel relieved to be free of fighting, since the war is over and peace has returned. His response is to doubt her implication before going on to remark that at least the war had given him something worthwhile to do, whereas now everything seems rather dull and boring.

It is not completely clear whether there is more than one subaltern involved here, although the title of the poem being plural would seem to indicate this. If this is the case, it certainly makes sense of the fact that the two male responses are somewhat contradictory, since the first recalls "icy memories", while the second seems to have more fond recollections, resenting the peace, rather than the war.

The format of this poem, with a question and answer, allows Daryush to create an automatic contrast within the piece as the man contradicts the woman's statements each time.

Daryush doesn't paint a very positive portrait of her own sex here, portraying the female character as insensitive and innocent to the ways of war, event at its end. Within the context of Jon Stallworthy's *Oxford Book of War Poetry*, it is quite difficult to compare this poem with those of other female writers, since only one other is included and that doesn't really bare any comparison with this piece, as their subject matters are completely at odds. It is more suitable to compare this piece with *Glory of Women* by Siegfried Sassoon, in which he initially and ironically portrays women in a similar, harsh light, decrying them for their delight in war and their wilful misunderstanding of reality. Only at the end of the poem does Sassoon allow for any other type of woman: the lonely mother who continues to knit socks for her dead son. In Kipling's *Epitaphs* the poet also makes several references to women and their role in the war, such as in *An Only Son, Shock, VAD (Mediterranean), Unknown Female Corpse,* and *Raped and Revenged*, although many of these are written from the perspective of a mother's relationship with her son, making them different to *Subalterns*.

MAY WEDDERBURN CANNAN

There are many people who could be said to be representative of a generation and May Cannan is one of them. In a quiet, understated way, she suffered great loss and sadness during the war and afterwards found that her life was changed forever. She felt angry and frustrated that everything she had dreamed of was gone and her overwhelming feelings were of sorrow and loneliness. Others might question why Vera Brittain - the customary spokesperson for the women who were damaged by the First World War - is missing from this anthology. I do not: May Cannan is, quite simply, the best ambassador for the female voice of war poetry.

BIOGRAPHICAL DETAILS

May Wedderburn Cannan was born on 14th October 1893, together with her twin sister Frances, in Oxford, although Frances died at the age of just two months. May was the middle of the three daughters of Charles and Mary Cannan and her father was a tutor in Classics. The family lived at Magdalen College, Oxford and May was educated initially at home, then at Wychwood School and finally at Downe House in Kent. In May's final year at Downe House, however, she became seriously ill, firstly with measles and then pneumonia, which resulted in her returning to Wychwood School to complete her education. It was at this stage that May first became acquainted with a young man named Bevil Quiller-Couch, whose father was a friend of the family.

When she turned 18 in October 1911, May took the examinations to join the Voluntary Aid Detachment, of which her mother was the local Commandant and, in addition, she helped out at her father's business - the Oxford University Press. As war approached, May's life became a strange combination of VAD work

- organising a new hospital for 60 patients - and the usual summer social activities of dancing, tennis and picnics. When war was declared, however, everything changed. Her hospital was organised and ready for its first patients within 2 days. However, she was soon notified that the authorities had changed their minds and no longer required the use of such establishments. In addition, Bevil - an army reservist - was mobilised and sailed for France on August 17th. He wrote to May very often but was disappointed that the proposal of marriage which he had intended making before his departure, would now have to wait.

With her nursing skills seemingly not required at present, May decided to stay on at the Oxford University Press to help her father, since most of the male workers had gone off to enlist. She was joined there by both of her sisters and their father always ensured that the families of his former workers, who had gone to fight, were well cared for. In April 1915, May and a friend, Lucie Raleigh, went to Rouen in France, to work in a canteen. Initially the girls could only stay for four weeks, but May was keen to remain, although she also knew that her father needed her at The Press, so she reluctantly returned home.

The summer of 1915 was very different from its predecessor: many of May's friends had been wounded, some killed; there were no lavish parties; what little spare time she had, she filled with war work. As the war progressed, May and Bevil continued to correspond and she also wrote poetry, publishing a volume entitled In War Time in 1917. Both of May's sisters were married in 1918, leaving May alone at The Press, contemplating an uncertain future. That summer, however, her life changed once again, when she was offered a job in a War Office department in Paris. She knew almost nothing about her new job, other than the fact that it was 'in intelligence' and only when she arrived in Paris did she discover that she would be working for MI5 in the Espionage department. She enjoyed her work, especially when she was promoted to the position of Acting Head of the Women's Espionage Unit.

Then, on the morning of the 11th November 1918, May was summoned to the office of the Colonel in charge of her unit, where she was instructed to take down a dictation of the Terms of the Armistice. She then returned to her office and typed out four copies of the document, before bursting into tears - the war was finally over.

A few days later, quite unexpectedly, Bevil arrived at her office - he had five days leave and they spent it together. Before returning to his unit, he proposed to May and she accepted. By early December she was back in England, anxiously awaiting Bevil's return. Their wedding date was fixed for 3rd June 1919. At the beginning of February, May received word that Bevil was seriously ill with influenza and before she could travel to him, he died. May felt that her life - forever changed by the war - was now over. In the immediate aftermath, loneliness engulfed her - along with anger and frustration.

By November, however, all had changed again: her father died following a stroke and her mother decided she and May should move to London. She eventually found work at the Athenaeum Club, as assistant Librarian: she was the first woman they had ever employed. She continued to write poetry and joined a writer's club. In 1924 she received an unsolicited, but intriguing letter, signed simply P.J.S. The writer said that he was a great admirer of her poetry and wondered if they could meet. May decided to accept this invitation - which was actually from a former infantry officer - Captain P. J. Slater. Before the year was out, May and P. J. Slater were married. Little is known of what happened to May in the following years. She died in 1973, leaving behind an unpublished manuscript which detailed her experiences of the First World War: her lost dreams and hopes; her anger and ultimate acceptance of her fate and, above all, the thoughts of a generation, whose lives would forever be different.

ROUEN

This poem offers a very evocative description of May's time at Rouen, working in a Canteen at the Rail Head. In it, she conveys the atmosphere both in and around her workplace; sights, sounds and smells are brought to life.

May wrote this poem in the form of questions about remembrances of a time which, for her, was very happy and fulfilling. For her this was a great adventure, as she had longed to be in France and taste the reality of war first hand.

Throughout the poem she describes various aspects of daily life in the canteen, from the sunrises she witnessed at the end of her shift (May worked mainly during the night), to the strange voices of the Indian soldiers who served during the war. One phrase which often provokes questions in this poem relates to tatties and why they would make a clicking sound. A tattie is the name given, in India, to a screen of grass fibres which was hung at a door or window opening. In India, this screen would have been kept wet to moisten and cool the air. We may, therefore, suppose that screens similar to these were used in the canteens. Either they would be caught in the wind, or as people passed through them, they would bang on the door frame, thus making the clicking sound referred to. May might have heard the Indian soldiers refer to the screens as tatties, or she might have already known about them, since she had some old Oxford friends who had gone out to India with the regular army before the First World War, and she may have picked up the word from them.

She describes the contrast between the still sleeping town, and the hoards of hungry soldiers, laughing over their coffee and sandwiches before going on towards the front. When the soldiers finish and their trains are ready to depart, they are called to attention and sing God Save the King.

Suddenly the canteen is quiet again, all the men have left, and although dawn approaches promising a new beginning, she perceives that the men are travelling to and from darkness. However, everything carries on: there is another shift of workers to hand over to; another train full of soldiers in need of refreshment and a smile. Having completed her own shift, May is now free to enjoy the cool calmness of the morning and to sleep.

In the final two verses, the tone of the poem changes, May is no longer asking whether others share her remembrances - she is telling us that she does remember. She is looking back to her time in Rouen and her adventures there, with an almost romantic air. Her pride in the soldiers is there in the final verse, in that her most abiding memory is of the trains carrying them towards the war. May perceived that the men were fighting gallantly for a worthy cause, and held the soldiers in high esteem.

The fondness of May's memories of that time is apparent in this poem. When she returned to Oxford after her month in Rouen, she felt that she would give almost anything to be able to return to France. She had a profound sense of belonging there: that she was, even only in a small way, doing 'her bit' for the war effort, and in doing so, she felt fulfiled.

PHILIP LARKIN

Although not born until after the First World War had ended, Larkin has captured the essence of the summer of 1914, often referred to as the 'golden summer', after which nothing would ever be the same again.

BIOGRAPHICAL DETAILS

Born on August 9th 1922 in Coventry, Philip Arthur Larkin was the only son of Sydney and Eve Larkin. Sydney was City Treasurer between 1922 and 1944. Philip attended King Henry VIII School in Coventry until he was eighteen years old, then went to St John's College, Oxford, from where he graduated in 1943, having gained a First Class Honours degree in English. He tried to enlist during the Second World War, but was rejected on account of his poor eyesight. After leaving university, he became a librarian and in 1946, he was appointed Assistant Librarian at the University College of Leicester. Four years later, Larkin became Sub-Librarian at Queen's University Belfast, before moving to the University of Hull in 1955. Throughout this time, Larkin continued to write poetry, much of which was published in small volumes or pamphlets. In 1964 he was awarded the Queen's Gold Medal for Poetry, followed by a CBE in 1975. Although Larkin never married, he had numerous relationships, indeed at one stage in his life, he was seeing three women simultaneously. These affairs were generally - although not always - sexual, and the most significant was probably with Monica Jones, who he met in 1950 and with whom he maintained a close friendship until his death in 1985.

MCMXIV

Published in 1960, the poem's title is the Roman numeral for 1914 - the year in which the First World War began. Larkin describes here the scenes, possibly from an old photograph or newsreels, in early August of that year, when young men, keen to enlist and 'do their bit' for their country, thronged into towns and cities, where they waited for hours, amidst vast crowd, for the opportunity to join up. He says that they look just like a queue, waiting for admission to a football or cricket match. His reference to the men acting as though they were involved in an 'August Bank Holiday lark' alludes to the fact that August 3rd 1914 was, in fact, a Bank Holiday, but also to the notion that in those day, Bank Holidays were far more significant, since most workers did not receive paid holiday, so they took advantage of every opportunity to enjoy a day out and have a 'lark'.

In the second verse, Larkin continues with this theme of joyous enthusiasm on the part of the general population and the reader may easily imagine the 'children at play' and a heady atmosphere of anticipation. These scenes were, however, not just restricted to the towns: the countryside was also different and servants from 'huge houses' were able to put on their 'best' clothes and enjoy a day out. In the final verse, the tone changes slightly as, rather than just describing the scene, Larkin begins to analyse it and to realise that these events could never be repeated. He asserts that there will never be 'such innocence' again. Never will men go so willingly to their deaths, leaving behind everything which they had loved, because now they would know what awaited them; now they would ask questions, rather than just going. The First World War changed everything about how people perceived their country and their duty towards it. Larkin appears to regret at least some of that change.

VERNON SCANNELL

Although Scannell became a much respected poet, his military background gives him a unique perspective on war.

BIOGRAPHICAL DETAILS

Vernon Scannell was actually born John Vernon Bain on 23rd January 1922 in Lincolnshire. His father was a photographer and the family moved a lot before settling in Aylesbury. Scannell left school at fourteen and went to work for a firm of accountants. He also took up boxing. In 1940, at the age of eighteen, he was called up and fought with the Gordon Highlanders. While serving in Tunisia, he went absent without leave and, when he was arrested as a deserted, he was sent to a military prison. In 1944, his sentence was suspended and he was released to take part in the D-Day landings. He was wounded in Normandy and while recovering, he went on the run again, this time changing his name to Vernon Scannell. He took up various jobs in his new guise, including professional boxing, but in 1947, the authorities caught up with him and he was arrested for desertion and briefly detained in Northfield Hospital, following a psychiatric assessment. Once released, he turned more seriously to writing and became a respected poet and author. He married Josephine Higson in 1954 and they had six children before they were divorced. Scannell died in Otley, West Yorkshire on November 16th 2007, at the age of 85.

THE GREAT WAR

There are tones of both anger and gratitude within this poem. The poet opens by making generalisations about his perspective of the conflict as a whole. He refers to the soldiers involved as being blindly murdered and describes the shattered landscape of the war. In this first section, there are underlying references to the works of some of the soldier poets, such as Owen and Rosenberg, who also described the barbed wire as being like a 'bramble' and personified the artifacts of war. In addition, Siegfried Sassoon, in his poem *Attack*, refers to the time which 'ticks blank and busy' on the wrists of the soldiers waiting to attack. The beginning of Scannell's poem echoes the tone and the anger of many of these other poets, especially after the Battle of the Somme. However, Scannell goes on to say that these imaginings 'are only part' of his thoughts, before he goes into more detail about specific places and people, songs, battles and trench life - in other words some of the more positive aspects, like comradeship and humour. Finally, he asserts that on Remembrance Day, he does not recall the Second World War in which he fought, but the earlier conflict, which ended before he was even born, but which is indelibly marked on this country's conscience.

TED HUGHES

Ted Hughes is probably responsible for writing the most famous poem about the conflict, by someone born after it had finished.

BIOGRAPHICAL DETAILS

Edward James Hughes was born on 17th August 1930 in Yorkshire, where his parents, William and Edith, ran a newagents. He attended the local grammar school and then did his two years of National Service with the RAF, before going to Pembroke College, Cambridge in 1951. Here he studied English, Anthropology and Archaeology and he also wrote poetry. In 1956, he met and married Sylvia Plath, an American poet who was attending Cambridge University on a Fulbright Scholarship. For the first few years of their marriage, they lived in America, returning to England in late 1959, where they initially settled into a small flat in London. Their first child, Frieda, was born the following year and in 1961, they moved to Devon, where their second child Nicholas was born in January 1962. Hughes, however, had begun an affair with Assia Wevill and later that year, he and Sylvia separated. In February 1963, Sylvia committed suicide. Hughes continued his relationship with Assia Wevill and they had a daughter, Shura, in 1967. A few years later, Wevill first killed her daugher and then herself, using the same method as Sylvia Plath. In 1970, Hughes married Carol Orchard, who raised Frieda and Nicholas as though they were her own children. He was appointed Poet Laureate from 1984 until his death in 1998. His son, Nicholas, also committed suicide on 16th March 2009.

SIX YOUNG MEN

This poem was inspired by a photograph of 'six young men' who had enlisted and were about to go and fight in the First World War. The photograph was taken near Hebden Bridge in West Yorkshire and all of the 'six young men' were killed in the conflict. The poem opens with the suggestion - in an echo of Laurence Binyon's *For the Fallen* - that the passage of time has not aged these men. Hughes goes on to describe features of each of these men, reiterating their familiarity both with each other and with their friends, before bluntly informing us that within six months, all six men were dead. Next, he turns to the landscape around the men, which in reality has not changed with the passing decades. This verse reminds the reader that although the photograph may seem to have preserved the men, they are in fact dead and buried, while everything at home has remained the same.

In the third verse, Hughes gives us the details - where known - as to how the men died. However, the tone of the poem changes completely in the fourth verse as the poet's anger begins to creep in. Now we can see his frustration regarding the waste of these young men's lives, transformed from their smiling photographic image, into 'mangled' and 'rotting' corpses. In the final verse Hughes draws the reader in, by relating the men in the photograph to present-day people, as well as 'prehistorical or fabulous beast[s]', reminding us that, while the men smiled because they did not know their fate, we who are left and understand what happened, should not simply look upon them as another piece of history.

DOUGLAS DUNN

Douglas Dunn was born during the Second World War, but in the poem which Jon Stallworthy has selected, he provides us with a late 20th century perspective of the aftermath of the earlier conflict.

BIOGRAPHICAL DETAILS

Born on 23 October 1942 in Renfrewshire, Douglas Eaglesham Dunn was educated at Renfrew High School and Camphill School in Paisley, before becoming a librarian. Following his marriage in 1964, he and his wife moved to America, where they lived for two years. Upon their return, Dunn took up a place at the University of Hull, reading English and graduated with First Class Honours in 1969. He has written poetry, short stories and play and received many awards, including an OBE in 2003

WAR BLINDED

Written 'more than sixty years' after the First World War, this poem is about the consequences of the conflict. The first subject of the poem has been blinded and now resides in a 'soldiers' hospital'. It would seem, according to the second verse, that the poet had first seen this man thirty years before writing the poem and that he had also been aware of the blind man's ability to weave baskets. He then imagines how the man might have felt when he was young and had joined up, possibly at a football ground, which had been turned into a makeshift recruiting office. However this image of youthful enthusiasm is then shattered by Dunn's description of the man lying 'across a parapet', with blood pouring from his wounded eyes.

The tone changes slightly in the fourth verse, as Dunn describes his own feelings when, many years later, he had first seen this blind man, pushing the wheelchair of a lame veteran of the conflict. In this way, the two ex-servicemen help each other - the lame man becomes the 'eyes' of the blind man, while he in turn provides the 'legs' to wheel the other around. Dunn, it would seem, had been struck by their 'dignity' which had, at the time, helped him to come to terms with his own problems. (This poem may have been written around the time of the death of Dunn's first wife).

The final verse, despite everything which has gone before, is somewhat dismissive, as Dunn states that the First World War is really too long ago for him to be able to empathise with the man, or his feelings. In a somewhat clichéd ending, Dunn forces the reader to call to mind the famous painting entitled 'Gassed' by John Singer Sargent which depicts a line of soldiers, each with their eyes bandaged, walking with one hand placed upon the shoulder of the 'man in front'.

This poem is also reminiscent of the work of Wilfred Owen, in that Dunn makes some use of Owen's trademark half-rhyme (or pararhyme) as in 'blind/wind' and 'at/parapet', as well as internal rhymes such as 'me/ferry/filigree'. In addition this poem also provides reminders of Owen's *Disabled* in which a young Scottish football player enlists to fight in the war, but ends up losing both of his legs and one arm. Owen describes the man's sacrifice in terms of him having 'poured' his blood away and paints a bleak picture of this once-popular man, whom people now shun.

In a way, Dunn's poem perpetuates and justifies Owen's anger in *Disabled*, in that those who gave everything would seem to be forgotten, either because people choose not to remember such unpleasantness, preferring to see men who were 'whole', or because, as Siegfried Sassoon once put it, they did not have 'sufficient imagination to realise'.

FURTHER READING
RECOMMENDATIONS FOR STUDENTS

Students are often expected to demonstrate a sound knowledge of the texts which they are studying and also to enhance this knowledge with extensive reading of other books within this genre. I have provided on the following pages a list of books, poetry, plays and non-fiction which, in my opinion, provide a good basic understanding of this topic. In addition, a small review of each book has been provided to help students choose which of the following are most suitable for them.

NOVELS

STRANGE MEETING by Susan Hill

Strange Meeting is a beautiful and moving book. It is the story of two young men, who meet in the worst circumstances, yet manage to overcome their surroundings and form a deep and lasting friendship. They are opposites: John Hilliard is quiet and reserved, while David Barton is outgoing and friendly. Despite their differences, their friendship blossoms, as the world around them disintegrates into self-destruction. Susan Hill writes so evocatively that the reader is automatically drawn into the lives of these men: the sights, sounds and even smells which they witness are brought to life. This is a book about war and its effects; it is also a story of love, both conventional and 'forbidden'; of human relationships of every variety. This is a tale told during the worst of times, about the best of men and is, quite simply, one of the best novels ever written about the First World War.

A VERY LONG ENGAGEMENT by Sebastien Japrisot

A story of enduring love, truth and determination. Refusing to believe that her fiancé can possibly have left her forever, Mathilde decides to search for Manech whom she has been told is missing, presumed dead. She learns from a first-hand witness, that he may not have died, so she sets out on a voyage of discovery - learning not just about his fate, but also a great deal about herself and human nature. Mathilde herself has to overcome her own personal fears and hardships and, out of sheer persistence and a refusal to accept the obvious, she eventually discovers the truth. Although this novel does not form part of the main syllabus reading list, it does make an interesting and fairly easy read and is useful from the perspective that it gives a French woman's viewpoint of the war.

REGENERATION by Pat Barker

This book is, as its title implies, a novel about the rebuilding of men following extreme trauma. Billy Prior is a young working-class officer - a 'temporary gentleman' - who finds himself at Craiglockhart Military Hospital in Edinburgh, having been damaged by his experiences on the Western Front. It is the job of Dr W. H. R. Rivers, to 'mend' Prior, and others like him, ready for them to return to the fighting, while wrestling with his own conscience at the same time. Interweaved into this central plot is the meeting, also at Craiglockhart, of poets Siegfried Sassoon and Wilfred Owen, who are both there to receive treatment. This mixture of fact and fiction within a novel has created some controversy, but it is a common feature within this genre and one which Pat Barker handles better than most. This is an immensely useful book - even if not read as part of the Trilogy - as it takes place away from the front lines, showing the reader the deep and long-lasting effects of battle upon men, whose lives would never be the same again. Due to some adult content, we recommend this book for A-Level students only.

THE RETURN OF THE SOLDIER by Rebecca West

Written in 1918, by an author who had lived through the conflict, this home-front novel gives a useful insight into the trauma of war and society's reaction, as seen through the eyes of three women. Chris Baldry, an officer and husband of Kitty, returns home mid-way through the war, suffering from shell-shock and amnesia. He believes that that he is still in a relationship with Margaret Allington

- his first love from fifteen years earlier. Kitty, Margaret and Chris's cousin, Jenny, must decide whether to leave Chris in his make-believe world, safe from the war; or whether to 'cure' him and risk his future welfare once he returns to being a soldier. A useful novel from many perspectives in that it was written right at the end of the war, and it gives a female, home-front view of the effects of the war on individuals and families.

ALL QUIET ON THE WESTERN FRONT by Erich Maria Remarque

Written from first-hand experience of life in the trenches, this novel is the moving account of the lives of a group of young German soldiers during the First World War. Remarque had been in the trenches during the later stages of the war and this poignant account of war is a must-read for all those who show an interest in this subject. His descriptions of trench-life and battles are second-to-none and his portrayal of the close friendships forged between the men make this an immensely valuable piece of literature. The fact that this, often shocking, story is told from a German perspective also demonstrates the universal horrors of the war and the sympathy between men of both sides for others enduring the same hardships as themselves.

A LONG LONG WAY by Sebastian Barry

Sebastian Barry's novel tells the a story of Willie Dunne, a young Irish volunteer serving in the trenches of the Western Front. Willie must not only contend with the horrors of the war, but also his own confused feelings regarding the Easter uprising of 1916, and his father's disapproval. Willie's feelings and doubts lead to great upheavals in his life, including personal losses and betrayals by those whom he had believed he could trust. This is an interesting novel about loyalty, war and love, although it does suffer from a degree of historical inaccuracy. In our opinion, due to the adult content of this novel, it is suitable only for A-Level students.

NOT SO QUIET... by Helen Zenna Smith

This novel describes the lives of women working very close to the front line on the Western Front during the First World War, as ambulance drivers. Theirs is a dangerous job, in harsh conditions, with little or no respite. Helen (or Smithy, as she is called by her friends), eventually breaks down under the pressure of the work and returns, briefly, to England. An excellent novel for studying the female perspective, as well as the home front.

POETRY

It is recommended that students read from a wide variety of poets, including female writers. The following anthologies provide good resources for students.

POEMS OF THE FIRST WORLD WAR -
NEVER SUCH INNOCENCE
Edited by Martin Stephen

Probably one of the finest anthologies of First World War poetry currently available. Martin Stephen has collected together some of the best known works by some of the most famous and well-read poets and mixed these with more obscure verses, including many by women and those on the home-front, together with some popular songs both from home and from the front. These have been interspersed with excellent notes which give the reader sufficient information without being too weighty. At the back of the book, there are short biographical notes on many of the poets. This is a fine anthology, suitable both for those who are starting out with their studies, and for the more experienced reader.

LADS: LOVE POETRY OF THE TRENCHES by Martin Taylor

Featuring many lesser-known poets and poems, this anthology approaches the First World War from a different perspective: love. A valuable introduction discusses the emotions of men who, perhaps for the first time, were discovering their own capacity to love their fellow man. This is not an anthology of purely homo-erotic poems, but also features verses by those who had found affection and deep, lasting friendship in the trenches of the First World War.

SCARS UPON MY HEART
Selected by Catherine Reilly

First published in 1981, this anthology is invaluable as it features a collection of poems written exclusively by women on the subject of the First World War.

Some of the better known female poets are featured here, such as Vera Brittain and Jessie Pope, but there are also many more writers who are less famous. In addition there are some poets whose work is featured, who are not now renowned for their poetry, but for their works in other areas of literature. Many of the poets included here have minor biographical details featured at the end of the anthology. This book has become the 'standard' for those wishing to study the female contribution to this genre.

UP THE LINE TO DEATH
Edited by Brian Gardner

This anthology, described by its editor Brian Gardner as a 'book about war', is probably, and deservedly, one of the most widely read in this genre. The famous and not-so-famous sit happily together within in these pages of carefully selected poetry. Arranged thematically, these poems provide a poet's-eye-view of the progression of the war, from the initial euphoria and nationalistic pride of John Freeman's 'Happy is England Now' to Sassoon's plea that we should 'never forget'. Useful biographical details and introductions complete this book, which is almost certainly the most useful and important of all the First World War poetry anthologies.

NON-FICTION

UNDERTONES OF WAR by Edmund Blunden

Edmund Blunden's memoir of his experiences in the First World War is a moving, enlightening and occasionally humorous book, demonstrating above all the intense feelings of respect and comradeship which Blunden found in the trenches.

MEMOIRS OF AN INFANTRY OFFICER by Siegfried Sassoon

Following on from *Memoirs of a Fox-hunting Man*, this book is an autobiographical account of Sassoon's life during the First World War. Sassoon has changed the names of the characters and George Sherston (Sassoon) is not a poet. Sassoon became one of the war's most famous poets and this prose account of his war provides useful background information.
(For a list of the fictional characters and their factual counterparts, see Appendix II of *Siegfried Sassoon* by John Stuart Roberts.)

THE GREAT WAR GENERALS ON THE WESTERN FRONT 1914-1918 by Robin Neillands

Like many others before and since, the cover of this book claims that it will dismiss the old myth that the troops who served in the First World War were badly served by their senior officers. Unlike most of the other books, however, this one is balanced and thought-provoking. Of particular interest within this book is the final chapter which provides an assessment of the main protagonists and their role in the conflict.

THE WESTERN FRONT by Richard Holmes

This is one of many history books about the First World War. Dealing specifically with the Western Front, Richard Holmes looks at the creation of the trench warfare system, supplying men and munitions, major battles and living on the front line..

LETTERS FROM A LOST GENERATION (FIRST WORLD WAR LETTERS OF VERA BRITTAIN AND FOUR FRIENDS) Edited by Alan Bishop and Mark Bostridge

A remarkable insight into the changes which the First World War caused to a particular set of individuals. In this instance, Vera Brittain lost four important people in her life (two close friends, her fiancé and her brother). The agony this evoked is demonstrated through letters sent between these five characters, which went on to form the basis of Vera Brittain's autobiography *Testament of Youth*.

1914-1918: VOICES AND IMAGES OF THE GREAT WAR by Lyn MacDonald

One of the most useful 'unofficial' history books available to those studying the First World War. This book tells the story of the soldiers who fought the war through their letters, diary extracts, newspaper reports, poetry and eye-witness accounts. As with all of Lyn MacDonald's excellent books, *Voices and Images of the Great War* tells its story through the words of the people who were there. The author gives just the right amount of background information of a political and historical nature to keep the reader interested and informed, while leaving the centre-stage to those who really matter... the men themselves.

BIBLIOGRAPHY

Grey Ghosts and Voices (May Wedderburn Cannan)

The Collected Poems of Edward Thomas (R George Thomas)

Anthem for Doomed Youth (Jon Stallworthy)

Violets from Oversea (Tonie and Valmai Hart)

Minds at War - The Poetry and Experience of the First World War (David Roberts)

The War Poets (Robert Giddings)

Poems of the First World War - Never Such Innocence (Martin Stephen)

Lads (Martin Taylor)

Siegfried Sassoon: The Making of a War Poet - A Biography 1886-1918 (Jean Moorcroft Wilson)

Siegfried Sassoon (John Stuart Roberts)

Siegfried Sassoon - Collected Poems 1908-1956

Siegfried Sassoon - The War Poems (Rupert Hart-Davis)

Siegfried Sassoon (Max Egremont)

Up the Line to Death: The War Poets 1914-1918 (Brian Gardner)

Stars in a Dark Night: The Letters of Ivor Gurney to the Chapman Family (Anthony Boden)

Wilfred Owen - War Poems and Others (Dominic Hibberd)

The Poems of Wilfred Owen (Edmund Blunden)

The War the Infantry Knew 1914-1919 (Captain J C Dunn)

Goodbye to all That (Robert Graves)

Robert Graves - The Assault Heroic 1895-1926 (Richard Perceval Graves)

Robert Graves - The Years with Laura 1926-1940 (Richard Perceval Graves)

Robert Graves and the White Goddess 1940-1985 (Richard Perceval Graves)

Undertones of War (Edmund Blunden)

Edmund Blunden - A Biography (Barry Webb)

Julian Grenfell (Nicholas Mosley)

The Winter of the World - Poems of the Great War (edited by Dominic Hibberd and John Onions)

Binyon, (Robert) Laurence (1869–1943)', (John Hatcher, Oxford Dictionary of National Biography, Oxford University Press, 2004)

OTHER TITLES

GREAT WAR LITERATURE STUDY GUIDE E-BOOKS:

NOVELS & PLAYS

All Quiet on the Western Front
Birdsong
Journey's End (A-Level or GCSE)
Regeneration
The Eye in the Door
The Ghost Road
A Long Long Way
The First Casualty
Strange Meeting
The Return of the Soldier
The Accrington Pals
Not About Heroes
Oh What a Lovely War

POET BIOGRAPHIES AND POETRY ANALYSIS:

Herbert Asquith
Harold Begbie
John Peale Bishop
Edmund Blunden
Vera Brittain
Rupert Brooke
Thomas Burke
May Wedderburn Cannan
Margaret Postgate Cole
Alice Corbin
E E Cummings

Nancy Cunard
T S Eliot
Eleanor Farjeon
Gilbert Frankau
Robert Frost
Wilfrid Wilson Gibson
Anna Gordon Keown
Robert Graves
Julian Grenfell
Ivor Gurney
Thomas Hardy
Alan P Herbert
Agnes Grozier Herbertson
W N Hodgson
A E Housman
Geoffrey Anketell Studdert Kennedy
Winifred M Letts
Amy Lowell
E A Mackintosh
John McCrae
Charlotte Mew
Edna St Vincent Millay
Ruth Comfort Mitchell
Harriet Monroe
Edith Nesbit
Robert Nichols
Wilfred Owen
Jessie Pope
Ezra Pound
Florence Ripley Mastin
Isaac Rosenberg
Carl Sandburg
Siegfried Sassoon
Alan Seeger
Charles Hamilton Sorley
Wallace Stevens
Sara Teasdale
Edward Wyndham Tennant
Lesbia Thanet
Edward Thomas

Iris Tree
Katharine Tynan Hinkson
Robert Ernest Vernède
Arthur Graeme West

*Please note that e-books are only available direct from our Web site at
www.greatwarliterature.co.uk and cannot be purchased through bookshops.*

NOTES

Printed in Great Britain
by Amazon

18634198R00138